BERNARD P. INDIK
} EDITORS
F. KENNETH BERRIEN

PEOPLE, GROUPS, AND ORGANIZATIONS

*HM
131
.P348*

TEACHERS COLLEGE PRESS   } TEACHERS COLLEGE
COLUMBIA UNIVERSITY
NEW YORK, NEW YORK

161792

Preface

In bringing together these papers, which were originally presented in a symposium at Rutgers — The State University in late 1966, it is our purpose to generate some cross-system conceptual integration. It seemed to us initially that links needed to be forged joining studies of individual characteristics to those of group phenomena and those of organizational features. Furthermore, as specialized languages have developed within these three levels, their users have grown less and less understandable to one another. Our second objective, then, was to help break down artificial semantic differences, and also to highlight real differences in points of view. We succeeded better perhaps in the latter than in the former. As one participant expressed it, we played a game: "You show me your conceptual model, and I'll show you mine."

Our efforts show three successive emphases. It is quite appropriate to deal first with taxonomic issues. General rules for classifying data of any kind and considerations for evaluating any taxonomy are presented in Altman's paper, after Sells and Indik have proposed several approaches to the domains under consideration.

Part Two of the book provides reviews of research and theory in the various subareas of concern in the understanding of organizational behavior. Popenoe deals with the communities and societies that are the environments of organizations, Etzioni with the analysis of organizations *per se,* with particular respect to control and compliance behavior. Berrien's analysis of groups and organizations is from the point of view of General Systems Theory. Golembiewski then offers a summary and review of the integration of small behavioral units into large formal organizations. Personality and organizational behavior are then related in Williams' survey of findings, with a particular focus on the use of a developmental model jointly applied to personality and organizational variables. In the final paper in Part Two, Seashore and Yuchtman explore the elements of organizational performance and, using an exemplary analysis of data available from seventy-five life insurance sales agencies, show how naive our prior conceptions of organizational performance have been.

Part Three of this volume begins with the consideration of methodology. McGrath deals with the problem of empirically testing a scheme for classifying individual, group, and organizational concepts, in particular, illustrating the applicability of multifacet analysis. Weick

v

also deals with methodological issues. He suggests modifications of experimental approaches from the psychological laboratory and brings a number of other methodological issues to our attention. Gump's chapter offers an approach in a perspective quite different from that of people, groups, organizations, and sociocultural environments. His suggestion of systematically observing "persons, settings and larger contexts" is based on more than a mere difference in semantics, for there are involved differences in conceptualization, in methods of approach, and in techniques of summarization, as well as differences in attending to the dynamics of actual behavior. In the final chapter in this volume Indik attempts to distill as well as to summarize the important questions raised by the earlier chapters and to indicate some of the answers or partial answers we have now obtained. He notes that much is yet to be learned, but that some significant first steps have been taken.

At this point we would like to acknowledge, with much gratitude, the help of all of the contributors to this volume and the financial support both of the Group Psychology Branch, Office of Naval Research and of the Institute of Management and Labor Relations of Rutgers — The State University, which made it possible for the contributors to meet and exchange views with their colleagues.

We would also like to express our appreciation for the competence and patience of our secretary, Louise Aerstin, who has worried with us through the many stages of this final product.

BERNARD P. INDIK
Associate Research Professor
Rutgers — The State University

F. KENNETH BERRIEN
Professor of Psychology
Rutgers — The State University

June 1967

Foreword

The need for an effective integration of knowledge concerning individuals, groups, and organizations is obvious; the means for doing this are presently obscure. This area is characterized presently by a plethora of issues, approaches, theories, nomenclatures, and findings which seemingly defy our efforts to distill and synthesize meaningful results. We can, in fact, legitimately ask whether it is reasonable or visionary to look for such integration now, since all of the social and behavioral sciences as well as the humanities, the life sciences, and physical sciences and engineering have staked out certain claims in these areas. It is not surprising, therefore, to find that many current issues in the study of groups and organizations have been perplexing social and behavioral scientists in general. Let me cite just a few instances.

How much of our research should be empirical and how much should be guided by theory, or what is the proper mix of basic and applied research? To what degree should we focus on laboratory experiments and to what degree on field research? Should we use the approaches and languages of sociology, or anthropology, or psychology, or management, or that of the systems engineers and theorists? How far can we generalize our findings from laboratory small-group research to real-life organizations or, for that matter, from a single industrial organization to academic, military, religious, or governmental organizations in general? Does this field have the clearly marked, stable first-order variables that are the necessary building blocks for a useful taxonomy? Needless to say, the present volume does not — and could not — provide answers to all these questions. It does, however, throw considerable light into many formerly dark corners and provide general guidance for fruitful future research.

The Office of Naval Research has, over the years, sponsored a substantial proportion of the research laboratory experiments involving group phenomena as well as field studies of groups and organizations in the hope that cross fertilization would produce a hybrid (interdisciplinary) synthesizing approach. The earlier research efforts sponsored by the Office of Naval Research tended to fall in the leadership area (Guetzkow, 1951; Likert, 1961; Petrullo & Bass, 1961; Sherif, 1962). The more recent ones emphasize mathematical methods, systems approaches, and models (Criswell, Solomon, & Suppes, 1962), and the interaction of different categories of variables — environmental and psychological in the case of Sells (1962); physiological and psychological in the instances of Leiderman and Shapiro (1964) and Appley and Trumbull (1967). The present volume happily combines these various disciplines and approaches (except the physiological) and provides an up-to-date summary of thinking about individuals, groups, and organizations that will inevitably influence this field greatly.

Given the fact that this volume summarizes thinking at the frontiers of research on organizations, what should we strive for in our future efforts? Certainly, like all other fields, we need better data banks and better information retrieval methods to prevent needless duplication of effort and to free the time of scarce research personnel for more creative functions than a literature search. This, in turn, seemingly would require at least minimal agreement on nomenclature to permit the use of keywords facilitating such information retrieval. That brings us back, obviously, to the subject of classification, and there is the rub. Can we agree, at this stage of development in the science of organizations, on a single nomenclature and taxonomy to replace the several that prevail, for example, Sells (1963), Indik (1963), & Haas, Hall & Johnson (1966)? Altman's chapter in the present volume is especially enlightening in this respect, showing that the more mature sciences experienced abortive attempts at taxonomy before arriving at those elaborated by Linnaeus and Mendeleev.

Certain risks inhere, of course, in consciously striving to construct a taxonomy — notably the danger of prematurely "freezing" our terms and our concepts. A good way of preventing this consists of regarding our taxonomic efforts the same way we look at theories: as something to be tested and, if found wanting, to be rejected and replaced by a better framework that its ability commands respect by virtue of its ability to generate new knowledge or to direct attention at missing information rather than merely codifying what we know already. In the meantime, our taxonomic efforts certainly bear some fruit in that they force us to consider the whole gamut of variables involved and thus help us to reject simplistic explanations such as those that have characterized — at times — both the scientific management approach and the human relations orientation to organizational research.

Like taxonomy, systems approaches deal with a large number of variables in an integrated manner. McGregor (1967) finds that the broad framework of thinking called *general systems theory* is increasingly involved in an attempt to describe, explain, and predict the structure and functioning of human organizations. Therefore, we may regard the organization as an assembly of interdependent parts which are open, organic, and sociotechnical. Professor Berrien's chapter in this volume nicely illustrates the application of systems approaches to the study of groups and organizations.

While subscribing to the general approach of the systems analysts, we must, nevertheless, recognize that human organizations — so far, at least — defy our efforts at systematic explanation because so many of the elementary relationships between even pairs of variables remain ambiguous. We need, consequently, many more studies devoted to relationships between two, three, four or more variables across a wide range of different organizations differing in size, function, goals, location, and so forth. Of course, such relationships must hold up both in the laboratory and in the field. Until we complete such research, we can expect continuing difficulty in adequately understanding human organizations.

Systematic scientific sampling of organizational phenomena will require allocation of large amounts of research money and manpower. This becomes even more apparent when we realize that research on organizations must involve an interdisciplinary, multimethod approach. Simultaneously we must increase our laboratory experiments on groups, our field studies of groups and organizations, and simulation studies like those of Guetzkow (1963) and the Romes (1963). Let us hope that society will make available the resources needed for large-scale research in this crucial area.

Recent research on the communication of scientific information (Garvey & Griffith, 1964) reinforces earlier mass media research showing the importance of face-to-face communication (Katz & Lazarsfeld, 1955; Klapper, 1960). Volumes like the present one constitute one of the best means of encouraging researchers really to understand each other's work and to experiment with different techniques, and one of the best means of obtaining social reinforcement for their labors. While this particular book has accomplished its purpose of integrating present knowledge, the information explosion and the accelerating progress of social and behavioral science fortunately ensure that there will be many more such stimulating adventures to anticipate.

BERT T. KING
Assistant Head, Group Psychology Branch
Office of Naval Research
Washington, D. C.

Bibliography

Appley, M. H., & Trumbull, R. *Psychological stress.* New York: Appleton-Century-Crofts, 1967.

Criswell, J., Solomon, H., & Suppes, P. *Mathematical methods in small group processes.* Stanford: Stanford University Press, 1962.

Garvey, W. D., & Griffith, B. C. Scientic information exchange on psychology. *Science,* 1964, 146, 1655–1659.

Guetzkow, H. (Ed.). *Groups, leadership and men.* Pittsburgh: Carnegie Institute of Technology, 1951.

Guetzkow, H., *et al. Simulation in international relations.* Englewood Cliffs, N. J.: Prentice-Hall, 1963.

Haas, E., Hall, R. H., & Johnson, N. J. Toward an empirically derived taxonomy of organizations. In R. Bowers (Ed.), *Studies on behavior in organizations.* Athens, Georgia: University of Georgia Press, 1966.

Indik, B. P. The study of organizational and relevant small group and individual dimensions. New Brunswick, N. J.: Rutgers – The State University, Technical Report 13, Contract Nonr-404(10), 1963.

Katz, E., & Lazarsfeld, P. F. *Personal influence.* Glencoe, Illinois: The Free Press, 1955.

Klapper, J. T. *The effects of mass communication.* Glencoe, Illinois: The Free Press, 1960.

Leiderman, P. H., & Shapiro, D. (Eds.). *Psychological approaches to social behavior.* Stanford: Stanford University Press, 1964.

Likert, R. *New patterns of management.* New York: McGraw-Hill, 1961.

McGregor, D. *The professional manager.* New York: McGraw-Hill, 1967.

Petrullo, L., & Bass, B. M. (Eds.). *Leadership and interpersonal behavior.* New York: Holt, Rinehart & Winston, 1961.

Rome, B. K., & Rome, S. C. Leviathan: An experimental study of large organizations with the aid of computers. In Bowers, R. (Ed.). *Studies on behavior in organizations.* Athens, Georgia: University of Georgia Press, 1963.

Sells, S. B. (Ed.). *Stimulus determinants of behavior.* New York: Ronald Press, 1963.

Sherif, M. (Ed.) *Intergroup relations and leadership.* New York: John Wiley & Sons, 1962.

Contents

I

Classification Systems for the Integration of Knowledge

II

Sociocultural Environments, Organizations, Groups, and Individuals

III

Methodological Suggestions and Theoretical Alternatives

PEOPLE, } GROUPS, AND } ORGANIZATIONS { **I**

CLASSIFICATION SYSTEMS FOR THE
INTEGRATION OF KNOWLEDGE

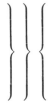

The Scope of the Problem and Some Suggestions toward a Solution[1]

BERNARD P. INDIK

Institute of Management and Labor Relations
Rutgers — The State University

The Present Major Problems

This symposium is faced with a major and significant problem. We have a tremendous research literature to cover, and we have an extremely significant and complex problem to understand with reference to that literature, that is: How may we organize this information so that we can adequately understand individual behavior in small groups which are in organizations embedded in a sociocultural environment?

First of all, the problem, as stated, is extremely complex in nature. One complexity comes from the necessity to deal with several levels of analysis: the individual, the group, the organization, and the sociocultural environment. The question here is twofold: First, why should we divide the problem according to these levels of analysis, and, second, what does this decision focus on and what does it omit? Another major problem has been the lack of an accepted general framework to guide research. This deficiency has led to the next several major problems that stand as barriers to progress in developing and integrating future research. Because of the lack of an accepted, clearly logical taxonomic framework, we have no clear understanding of what basic criteria set the specific variables to be studied. We have no long-run basis for organizing information available from past research, no basis for specifying which variables should be relevant for study when a given problem

[1] This chapter has been prepared under Contracts Nonr-404(10) and Nonr-0001, Group Psychology Branch, Office of Naval Research, Washington, D. C. Reproduction, translation, publication, use and disposal in whole or in part by or for the United States Government is permitted.

is proposed. We have no basis for deciding which of several overlapping terms should be used as definitions of the variables to be considered, or which of a myriad of operational definitions should be used.

Without an acceptable basic rationale for an underlying systematic taxonomic framework, knowledge in the area of organizational behavior will continue to proliferate in a fragmentary and unorganized manner. It will continue to seem too massive in its amount, contradictory in substance, simple-minded, fragmentary, and ungeneralizable. What then can be proposed as a possible approach to help resolve these basic problems?

Requirements of a Classification System

One basic requirement for a classification system that may help resolve these problems is to specify the levels of analysis that are necessary. It is useful to identify four levels of analysis: first, the individual; second, the group; third, the organization; and fourth, the organizational context — that is, the cultural climate, mores, implicit values, and technology — in which the individuals, groups, and organizations exist. Each of these levels of analysis reflects a social system — that is, individuals, groups, and organizations are social systems, and the organizational context is, or can be considered, a social system of a more complex nature than any of the prior three systems. In theory, one could specify several more levels of social systems that could be generated from the organizational context, but for the purposes of consideration here it is not necessary to be more detailed.

Within each of these levels of analysis it has been useful to subcategorize the variables to be considered in terms of those variables that are structural in nature as contrasted to those variables that are dynamic in nature. This basic division has been demonstrated as useful by the studies reported by McGrath (1963), Indik (1963), and Altman (1966). Miller (1965a) has also demonstrated further theoretical reasons for making this kind of distinction. For our present purposes, we may consider that individuals, groups, and organizations are various subcategories of systems, and by this we mean that, following Miller (1965a), we are interested in living systems which, of course, are a special subset of all possible systems that have the following kinds of characteristics.

Living systems are open systems; they maintain a steady state of negentropy even though entropic changes occur in them — as, of course, they do everywhere else. Living systems take in inputs of matter-energy higher in complexity of organization or in negative entropy (that is, lower in entropy) than their outputs. Furthermore, they restore their own energy from both external and internal sources and repair breakdowns in their own organization. Then, we may see that a system has a certain minimum degree of component complexity. There is some kind of basic blueprint of the structure of the system and a basic program for the development of their processes from the moment of their origin. These kinds of living systems are largely composed of protoplasm and its derivatives. These systems are integrated to form actively self-regulating developing systems with specific purposes and goals. They can exist only in a specific range of environments. Furthermore, these systems are encompassed by a recognizable boundary. This boundary is permeable.

For our present purposes we may define an *individual* as a human being functioning in a group or an organizational setting. A *group* is a social system containing a set of two or more individuals who have some systematic interaction relationship to each other and who have some common basis for their association with each other. An *organization* is a social system containing a set of two or more interrelated groups having a common status and control hierarchy and collective identity, devoted primarily to the attainment of specific goals by a program of activity. It is clear from the above that individual, group, and organization are progressively more inclusive. That is, an individual is a subsystem of a group which is a subsystem of an organization. It is apparent also that individuals, groups, and organizations are embedded in environments, the attributes of which influence the degree, manner, and nature of relationships that exist among these individuals, groups, and organizations.

Returning now to the distinction between structure and process, *structure* is used in a straightforward manner. *Structure* refers to the arrangement of a system's subsystems and components in social psychological and physical space. Here we are concerned mainly with those characteristics that tend to remain constant over time. Such structural characteristics tend to deal with distinctions associated with shape, pattern, number of components or description of other constituent materials that are basic aspects of the system. Common process classifications tend to be in terms of the variables and relationships that maintain the system in a steady state, or that deal with the adjustment processes that are mobilized to maintain those steady states. Process taxonomies may also be in terms of the system's irreversible changes or history — that is, the period of growth or decline, retardation or advancement and development as compared to other types of systems. Miller (1965b), for example, has hypothesized that systems tend to contain certain kinds of structural components in order to carry out basic functional processes. These basic structures are of three categories: those subsystems that process both matter-energy and information; those that deal only with processing matter-energy; and a third kind that deal only with processing information.

A further set of requirements of this system of variables focuses within a given subclass at a particular level of analysis either structural or process in nature and asks what should be characteristic of each of these subclasses of variables. First, each subclass of variables should be relevant to the study of individuals or small groups or organizations, or their environments. Second, each subclass of variables should be definitionally mutually exclusive from each other class of variables in the taxonomic scheme. Third, each class of variables should be related in a specific way to each other class of variables. Fourth, each class of variables should contain variables that are homogeneous in the characteristics under which they are classified.

The next basic question is: Specifically, what should the classes of variables be? Inkeles and Levinson (1963) take the position that there are basically two levels of analysis that are appropriate — the sociocultural system and the personality system — and that the analysis of their interrelationships can be made through the testing of hypotheses as to their isomorphisms. While this looks to be a rather fruitful approach, it is somewhat limited in its power to organize knowledge, since this approach cannot deal with how the classes of variables that they consider at either level of analysis are related to each other. Furthermore, they cannot deal with emergent phenomena that occur at each new level of analysis. Finally, the Inkeles-Levinson approach cannot, as yet, deal with the fact that individuals and small groups are embedded in organizational settings. The organizations are also embedded in their environments.

Sells (1962) takes a more expansive view. In his view the consideration should be more multidimensional:

(A) Organizations are behaving organisms whose behavior is represented by the coordinate composite action of their members functioning in their roles as organizational members; (B) the behavior of organizations with respect to any task or index is a predictable function of three major sources of variance, which may be referred to as (1) characteristics of the individuals participating (abilities, motivational and stylistic personality traits, background, past experience, and training, ethnic factors, etc.); (2) organizational characteristics (goals, tasks, group structure, facilities, procedures, etc.); and (3) characteristics of the physical and social environment. It is assumed that the significant portions of the variance of organizational behavioral criteria will be accounted for by factors representing these separate sources as well as by other factors representing interactions of these sources.

His general view follows the notion that the stimulus situation in its complexity and the individual in his complexity interact such as to explain the variance in the behavior of that individual. Both the individual variables and the environmental variables and their interaction affect organizational behavior variance. Our focus in this chapter will be similar to that of Sells; however, we intend to include consideration of variables at the group level as well as those that Sells has considered. We should expect also that the taxonomic system that we developed should generate systematic hypotheses that are consistent with the present findings, and should also be explanatory of future findings, much in the same way that Miller's article (1965b) on living systems generates cross-level hypotheses that are consistent with present findings and potentially fruitful for future hypothesis testing.

A Suggested Classification System

At this point it is useful to turn toward a suggested solution. The present scheme that I am dealing with has been outlined somewhat earlier (Indik, 1963), but may be more clearly specified at this time. There are seven basic classes of variables. These include the following panels:

    I. Variables associated with organizational structure.
    II. Variables associated with organizational process and function.
    III. Variables associated with small group structure.
    IV. Variables associated with small group process and function.
    V. Organizationally relevant individual attitudes, perceptions, abilities, temperaments, ascriptive dimensions and motivations.
    VI. Organizationally relevant individual behavior.
    VII. Organizational environment.

Panel I: Organizational Structure Variables

This classification area is concerned with those attributes of organizations that are relatively static in time. Such variables as the following are considered as being within this category.

A. *Size.* The number of individuals who are members of the organization by organizational criteria.

B. *Span of control.* The average number of individuals who are responsible to a supervisor.

C. *The number of hierarchical levels in the organization.* The number of layers of authority between the highest and the lowest member of the organization.

D. *The authority structure.* The pattern of influence present in the organization with reference to organizational activities.

E. *The communication structure.* The pattern of one-way and two-way information passing connections between individuals.

F. *The degree of task specification.* The extent to which the roles and tasks within the organization are described and formalized.

G. *The degree of task interdependence.* The extent to which the tasks of the different roles are interrelated with each other.

H. *Task specialization.* The extent to which jobs are fragmented and made smaller parts of the whole function of the organization.

I. *The status and prestige structure.* The distribution pattern of status and prestige attributed to role occupants in the organization.

J. *The psychological distance between the decision makers and the operating level in the organization.*

Panel II: Organizational Function or Process Variables

A. *Communication.* The process by which individuals send and receive information to and from other individuals within the organization (Bales, 1950).

1. The average amount of communication interaction within the organization.
   - The amount of task-oriented communication.
   - The amount of socioemotional communication.
   - The amount of inappropriate communication (to the organization).
2. The distribution of communication interaction within the organization.

B. *Control.* The process by which individuals or groups influence each other within the organizational setting.

1. The average amount of influence exerted by members in the organization.
2. The distribution of influence exerted by members in the organization.
3. The discrepancy between the actual distribution of influence and the desired distribution of influence in the organization.

C. *Coordination.* The process by which the parts of the organization are geared and articulated toward the objectives of the whole organization.

1. The extent to which the parts of the organization are geared and articulated toward the objectives of the organization.
2. The clarity of understanding of the goals of the organization by the members.

3. The extent to which the parts of the organization are articulated in time sequence toward the objectives of the organization.

D. Organizational socialization-integration processes. The processes by which the organization obtains members to replace and/or increase its size and adapt these members for behavior valuable to the system by differential reward values such as pay, promotions, and status.

1. Recruitment process. The process by which and the extent to which members are selected from the population available and placed in the roles allocated by the organizational system.

2. Orientation and adaptation process. The process by which and the extent to which members are oriented (and/or conditioned) to the needs of the organization.

3. Reward process. The process by which and the extent to which members are rewarded (with pay, status, and promotions) for attitudes and behavior desired by the organization.

E. Supervision. The process by which and the extent to which managers facilitate the objectives of the organization through the use of their administrative, human-relations, and technical skills.

1. Initiating structure. The extent to which supervision facilitates task performance by allocating tasks clearly and understandably.

2. Consideration. The extent to which supervision facilitates satisfaction of the socioemotional needs of the members.

3. Leadership style. The extent to which the approach of supervision is distributed closer to the authoritarian or democratic (participative) end of the continuum (or possibly the "laissez-faire" corner if the continuum should be considered a triangle).

4. Supervisory skill mix. The distribution of supervisory skills (administrative, human relations, and technical) operating in the organization.

F. Adaptability to change. The extent to which the organization and its members can adjust to internal and external changes in a manner that promotes the survival and development of the organization.

1. Adaptability to internal changes.
2. Adaptability to external changes that are relevant to the organization.
3. Rate of change.

G. Conflict control process. The extent to which conflicts of needs or interests are resolved toward the more effective operation of the organization toward its objectives.

1. The amount of tension and conflict.
2. The amount of conflict resolution and tension reduction.
3. The discrepancy between G1 and G2.

H. The mutual understanding of reciprocal role relations. The degree to which role expectations in the organization are clear to those who are interdependent in their relationships.

I. The degree of bureaucracy. The proportion of behavior that is controlled by specified rules and regulations of the organization.

J1. Amount of communication interaction by members of the organization with nonmembers for organizational purposes.

J2. Distribution of communication interaction by members of the organization with nonmembers for organizational purposes.

It can be seen from the above listings of variables within these first two panels of variables that they are not sets of mutually exclusive variables. Ideally, they should be such; however, the present state of the field only allows us the possibility to enumerate a wide range (possibly not inclusive enough) of variables within the two organizational panels. It remains for our future research ventures to measure adequately the variables in these domains and clarify and indicate which are the genotypic categories that should be used in our research schema. The same problems exist to a greater or lesser degree in all seven of the panels under study here.

Panel III: Small-Group Structure Variables

This domain is concerned with those variables of groups that are relatively static in time. Such variables as the following are seen as being in this category:

A. Size of the group. The number of individuals who are members of the group by the group's criteria of membership.

B. The authority and influence structure of the group. The pattern of interpersonal control present in the group with reference to group activities.

C. The communication structure of the group. The pattern of one-way and two-way information passing connections between individuals in the group.

D. The degree of task specification. The extent to which the roles and tasks within the group are proscribed and formalized.

E. The degree of task interdependence. The extent to which the tasks of the different roles are interrelated with each other.

F. The degree of task specialization. The extent to which jobs are fragmented and made smaller parts of the whole function of the group.

G. The status and prestige structure of the group. The distribution pattern of status and prestige attributed to role occupants in the group.

H. The psychological distance between the leader(s) of the group and the rest of its members.

Panel IV: Group Function or Process Variables

A. *Communication.* The process by which individuals send and receive information to and from each other within the group (Bales, 1950).

   1. The average amount of communication interaction.

   2. The distribution of communication interaction.

   3. The proportion of socioemotional negative communications.

   4. The proportion of socioemotional positive communications.

   5. The proportion of "ask for information" communications.

   6. The proportion of "giving information" communications.

   7. The amount and distribution of communications by members of the group with the larger system in the organization.

   8. The amount, proportion, and distribution of communication interaction by members of the group with nonmembers of the organization.

B. *Control.* The process by which individuals influence each other within groups.

   1. The average amount of influence exerted by members in the group.

   2. The distribution of influence exerted by members in the group.

   3. The discrepancy between the actual distribution of influence and the desired distribution of influence in the group.

   4. The amount of influence from the larger system.

C. *Coordination.* The process by which the parts of the group are geared and articulated toward the objectives of the whole organization.

   1. The extent to which parts of the group are geared and articulated toward the objectives of the organization.

   2. The clarity of understanding of the goals of the group by the members.

   3. The extent to which the parts of the group are articulated in time sequence toward the objectives of the larger organization.

D. *Group socialization-integration processes.* The processes that provide for the needs of the group by bringing in members and developing norms and rewarding the members for behavior valuable to the system by differential reward values such as pay, promotions, and status.

   1. Recruitment process. The process by which and the extent to which members of the group are selected from the population available and placed in the roles allocated by the group.

   2. Orientation and adaptation process. The process by which and the extent to which members of the group are oriented (trained and/or conditioned) to the needs of the group.

   3. Reward process. The process by which and the extent to which

members are rewarded (with pay, status, and promotions) for attitudes and behavior desired by the group.

E. Supervision. The process by which and the extent to which supervisors (leaders) of groups facilitate the objectives of the group through the use of their administrative, human relations, and technical skills.

1. Initiating structure. The extent to which supervision (leaders) facilitates task performance by allocating tasks clearly and understandably.

2. Consideration. The extent to which supervision (leaders) facilities the satisfaction of the socioemotional needs of the group members.

3. Leadership style. The extent to which the approach of supervision (leadership) is distributed either closer to the authoritarian or democratic (participative) end of the continuum (or possibly the "laissez-faire" corner, if the continuum should be considered a triangle).

4. Supervisory skill mix. The distribution of supervisory (leadership) skills (administrative, human relations, and technical) operating in the group.

F. Adaptability to change. The extent to which the group and its members can adjust to internal and external changes in a manner that promotes the survival and development of the group.

1. Adaptability to internal changes.

2. Adaptability to external changes that are relevant to the group.

3. Rate of change.

G. Conflict control processes. The extent to which conflicts of needs or interests are resolved toward the more effective operation of the group toward its goals.

1. The amount of tension and conflict.

2. The amount of conflict resolution and tension reduction.

3. The discrepancy between G1 and G2.

H. The mutual understanding of reciprocal role relations. The degree to which role expectations in the group are clear to those who are interdependent in their relationships.

I. The degree of bureaucracy. The proportion of behavior that is controlled by specified rules and regulations of the group.

J1. Amount of communication interaction by members of the group with nonmembers for organizational purposes.

J2. Distribution of communication interaction by members of the group with nonmembers for organizational purposes.

It can be seen, once again, from the above listings of variables within the third and fourth panels of variables, that they are not sets of mutually exclusive variables. Ideally they should be such; however, the present state of the field only allows us the possibility to enumerate a wide range (possibly not inclusive enough) of variables within the two small group panels.

Panel V: Organization and Group-Relevant (Nonbehavioral) Individual Variables

In this panel we are going to attempt to place those nonbehavioral psychological variables that have relevance to and mediate between the organizational variables and individual behaviors in these organizational and small group settings. While any arbitrary set of variables considered might be inexhaustive of this domain, our intention will be to include as many separable and relevant variables as seem appropriate. We will let subsequent empirical analysis and present conceptual criteria govern our choices.

A. *Motivational variables.* This subcategory of variables will reflect the forces that impel responses toward or away from a class of goal objects, persons, or ideas generally found in small group and organizational settings (see Murray, 1955).

1. Need for achievement. The degree to which an individual wants to perform at a high degree of excellence.

2. Need for affiliation. The degree to which an individual wants to be included and feels that he belongs in a group or organization. The converse of this is the need for independence, that is, the degree to which he wants to be autonomous.

3. Need for power. The degree to which an individual desires to control others and the converse, that is, to be controlled by others. This is related to authoritarianism.

4. Need for ego support, status, and recognition. The degree to which the individual wants to be appreciated and receive positive evaluations of himself in the group and organizational setting.

5. Need for affection. The degree to which an individual wants to like others and be liked by others.

6. Need for acquisition. The degree to which an individual wants material things, that is, money.

B. *Attitudinal variables.* An enduring system of positive or negative evaluations, emotional feelings, and pro or con action tendencies with respect to a social object, position, person, or system. (Krech, Crutchfield, & Ballachey, 1962).

1. Attitude toward the organization. The enduring system of positive or negative evaluations, emotional feelings, and pro or con action tendencies with respect to the work organization and its top management.

2. Attitude toward supervision. The enduring system of positive or

negative evaluations, emotional feelings, and pro or con action tendencies with respect to his immediate supervisors or superiors.

3. Attitude toward the work group. The enduring system of positive or negative evaluations, emotional feelings, and pro or con action tendencies with respect to the work group in which the individual finds himself.

4. Attitude toward the job. The enduring system of positive or negative evaluations, emotional feelings, and pro or con action tendencies with respect to the work position the individual fills in the organization.

Intrinsic job satisfaction. The degree to which an individual feels his needs satisfied by the activities performed on his job.

Extrinsic job satisfaction. The degree to which an individual feels his needs satisfied by the rewards and punishments associated with his job performance.

5. Attitude toward influential ancillary organizations. The enduring system of positive or negative evaluations, emotional feelings, and pro or con action tendencies with respect to influential ancillary organizations such as unions or professional organizations, or trade and fraternal associations.

C. *Perceptual role relations variables.* This category of variables includes those variables reflecting aspects of the organizational environment that impinge on the individual and are perceived by the individual but that have not been covered in other categories so far.

1. Discrepancies between the organizationally relevant expectations of the individual and his experiences as he sees them.

2. Job-related stress. A set of forces that impinge on an individual on the job as seen by the individual.

3. Role conflict (taken from Wolfe & Snoek, 1962). This occurs when two or more sets of role pressures are incompatible with each other.

D. *Aptitude variables.* The variables in this subcategory reflect the capacities of the individuals to perform organizationally relevant behaviors, and in this sense form upper and lower limits on their behavioral tendencies. A capacity can only be exercised to the degree it is present.

1. Perceptual. The senses of vision, audition, taste, smell, cutaneous senses, kinesthesis, and equilibrium are considered in this category.

    Color sensitivity
    Attention
    Length estimation
    Sensitivity to visual movement
    Auditory sensitivity (range of frequencies)
    Pitch discrimination
    Loudness discrimination
    Auditory integral (tone duration discrimination)
    Kinesthetic sensitivity

Balance control
Taste
Smell
Cutaneous senses

2. Psychomotor dimensions are from Guilford (1959).
- Strength
  (1) General strength
  (2) Trunk strength
  (3) Limb strength
- Impulsion
  (1) General reaction time
  (2) Limb thrust
  (3) Tapping
  (4) Articulation speed
- Motor speed. This subcategory can be distinguished from the impulsion subcategory by the fact that it tends to emphasize the rate of movement after it has been initiated.
  (1) Arm speed
  (2) Hand speed
  (3) Finger speed
- Static precision
  (1) Static balance
  (2) Arm steadiness
- Dynamic precision
  (1) Dynamic balance
  (2) Arm aiming
  (3) Hand aiming
- Coordination. The variables in this subcategory involve the use of patterns of muscles in combination and in sequence.
  (1) Gross body coordination
  (2) Hand dexterity
  (3) Finger dexterity
- Flexibility. This subcategory, finally, includes variables reflecting upon the looseness of the joints and determining the range of movements of parts associated with the trunk and the legs.
  (1) Trunk flexibility
  (2) Leg flexibility

3. Intellectual abilities, also from Guilford (1959) include a group of memory abilities and a group of thinking abilities. The list of **memory abilities** follows.
- Substantive memory variables
  (1) Visual memory
  (2) Auditory memory
  (3) Memory span
  (4) Memory for ideas

- Associative memory variables
    - (1) Rote memory
    - (2) Meaningful memory
- Memory for systems variables
    - (1) Memory for spatial position
    - (2) Memory for temporal order

There is a larger group of **cognitive factors.**

- Factors for knowing units
    - (1) Visual cognition
    - (2) Auditory cognition
    - (3) Symbolic cognition
    - (4) Verbal comprehension
- Factors for knowing classes
    - (1) Figural classification
    - (2) Semantic classification
- Factors for knowing relations
    - (1) Eduction of figural relations
    - (2) Eduction of symbolic relations
    - (3) Eduction of semantic relations
- Factor for knowing patterns or systems
    - (1) Spatial orientation
    - (2) Eduction of symbolic patterns
    - (3) General reasoning
- Factors for knowing implications
    - (1) Perceptual foresight
    - (2) Conceptual foresight
- Convergent thinking factors
    - (1) Factors for producing names
        - Object naming
        - Concept naming
    - (2) Factors for producing correlates
        - Eduction of symbolic correlates
        - Eduction of semantic correlates
    - (3) The ordering factor for the production of system
    - (4) Factors for the production of transformation
        - Visualization
        - Symbolic redefinition
        - Semantic redefinition
    - (5) Factors for production of unique implications
        - Symbol substitution
        - Numerical facility
- Divergent thinking factors
    - (1) Factors involving production of units
        - Word fluency
        - Ideational fluency

   (2) Factors involving spontaneous shifts of classes
         Semantic spontaneous flexibility
         Figural spontaneous flexibility
   (3) Factor of associational fluency, for producing correlates
   (4) Factor of expressional fluency, for production of systems
   (5) Factors involving divergent transformations
         Figural adaptive flexibility
         Symbolic adaptive flexibility
         Originality
   (6) Factor involving varied implications
         Elaboration

● Evaluative factors, having have to do with testing information and conclusions as to their suitability, acceptability, goodness, or correctness.
   (1) Factors involving judgments of identity
         Figural identification
         Symbolic identification
   (2) Factors involving judgments of relations
         Logical evaluation
         Symbolic manipulation
   (3) Factors for judging in terms of systematic consistency
         Experiential evaluation
         Judgment, the ability to make wise choices of action in a somewhat ambiguous situation
   (4) Factor involving judgments of goal satisfaction
         Sensitivity to problems, recognizing that a problem exists

It is clear that organizational and small-group variables do not affect these ability variables in the same sense that they may influence the other variables in this panel (except that a number of group variables do seem to affect individual judgments in group situations). In this case we feel justified in placing an ability or aptitude set of categories in the overall picture for two reasons. First, the organizational requirements of role performers, both in the group and in the organization, affect the ability mix that is found in a particular group or organization through the processes of selection, promotion, attrition, and so forth. Secondly, the organizational and group structure and processes influence the exercise of these abilities and aptitudes. As well, these abilities and aptitudes affect organizationally relevant behavior. Clearly much taxonomic research has been done in abilities and aptitudes, but more research needs to be done on how these abilities variables fit into the larger picture.

    E. Dimensions of temperament. Temperamental traits have to do with the personality tendencies of the individuals. We are concerned here with the characteristics of the dispositions of the individuals in the groups in the organizational settings. This area is less clearly organized than the abilities area, but there is some clear evidence that supports a breakdown such as the one that follows (Guilford, 1959). Further, it is relevant to consider temperament in this general panel of variables, since it is a nonbehavioral characteristic of individuals in organizational and small-group environments that is influenced by these environmental factors and is in turn influential on organizationally relevant individual behavior.

1. Factors of general disposition.
   Confidence vs. inferiority feelings
   Alertness vs. inattentiveness
   Impulsiveness vs. deliberateness
   Restraint vs. rhathymia. This dimension can be described in terms of the comparison of the self-controlled, serious, and conscientious disposition and the happy-go-lucky and carefree disposition.
   Objectivity vs. hypersensitivity
2. Factors of emotional disposition.
   Cheerfulness vs. depression
   Emotional immaturity vs. maturity
   Nervousness vs. composure
   Stability vs. cycloid disposition
   Poise vs. self-consciousness
3. Factors of social disposition.
   Ascendance vs. timidity
   Socialization vs. self-sufficiency. This dimension is definable in terms of dependency vs. independence.
   Social initiative vs. passivity
   Friendliness vs. hostility
   Tolerance vs. criticalness
4. Masculinity vs. femininity.
5. Personal tempo, rate of movement.
6. Perseveration. Mental inertia or lag (rigidity) vs. quickness and originality.
7. Oscillation. The tendency for an individual to be variable in his behavior vs. the tendency to be stable.
8. Suggestibility.
   Primary suggestibility. This involves motoric reactions consequent to verbal suggestions.
   Secondary suggestibility. This involves unwarranted or illusory sensory or perceptual outcomes consequent to verbal suggestion.
   Prestige suggestibility. How strongly the individual accepts the opinions of authorities or peers.

   F. Ascriptive dimensions. Descriptive characteristics that place persons in specific categories relative to the positions they may hold in organizations.

1. Age
2. Sex
3. Level of formal education
4. Race
5. General physical condition
6. Past training
7. Ethnicity
8. Religion

Panel VI: *Organizationally Relevant Individual Behavior Variables*

A. *Member job outputs.* This category of variables is concerned with both the quantity and quality of behavior in job output units. Job outputs can range from the number and quality of "widgets" assembled by an assembler to the number and quality of plans made by a corporate board chairman or a university president. Included in this category are leadership behaviors as well as other organizationally relevant performances.

1. Relative number of job cycle units per unit time (repetitive jobs). The relative number of behavior cycles completed per unit time to produce a unit of organizationally relevant behavior.

2. Relative quality of job performance in repetitive type jobs. Quality is determined in and by organization criteria.

3. Relative amount of job performance of unequal units of job performance in complex jobs. The relative number of job performances of varying units of behavior including planning, decision-making, organizing, and influencing the behavior of others. This category is guided by a relativistic view of the distribution of this kind of behavior. That is, any given organization or group may have changing requirements over time. The consideration here is how well the distribution of this behavior reflects the needs of the system.

4. The relative quality of performance of unequal units of job performance in complex jobs. The qualitative complement to 3.

B. *Member Participation.* The relative frequency of attendance when attendance is expected by the organization. This variable may be indicated by such measures as:

1. Attendance rates (one minus absence rates)
2. One minus turnover rates
3. One minus lateness rates

C. *Strain symptoms.* This category of variables refers to the behavioral forces generated within a system in response to stress. Phenomenologically they are indicated by discomfort and malfunction.

1. Rate of behavior inappropriate to the organization. Frequency of dysfunctional behavior relative to the organization's requirements.

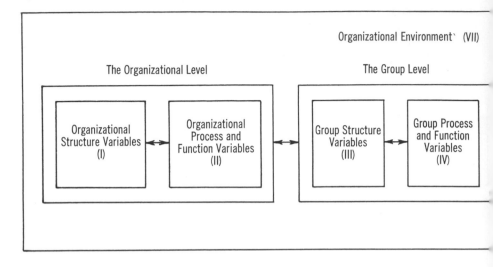

2. Rate of behavior inappropriate to the individual.
3. Rate of behavior inappropriate to the group.

Panel VII: Organizational Environment Variables

Recently Sells (1963) has attempted to develop a classification listing of aspects of the "total stimulus situation" for the individual. We are here attempting to develop such a classification system for the organization. That is, we are intending to develop a category scheme for the variables that impinge on the organization from its environment.

A. *Natural aspects of the environment.*

1. Weather in which the organization exists.
2. Gravity.
3. Terrain (rivers, lakes, deserts, altitude).
4. Natural resources.

B. *Availability of resources needed by the organization.*

1. Personnel resources.
2. Material resources.
3. Financial resources.
4. Market resources.
5. Technological resources.

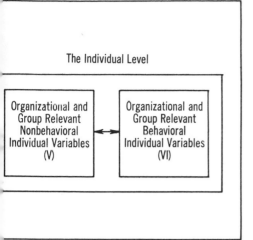

The Individual Level

Organizational and Group Relevant Nonbehavioral Individual Variables (V) ←→ Organizational and Group Relevant Behavioral Individual Variables (VI)

Figure 1. Relation of variables in a basic classification structure. Those variables most likely to be studied together are paired by means of arrows. Each of variables I–VI may be studied in conjunction with organizational environment (VII).

C. Structure and relations with social environment.

1. Technological structure.
2. Amount of contact with nonorganizational personnel.
3. Dependence on social environment.
   a. Degree to which the social environment provides consumers of organizational products or services
   b. Degree to which the environment provides integration of the organization to the larger social system
4. The other characteristics of the social environment that influence tionship and behavior in the systems (urban-rural location, and so forth).

What does this basic classification structure imply? Figure 1 points out that variables in Panels One and Two are at the level of organizations. Variables in Panels Three and Four are at the level of the group, and variables in Panels Five and Six are at the level of individuals embedded in, and affected by, the variables found in Panel Seven, the organization environment, which variables relate to variables in the other six panels.

Figure 1 reflects several classes of hypotheses and something of the structure of the classificatory system. Ideally, variables within each of the seven panels should be mutually exclusive of each other and exhaustive of their panels. At present this is not the case, but I think we should work toward that end for the sake of clarity and parsimony. It is intended that each of the seven panels is relevant to the study of individuals in groups in organizations that are embedded in their sociocultural and economic environment.

The first six panels are considered paired in Figure 1, because it is expected that the variables in the paired panels (I and II, III and IV, V and VI) are more likely to be directly and consistently related to each other since they are at the same level of analysis. There are, however, expectations that variables in panels close to each other are more closely related than are variables in panels that are farther apart. Furthermore, it is expected that variables in Panel One are related to variables in Panel Six through their effects on variables in Panels Two, Three, Four, and Five and are conditioned by attributes of Panel Seven. That is, it is not likely that Panel One variables directly affect Panel Six variables but that they work their effects through their resultant effects on Panel Two variables, which in turn affect Panel Three variables, which affect Panel Four variables, and so forth. Furthermore, it is implied that relationships between any two variables of differing panels should be cast in the present larger framework. That is to say, the present formulation does not expect to find any relationship of exactly the same size between a variable in one panel and a variable in another panel.

Specifically, we expect larger relationships to occur between variables in panels closer together in the schema. For example, organization size, a Panel One variable, should be more clearly related to variables of organization function or process such as communication, control, or coordination than to Panel Five variables such as attitude toward the organization, attitude toward the work group, and achievement motivation. Furthermore, we would expect that any connection between organization size and these Panel Five variables would be mediated by variables found in Panels Two, Three, and Four, and as well, be conditioned by variables in Panel Seven. There will be tendencies for variables to be positively or negatively related, but the amount of that relationship and sometimes the sign of that relationship will be dependent on the conditions, relations, and interactions of other variables in those particular panels concerned, as well as variables from other panels.

Some General Reflections

Recent empirical studies such as those of Indik (1965), McGrath and Altman (1966), Stogdill (1965), and Indik *et al.* (1968) reflect very significantly on this scheme. Furthermore, there are a number of publications that reflect on the basic question of what sort of taxonomic scheme makes sense at the level of organizations. Let us take a brief look at several.

Hughes (1952) notes that in modern society there seem to be five major organizational models: the voluntary association, the military organization, the philanthropic organization, the corporation, and the family business organization. Parsons (1956) classifies organizations by the social needs towards which the organization is directed. He suggests that a useful classification scheme would divide organizations into those: (a) oriented toward economic production; (b) oriented toward political goals; (c) concerned with social integration; and (d) concerned with pattern maintenance. This initial scheme has been elaborated by Parsons and also by Eisenstadt (1958), Scott (1959), and Gordon and Babchuk (1959); but the goal orientation of the classification scheme is basic.

Blau and Scott (1962) have worked out an approach to classification based on who benefits. They point out that four populations can be discussed with reference to any given large-scale organization. They are the rank and file participants or members, the owners or managers, the clients, and the public at large.

Blau and Scott include organizations in which the prime beneficiary is:

(a) the membership. (Mutual benefit associations, for example, unions, political parties, or professional associations.)

(b) the owners. (Business concerns, for example, banks, retail stores, and industrial firms.)

(c) the clients. (Service organizations, for example, schools, hospitals, or social agencies.)

(d) The public at large. (Commonweal organizations, for example, armies and police departments.)

This technique of classification is interesting, but, as with many other unidimensional schemes, it has very much oversimplified the problem.

Etzioni (1961) has proposed a classification scheme based on the predominant pattern of compliance, that is, whether coercive, utilitarian, or normative compliance is predominant. He finds four major groups: (a) those that are predominantly coercive, (b) those that are predominantly utilitarian, (c) those that are predominantly normative, and (d) those that have dual structures, being normative-coercive (for example, combat units), utilitarian-normative (for example, the majority of unions), and utilitarian-coercive (for example, some early industries, some farms, company towns, and townships).

Van Riper (1966) has attempted to use the relative strength of power relations of the few over the many — a totalitarian versus an anarchistic dimension as a basic classification device. He illustrates six prototypes: (1) control organizations (ancient empires), (2) production organization (bureaucratic Weberian type), (3) bargaining organizations (manufacturer-dealer systems, where the lesser units have clear "rights"), (4) representative organizations (where the members band together to employ one or more persons to represent them and to do their bidding), (5) research organizations (any organizations especially dedicated to novelty, most typically being cellular organization with very flexible communication systems), and (6) communal organizations (a Quaker "sense of the meeting" endeavor). Haas, *et al.* (1966) and Caplow (1964) have attempted to develop lists of types of organizations: the first through the use of empirical analysis and the latter from a more exhaustive listing of identifiable organizations in the U.S. in the twentieth century.

All of these typologies suffer from two serious problems. They are too simple in that they are based on one or two salient factors rather than the more complex reality, and they are based only on data at the level of the organization. In order to understand human behavior in organizations, not only is it necessary to study organizations *per se,* but also to look at the groups and the individuals within them and, as well, consider the attributes of the environment in which organizations are found.

What We Are Attempting

In approaching the present series of papers several objectives ought to be considered. First, we are trying to develop an integrated approach to the study of available information related to the understanding of human organizational behavior. We are going to propose several approaches to this problem and then focus on systems of classifying knowledge in this and related fields.

One of the major problems to be faced is how to evaluate a classification system. Karl Deutsch (1966) has developed a number of evaluative criteria which he notes should be applicable to any taxonomic scheme. In his discussion of these criteria, Altman helps us make conscious decisions about the classification of knowledge relevant to understanding organizationally relevant individual behavior.

Another important problem that can be ameliorated by a scheme like that which is presented here is the reduction in the amount of semantic confusion engendered by calling the same variable by different names and by using the same names for different variables. The presently inadequate communication system among scientists would thus be facilitated, and the burgeoning number of studies that have been made could be more meaningfully integrated.

It is also useful to juxtapose seemingly unrelated material to see how meaningful their real relationships might be. For too long, the paper walls of the various disciplines have acted as dividing lines of major consequence. It seems to me that this phase has more than outlived its usefulness and ought to be put in a more reasonable perspective.

Bibliography

Altman, I. The small group field: Implications for research. In Bowers, R. (Ed.), *Studies on behavior in organizations*. Athens, Georgia: University of Georgia Press, 1966.

Bales, R. F. *Interaction process analysis*. Cambridge, Mass.: Addison-Wesley, 1950.

Blau, P. M., & Scott, W. R. *Formal organizations: A comparative approach*. San Francisco: Chandler, 1962.

Caplow, T. *Principles of organization*. New York: Harcourt, Brace & World, 1964.

Deutsch, K. Communicating codes for organizing information. *Behavioral Science*, 1966, 11, 1, 1–17

Eisenstadt, S. N. Bureaucracy and bureaucratization. *Current Sociology*, 1958, 7, 99–124.

Etzioni, A. *A comparative analysis of complex organizations*. New York: Free Press, 1961.

Gordon, C. W., & Babchuk, N. A typology of voluntary associations. *American Sociological Review*, 1959, 24, 1, 22–29.

Guilford, J. P. *Personality*. New York: McGraw-Hill, 1959.

Haas, J. E., Hall, R. H., & Johnson, N. J. Toward an empirically derived taxonomy of organizations. In R. Bowers (Ed.), *Studies on behavior in organizations*. Athens, Georgia: University of Georgia Press, 1966.

Hughes, E. C. Memorandum on going concerns. *Society for Applied Anthropology*, 1952 (unpublished paper).

Indik, B. P. *Three studies of organizational and individual dimensions of organizations*. Technical Report 15, Nonr-404(10). New Brunswick, N. J.: Rutgers – The State University, 1965.

———. *The study of organizational and relevant small group and individual dimensions*. Technical Report 13, Nonr-404(10). New Brunswick, N. J.: Rutgers – The State University, 1963.

———, Hockmeyer, M., & Castore, C. *A compendium of measures of individuals, groups and organizations relevant to the study of organizational behavior*. Technical Report 16, Nonr-404(10). New Brunswick, N. J.: Rutgers – The State University, 1968.

Inkeles, A., & Levinson, D. J. The personal system and sociocultural system in large-scale organizations. *Sociometry,* 1963, 26, 2, 217–229.

Krech, D., Crutchfield, R. S., & Ballachey, E. L. *Individual in society.* New York: McGraw-Hill, 1962.

McGrath, J. E. Systems of information in small group research studies. *Human Relations,* 1963, 16, 3, 263–277.

McGrath, J. E., & Altman, I. *Small group research.* New York: Holt, Rinehart & Winston, 1966.

Miller, J. G. Living systems: Basic concepts. *Behavioral Science,* 1965a, 10, 3, 193–237.

————. Living Systems: Cross-level hypotheses. *Behavioral Science,* 1965b, 10, 4, 380–411.

Murray, H. A. Types of human needs. In D. C. McClelland (Ed.), *Studies in motivation.* New York: Appleton-Century-Crofts, 1955.

Parsons, T. Suggestions for a sociological approach to the theory of organizations. *Administrative Science Quarterly,* 1956, 1, 63–85.

Scott, F. G. Action theory and research in social organization. *American Journal of Sociology,* 1959, 64, 4, 386–395.

Sells, S. B. *Toward a taxonomy of organizations.* Technical Report 2, Fort Worth, Texas: Texas Christian University, 1962.

————. *Approaches to the taxonomy of situations: Task or situation.* Technical Report 4, Fort Worth, Texas: Texas Christian University, 1963.

Stogdill, R. M. *Managers, employees, organizations.* Columbus, Ohio: Bureau of Business Research, Ohio State University, 1965.

Van Riper, P. P. Organizations: Basic issues and a proposed typology. In R. Bowers (Ed.), *Studies on behavior in organizations.* Athens, Georgia: University of Georgia Press, 1966.

Wolfe, D. M., & Snoek, J. D. A study of tensions and adjustment under role conflict. *J. Social Issues,* 1962, 18, 3, 102–121.

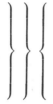

General Theoretical Problems Related to Organizational Taxonomy: A Model Solution[1]

S. B. SELLS

Institute of Behavioral Research
Texas Christian University

Introduction

The problem to which this paper is addressed is related to the tradition of "discriminatory analysis" (Hodges, 1950; Sells, 1955) and is illustrated by studies of craniotomy and physical anthropometry (Fisher, 1936; Harrower, 1928; Hasluck and Morant, 1929; Hooke and Morant, 1926; Morant, 1926; Pearson, 1926; and others). The multivariate methods implied by discriminatory analysis are useful both for establishing discriminable categories among populations of attribute profiles for organisms, objects, and also organizations, and for the critical problem of classifying individuals into established categories on the basis of tests of best fit.

My long-standing concern with these issues was recently intensified in a NASA study directed toward formulation of principles and guidelines related to group organization and interaction of crews of multiman, extended duration space ships, such as on the Mars mission. In the course of planning the selection of references for a critical review, the relevance of literature from a variety of sources was questioned. Relevance is necessary for generalization of past observations and research results to new problems and depends on the similarity of

[1] A report of the Office of Naval Research Contract No. Nonr-3436(00). Reproduction, translation, publication, use, and disposal in whole or in part by or for the United States Government is permitted.

critical conditions at the source to those in the new situation. Similarity, as a determiner of relevance, can be measured only in terms of some concept of what the critical conditions are. In regarding studies of isolation, confinement, and stress in various organizational settings, such as mental hospitals, prisons, remote duty stations, disasters, mountain climbing expeditions, and the like, as possible sources for generalization to the space ship, variations among types of group situations, in personnel, task, training, goals, and other aspects, loomed very large. The need for selection and systematic ordering of systems characteristics was apparent and led to the development of a social system model that might be used as a means of comparative study. This is presented below.

The significance of system variation may be illustrated by an oversimplified example, for which I am indebted to Dr. W. A. Wilbanks. The problem is to compare the products of two typists who took down and transcribed a round-table discussion. Typist A recorded the discussion directly on a typewriter, edited the copy, and then retyped the final copy. Typist B recorded the discussion on a tape recorder, typed a draft by replaying the tape, edited the draft, and then retyped the final copy. It is apparent that the difference between the roles of the two typists, expressed by their linkages in the two systems, make any direct comparisons futile, even if they were matched on skill, experience, motivation, and other factors.

System Concepts Applied to Organizations

In their impressive contribution to *The Social Psychology of Organizations*, Katz and Kahn (1966) characterized human organizations as *open systems* with the common characteristics of importation of energy, throughput, output, cycles of events, negative entropy, information processing, steady state and dynamic homeostasis, differentiation, and equifinality.

A major feature of the system formulation is provision for the continuing transactions with the environment, which have been neglected in many earlier analyses. Katz and Kahn have ably exploited the dependency of organizations on the social, "peopled" environment, but have neglected the physical environment, which also accounts for significant variance in organizational behavior. Perhaps because of my own interest in space ships and military organizations, mentioned below, which operate under extreme environmental conditions, the omission is more striking than it might be otherwise. Nevertheless, variables representing the physical environment are included in the system model presented here, in addition to others, to be discussed.

In terms of the open system model, all organizations are character-ized by Katz and Kahn as a type of subclass of social systems, which have in common the following five component characteristics:

1. Production, production support, and maintenance structures.
2. An elaborated formal role pattern.
3. A clear authority structure.
4. Adaptive structures.
5. An ideology to support system norms.

Much understanding is achieved by these analyses of the common characteristics of organizations, as is amply illustrated in this book. The question of organizational taxonomy, however, implies a need for further clarification of systematic, perhaps lawful variations within the general model.

That major variation occurs will perhaps not be questioned. Hemphill (1956), the present writer (Findikyan & Sells, 1966), and others have found disturbing variations in intercorrelations of "organiza-tional dimensions" measured by questionnaires administered to mem-bers of student, military, university department faculty, and various industrial work groups. It is believed that such variations may be explained by differences in roles, values, and norms of persons of differ-ent ages performing different tasks or functions, with different invest-ments and motivations, and different rewards and risks. A taxonomic study of organizations may reveal that different classes of organizations show systematic variations related to critical components of the organi-zational profiles on some common set of characteristics. The justifica-tion for this paper is the belief that this is the case.

Katz and Kahn have expressed proper skepticism concerning published objectives and philosophies of organizations and have em-phasized the distinction between idealized statements of intents and empirically observed operations, which are often quite different. Yet their *typology of organizations* (Katz & Kahn, 1966, Ch. 5) is not based on empirical study, but is rather an armchair analysis which assumes four genotypic classes: productive or economic organizations, main-tenance organizations, adaptive structures, and managerial or political organizations, and further subdivides on the basis of a number of insightful second-order characteristics.

My own experience in attempting to classify organizations on the basis of Hemphill's dimensions (Findikyan & Sells, 1966) and our own revisions of these dimensions do suggest that the classification of organizations should be, at least in part, an empirical problem. The model presented here for such an effort includes many of the Katz and

and Kahn second-order characteristics, although they were arrived at independently, but is organized differently.

The Organizational Unit

There appears to be some difference of opinion with reference to the organizational unit denoted by the term *organization*. Dr. Indik appears to include both informal groups and formal organizations in his concept of organization, regardless of size, historic development, complexity of structure, or other factors, accepting any unit that has a discriminable identity. I have followed the same approach. On the other hand, others have limited the term organization to large, formal, usually business organizations, such as business corporations. From the point of view of taxonomic study, I prefer the widest possible sampling of organizations. The search for characteristics of types, classes, or subgroups of the population of organizations would be most appropriate, in my judgment, after a viable taxonomy is achieved.

Apart from the logical argument in the foregoing paragraph, there are two other propositions in favor of inclusion of *informal* groups in the general discussion. The first is that the informal group is the *natural* group, a result of efforts of man to strive cooperatively with his fellowmen to attain jointly the satisfaction of common needs which neither is able to satisfy alone. The natural group reflects "human nature" in operation and should have much value as a model in the study of human organization, as other natural models have in other scientific areas. Second, it is generally recognized that formal group structure is only a plan or blueprint or strategy for design and control of an organization. The actual group, in operation, deviates from the plan as informal structure develops, with the formal matrix as only one determiner. I have often thought that an optimal strategy for the planning of formal structures is to exploit in their design, as extensively as possible, principles of informal group development and process. If for no other reasons, it seems highly desirable to incorporate a variety of informal groups in the taxonomic study.

General Approach

In 1962, at a similar conference at the Carnegie Institute of Technology, the writer (Sells, 1964) presented an approach to the taxonomy of organizations based on a multivariate model in which the total variance of any criteria of organizational behavior could be expressed in terms of weighted combinations of variables derived from three universes — persons, organizations, and environmental setting — which were assumed to afford a comprehensive basis for such analysis.

Further research, thought, and study on this problem, during the intervening years, have raised some fundamental questions about this model and the opportunity to participate in the present symposium was welcomed as an occasion for clarification and revision.

While still convinced of the general validity of the multivariate approach to the problem and of the practical usefulness of multivariate computer programs that we have used for such problems, I have two specific, but related objections to the regression model presented at the Carnegie Tech meeting. These are related to the criteria selected as dependent variables for the regression analysis and to the inclusion of interaction variables in the schedule of predictors.

First, it now appears erroneous to me, and I wish to correct my previous recommendation on this point, that measures of organizational behavior, whether of production, participation, attendance, or whatever, should be used as a focal dimension for classifying profiles of organizational descriptors. Such criterion measures more properly reflect *organizational states* rather than types or classifications of organizations, which are more appropriately described by organizational goals and objectives. And second, objections may properly be raised at including interaction process variables in the pattern of descriptors. A distinction must be made beween the broad dimensions of different types of social situations in which people interact and the modes of interaction exemplified in their behavior. The former, which include organizational goals in the descriptor pattern, appear appropriate as a basis for a useful taxonomy, while the latter again reflect varying states and relate more to the understanding of interaction process than classification.

If these objections are accepted, the approach to a taxonomy of organizations should focus on the general system characteristics, including goals, personnel composition, organizational structure, technology, and environment, of classes of organization. Criteria of performance and measures of interaction process, reflecting varying states of individual organizations, are most relevant to the study of factors accounting for variation within classes.

A General Social System Model

The aim of this discussion is to present a formulation leading to a standard set of system characteristics that can be applied generally as a means of ordering a wide range of human organizations, groups, and microsocieties according to their similarity to each other. The tentative model outlined here is linear and does not account for interdependencies, which are observable, nor for differential weighting of components or of varying system states. However, multivariate methodology is available for differential weighting and offers an attractive prospect for such research.

The general microsociety or organizational model to be presented is a modification of one developed for the analysis of the social system of the multiman, extended-duration space ship, such as one on a voyage to Mars (Sells, 1966a), and involves the following eight major categories of description, each of which is represented by a pattern of quantitative or categorical variables.

      I. Objectives and Goals
     II. Philosophy and Value Systems
    III. Personnel Composition
    IV. Organizational Structure
     V. Technology
    VI. Physical Environment
   VII. Social-Cultural Environment
  VIII. Temporal Characteristics

Although these categories overlap, each involves important factors which can be classified or ordered to some extent on continua conducive to comparative analysis. These major components and subcomponents are developed in the discussion below.

The spaceship model did not include Category VII, Social-Cultural Environment, for the simple reason that this was not expected to vary in the context for which that model was developed. However, in the present frame of reference it is regarded as a major source of variance.

I. Objectives and Goals

This category should be represented by a set of variables of broad generality that might be the basis for differential description of every type of human group or organization. For the purpose of distinguishing the space ship from other microsocieties with common characteristics of isolation, confinement, and stress, the following seven variables were mentioned.

    1. Formal (vs. informal) designation.
    2. Mandatory vs. permissive or voluntary.
    3. Use of formal authority.
    4. Degree of polarization toward its goals.
    5. Remoteness of goals.
    6. Criteria of successful goal attainment.
    7. Success uncertainty (risk).

To these, which may be sufficient within the class of organizations mentioned, at least three other characteristics should be added to achieve broad generality. These are:

8. Unitary vs. multiple goals.
9. Degree of competition involved (with other organizations).
10. Emphasis on growth.

It is possible that this list should include some means of characterizing the content or nature of the activities to which the goals refer, but at present this does not seem necessary, as this is covered fully by the other categories.

II. Philosophy and Value Systems

In the case of the spaceship, the aspect of organizational philosophy considered to be most important involved the values accepted with respect to the relative importance attributed to alternative goals and alternative means, costs, and risks related to the attainment of the preferred goals. Whether formal or informal, every group or organization is guided by some governing value system, which may range in acceptance by members from consensus to conflict, and which may be conspicuous, as in the case of religious institutions, or covert. With the exception of formal religious organizations, the governing value systems are rarely available in documentary form, but must be inferred from a variety of sources, such as the record of critical decisions made, key appointments, speeches, directives, and correspondence of responsible leaders, and the like.

On the basis of general background, our space ship model listed six items in the Philosophy and Value Systems category, as follows:

1. Obedience to command.
2. Mission emphasis.
3. Respect for individual lives.
4. High national priority.
5. Military tradition in personnel attitudes.
6. Acceptance of the "American way of life."

Although the taxonomic model requires system components of broad generality rather than the specifically tailored items listed in the spaceship analysis, consideration of these items does indicate greater generality than may seem apparent at first glance. For example, *obedience to command* is an expression of *control of member behavior by group authority; mission emphasis* reflects the *cost* that the organizational management is willing to incur to assure goal attainment; *respect for individual lives* could be stated more broadly as *the value accorded the individual,* which may include other factors, but in the same general value scale; *national priority* could be broadened in terms of preeminence in social esteem; the *military tradition* reflects a set of attitudes regarding acceptance of discipline, respect for rank, acceptance of personal hardships and austerity, masculinity, and patriotism; and, similarly, the "American way of life" implies conformity with the dominant mores and values of the society.

Further study is necessary to arrive at a nuclear set of values that would apply to a wide range of organizations. At present, I would add the "golden rule"; respect for women, children, and aged persons; competitiveness; the "Protestant Ethic"; concepts of fairness, honesty, loyalty, responsibility, and of the "good life"; and attitudes toward wealth, power, possessions, comfort, and status.

It is apparent that many of the values suggested or specified here are interrelated with the items outlined below under *personnel composition*. And it is evident that this overlap might be reduced by multivariate analysis. Nevertheless, in specifying the model, it is desirable to distinguish explicitly between values subscribed to by organizations, in their respective formal documents or traditions, and those held by their members, even though convergence is expected in normal experience.

III. Personnel Composition

The historic preoccupation of psychologists with individual differences has made the specification of characteristics of members of organizations the least difficult task in the construction of this model. Indeed, the items listed for the spaceship can be carried over virtually without change and can also, in most cases, be measured with fair confidence.

The spaceship model listed thirteen descriptors of personnel comprising various types of groups, referring to distributions with respect to:

1. Intellectual level.
2. Educational level.
3. Extent of relevant training.
4. Extent of relevant experience.
5. Personality profiles.
6. Moral traits.
7. Physical characteristics.
8. Possession of requisite skills.
9. Motivation to participate.
10. Sex.
11. Age.
12. Division into separate caste groups (e.g. crew, passengers, owner, employee, in-group, other).
13. Rank or status.

IV. *Organization*

The spaceship model included eleven items of varying degrees of redundancy and generality, which served well for comparison of the spaceship social system with others of some degree of similarity. However, this list, enumerated below, may require extensive revision for the present purpose.

The eleven items of organization in the spaceship model are:

1. Formal structure.
2. Prescribed roles.
3. Command structure.
4. Centralized authority.
5. Chain of command with provision for succession.
6. Extensive back-up organization.
7. Low autonomy in regard to goals.
8. Group size (8–12).
9. Prescribed discipline.
10. Low prescribed social distance among crew.
11. Congruency of rank and status.

A revised outline, phrased more appropriately for the taxonomic task, involves five major components and twenty subcomponents, as follows:

1. Size.
2. Differentiation.
   a. By subgroups
   b. By levels
   c. By existence of an in-group
3. Autonomy.
   a. Dependence on outside control
   b. Dependence on outside support
4. Control.
   a. Centralization
   b. Degree of control of member behavior
   c. Span of control
   d. Sanctions available
   e. Flexibility
   f. Communication channels
   g. Communication facilities
   h. Openness of expression
5. Role structure.
   a. Degree of formalization
   b. Stratification by rank or status levels

    c. Hierarchical relations
    d. Succession
    e. Status congruency
    f. Interpersonal distance
    g. Participation in organizational affairs
    h. Permeability of entrance and exit rules

Inasmuch as neither the terminology nor the dimensionality of organizational structure is standardized, the foregoing list of organizational components is highly tentative. However, it may serve to exemplify the type of system structure required.

V. Technology

The spaceship is technologically highly complex in the tradition of high-altitude, high-performance aviation. It makes extensive use of simulators and other technical training devices, depends on exhaustive training for every mission, uses highly technical language in execution of its missions, including a recondite jargon of abbreviations and acronyms, requires painstaking physical preconditioning of equipment and personnel for missions, and depends on scientific principles throughout. The spaceship model was tailored to these distinctive features.

For the taxonomic study, the subcategories of technology must be expanded to embrace a wide range of development, in which the spaceship may well represent one extreme. Here again, overlap with personnel requirements is apparent, but essential for specification of the model.

To accomplish an adequate specification of the range of technology in modern industrial society, it is necessary to define broad areas by content as well as complexity. This is suggested in the following list, but the details are not presented. Further consultation will be required before this list can be completed. The tentative breakdown of technology is as follows.

    1. Functions involved
       (for example, power, transportation, trade, manufacturing).
    2. Products or services involved.
    3. Types of equipment employed.
    4. Degree of technologic complexity.
    5. Use of specialized principles
       (for example, science, mathematics, and artistic or aesthetic principles).
    6. Use of specialized terminology.

7. Special conditions of operation
(for example, simulatory, technical training devices, physical preconditioning, and extensive preparation for events).

VI. *Physical Environment*

The physical environment is more prominent in the case of activities involving hazard, isolation, and various extreme conditions, than in more commonplace activities. Nevertheless, the effects of climate, terrain, distance from significant associates, limitation on mobility, visibility of surrounds, and other aspects of the physical environment account for more behavioral variation than is commonly recognized. Geographic factors have long been recognized in human ecology and must be incorporated in the description of social systems. An extensive taxonomic outline of physical environmental variables has been presented by the writer (Sells, 1963) elsewhere, with the following items: gravity; weather (temperature, humidity, oxygen, atmospheric pressure, climate, and atmospheric changes producing storms, rain, showers, hurricanes, typhoons, and so forth); terrain (rivers, lakes, mountains, valleys, deserts, altitude, erosion, stability-earthquakes, and so forth); and natural resources, including sources of food, shelter, clothing, minerals, and timber. These are incorporated in the model along with additional items carried over from the model for the space ship. The resulting outline is as follows.

1. Gravity.
2. Weather.
3. Terrain.
4. Natural resources.
5. Requirements for life support or physiologic protection.
6. Remoteness of site.
7. Presence of environmental hazards (known and unknown).
8. Confinement.
9. Endurance demands.
10. Restriction of communication.
11. Social isolation.
12. Mobility permitted.
13. Embedded environmental stresses.
14. Types of structures.
15. Types of furnishings.

This list includes items referring to the locale of the organization as well as the site. For some purposes it might be indicated to specify extensive detail under the category headings, while for a broad survey considerably less detail may be appropriate. This point is discussed below.

VII. Social-Cultural Environment

This component of the system was omitted in the space ship model, as mentioned earlier, on the grounds that it represented a source of variation held more or less constant in the context of that study. On reflection, I believe that this can be defended, but the dimensions of the social and cultural environment are certainly of major importance for the broad taxonomic study.

For any comprehensive analysis, it should be noted that Murdock and his associates (1961) distinguished eighty-eight significant categories in their *Outline of Cultural Materials* for the Human Relations Area Files developed at Yale University. These include *language, demography, history and culture change, total culture, communication, records, food quest, animal husbandry, agriculture, food processing,* and other categories pertaining to the modes of living, industrialization, economy, education, art, religion, organization, stratification, and other important aspects of cultures over the world.

For studies within a culture, many of these might be eliminated. However, the complete list is instructive as a guide to the complexity of the social-cultural environment which may influence organizations and their system characteristics. The following list of social-cultural characteristics has been adapted from Murdock et al. (1961). Although it is subject to refinement for the present purpose, it well illustrates the approach proposed.

1. Geography.
2. Human biology.
3. Behavior process and personality.
4. Demography.
5. History and cultural change.
6. Total culture.
7. Language.
8. Communication.
9. Records.
10. Food quest.
11. Animal husbandry.
12. Agriculture.
13. Food processing.
14. Food consumption.
15. Drink, drugs, indulgence.
16. Leather, textiles, fabrics.

17. Clothing.
18. Adornment.
19. Exploitative activities.
20. Processing of basic materials.
21. Building and construction.
22. Structures.
23. Equipment and maintenance of buildings.
24. Settlements.
25. Energy and power.
26. Chemical industries.
27. Capital goods and industries.
28. Machines.
29. Tools and appliances.
30. Property.
31. Exchange.
32. Marketing.
33. Finance.
34. Labor.
35. Business and industrial organization.
36. Travel and transportation.
37. Land transport.
38. Water and air transport.
39. Living standards and routines.
40. Recreation.
41. Fine arts.
42. Entertainment.
43. Individuation and mobility.
44. Social stratification.
45. Interpersonal relations.
46. Marriage.
47. Family.
48. Kinship.
49. Kin groups.
50. Community.
51. Territorial organization.
52. State.
53. Government activities.
54. Political behavior.
55. Law.
56. Offenses and sanctions.
57. Justice.
58. Armed forces.
59. Military technology.

60. War.
61. Social problems.
62. Health and welfare.
63. Sickness.
64. Death.
65. Religious beliefs.
66. Religious practices.
67. Ecclesiastical organization.
68. Numbers and measures.
69. Exact knowledge.
70. Ideas about man and nature.
71. Sex.
72. Reproduction.
73. Infancy and childhood.
74. Socialization.
75. Education.
76. Adolescence, adulthood, and old age.

Although many of these items apply to social systems and culture viewed in "macroperspective," it seems advisable to include them in the complete list. Furthermore, examination of the list suggests that many of these have significant analogs in a "microperspective," as well.

VIII. Temporal Characteristics

The spaceship model assumed a "total organization" in the sense that the term has been used by Goffman (1957), of occupying the total time of its members during their periods of participation. This was referred to as "total participation," which is the upper extreme of a continuum that must be permitted to vary in the more general model. This item has been restated to represent the proportion of daily time time required in participation. With this change, the temporal items are as follows:

1. Duration of participation.
2. Amount of daily participation required.
3. Remoteness of goals.

System Taxonomy and Organizational Classification

A methodological model for the taxonomic problem of grouping organizations according to profile similarity on a set of system characteristics was presented by Findikyan and Sells (1966) in a study of the similarity of campus student organizations assessed through a hierarchical grouping procedure. In this study, two sets of profiles were used, one consisting of thirteen group dimensions measured by the Hemphill Group Dimensions Description Questionnaire, and the other, from factor scores derived from the thirteen Hemphill dimensions. Both profiles were quite limited in comparison with the full range of the social system model presented above, but the hierarchical grouping method is based on analysis of D^2 matrices and is applicable equally to profile distance measures computed over system profiles, as suggested in this paper. The clustering procedure involves the use of a computer program which groups by an iterative hierarchical grouping procedure applied to matrices of interprofile distance measures (D^2) between the profiles of each organization and every other organization in the sample.

The Similarity Index (D^2)

The D^2 statistic is well known and requires no expository discussion in this paper.[2] However, as we discovered in this study, in which two D^2 matrices were analyzed, the values of D^2 obtained and the intercluster distance values obtained depend on the metric of the measures in the profiles and the numbers of variables in the profiles. Concerning metric, it is desirable to use standard scores when the metric varies. For any study, it is desirable to use the same variables throughout. However, comparison of results of studies with different numbers of variables presents a problem for which there is no easy solution.

Another problem affecting any measure of interprofile distance occurs when variables in the profiles are correlated. The D^2 measure tends to weight the salient factors heavier than others. While this may be acceptable for many purposes, it is a fact that should be recognized.

Hierarchical Grouping

Hierarchical grouping is generically a method of hierarchical cluster analysis which obtains an optimal grouping of a set of entities (for example, organizations) such that the average distance within a cluster is at a minimum at each stage of iteration. For any large matrix (of 50 or over) analysis of a matrix of distance measures without a computer would be unwieldly, if not impracticable. However, such analyses can be performed by computers with relative facility and amazing speed.

The iteration starts with a search for the minimum distance in the N (N-1) /2 matrix of distance measures. The two organizations having

---

[2] See Cronbach and Gleser (1953), Sawrey, Keller, and Conger (1960), Findikyan and Sells (1966) and others.

TABLE 1. Comparison of Social System Profiles of Eleven System Patterns with that of the Extended Duration Space Ship

System Characteristics	Comparison System										
	1	2	3	4	5	6	7	8	9	10	11
I. Objectives and Goals											
1. Formally prescribed	1	2	2	2	2	2	2	0	1	1	1
2. Mandatory	1	2	2	2	2	1	1	0	1	1	1
3. Formal authority	1	2	2	2	2	1	1	0	1	1	1
4. Polarization	2	1	1	2	1	2	1	0	0	0	0
5. Remoteness of goals	1	2	2	0	2	1	1	0	2	0	0
6. Success criteria	2	2	1	2	0	2	1	0	2	1	1
7. Success uncertainty	2	2	2	2	1	2	1	2	2	0	0
II. Value Systems											
8. Obedience to command	1	2	2	2	2	1	1	0	1	0	0
9. Mission emphasis	1	2	2	2	2	1	1	0	0	0	0
10. Respect for individual lives	2	2	2	2	2	0	1	0	1	0	1
11. High national priority	0	1	1	1	1	0	0	0	0	0	0
12. Military tradition in personal attitudes	0	2	2	1	1	0	0	0	2	0	0
13. Acceptance of American way of life	0	2	2	1	1	0	0	0	0	0	0
III. Personnel Composition											
14. Intellectual	1	1	0	0	0	0	0	0	0	0	0
15. Educational level	1	1	0	0	0	0	0	0	0	0	0
16. Extent of relevant training	1	1	1	0	1	1	1	0	1	0	0
17. Extent of relevant experience	2	1	1	0	0	1	1	0	0	1	0
18. Personality selectivity	1	1	0	1	0	0	0	0	0	0	0
19. Moral selectivity	1	1	0	1	1	0	0	0	0	0	0
20. Physical selectivity	1	1	1	1	1	1	0	0	1	0	0
21. Possession of requisite skills	2	1	1	1	1	2	1	0	0	0	0
22. Motivation to participate	2	1	0	0	0	1	0	0	0	0	0
23. Sex of participants	2	2	2	2	2	2	0	0	2	0	0
24. Age range	1	1	0	0	0	2	0	0	0	0	0
25. Presence of non-crew personnel	2	1	0	0	0	0	0	0	0	0	0
26. Rank distribution (all "officers")	1	0	0	0	0	0	0	0	0	0	0
IV. Organization											
27. Formal structure	1	2	2	2	2	1	1	0	1	0	0
28. Prescribed roles	2	2	2	2	2	1	1	0	1	0	0
29. Command structure	1	2	2	2	2	1	0	0	1	0	0
30. Centralized authority	1	2	2	2	2	1	0	0	0	0	0
31. Chain of command with provision for succession	1	2	2	2	2	0	0	0	1	0	0
32. Extensive back-up organization	1	2	2	2	2	0	0	0	1	0	0
33. Low autonomy re goals	1	2	2	2	2	0	1	0	0	0	0
34. Group size (8–12)	0	0	0	0	0	0	0	0	0	0	0
35. Prescribed discipline	1	2	2	2	2	1	0	0	1	2	1
36. Low prescribed social distance among crew	2	0	0	0	2	0	0	0	0	0	0
37. Congruency of rank and status	2	2	1	1	1	0	0	0	0	0	0

V. Technology

38. High technologic complexity	1	2	1	1	1	0	0	0	0	0	0
39. Relation to aviation tradition	0	1	1	1	2	0	0	0	0	0	0
40. Use of simulators and other technical training devices	0	1	1	1	1	0	0	0	0	0	0
41. Extensive preparation for missions	2	1	1	1	0	1	0	0	0	0	0
42. Use of technical language in execution	2	2	1	1	1	1	0	0	0	0	0
43. Physical preconditioning	1	1	1	1	0	1	0	0	0	0	0
44. Scientific principles involved	1	1	1	1	1	0	0	0	0	0	0

VI. Physical Environment

45. Required physiological protection and life support	1	2	0	0	0	0	0	0	0	0	0
46. Extreme remoteness from base	1	1	1	1	1	0	0	1	2	1	1
47. Presence of unknown environmental hazards	2	1	1	1	0	0	0	2	2	0	1
48. Extreme confinement in capsule	0	1	0	0	1	0	0	0	2	2	2
49. High endurance demands	2	1	0	0	0	1	0	2	2	0	0
50. Reduced communication	1	1	1	1	1	0	0	2	2	2	2
51. Social isolation	1	1	1	1	1	0	0	2	2	2	2
52. Maneuvering situation	2	1	1	1	0	1	0	0	0	0	0
53. Embedded environmental stresses	2	2	1	1	1	0	0	0	2	0	1

VII. Temporal Characteristics

54. Long duration of exposure	1	1	1	1	1	0	0	0	2	2	2
55. Total environmental situation	2	2	0	0	2	0	0	0	2	2	2
56. Remoteness of goals	1	1	1	1	1	1	0	0	2	2	2

Comparison systems 1–11 are identified in Table 2 below. Ratings indicate degree of similarity to the Extended Duration Space Ship social system on the following basis: 2 (highly similar), 1 (moderately similar), 0 (dissimilar or unrelated).

TABLE 2. Analysis of System Similarities by Descriptive Category

	System Characteristics						
Comparison Systems	I	II	III	IV	V	VI	VII
1. Exploration parties	2	1	1	1	1	1	1
2. Submarines	2	2	1	2	1	1	1
3. Naval ships	2	2	0	2	1	1	0
4. Bomber crews	2	2	1	2	1	1	0
5. Remote duty stations	2	2	0	2	1	0	1
6. Professional athletic teams	2	0	1	0	0	0	0
7. Industrial work groups	1	0	0	0	0	0	0
8. Shipwrecks and disasters	0	0	0	0	0	1	0
9. POW situations	1	1	0	0	0	2	2
10. Prison society	0	0	0	0	0	1	2
11. Mental hospital wards	0	0	0	0	0	1	2

Systems descriptions I–VII are identified in Table 1 above. Ratings indicate degree of similarity on the following basis: 2 (over 70 per cent of the items in Table 1 match), 1 (31 to 70 per cent of items match), 0 (less than 30 per cent of items match).

the smallest D^2 measure form the nucleus of a cluster. At each succeeding iteration an organization or cluster of organizations is sought which would have the smallest average distance from any of the clusters already formed. If at any point a cluster of organizations already formed is discovered to have a smaller average distance to another cluster than to any single organization not already clustered, the two will be combined into a single cluster. As this procedure progresses, average intracluster distances increase, until at the end, the entire sample becomes one heterogeneous cluster.

At this time, there are no mathematical tests of optimal intercluster and intracluster distance. However, in the studies we have done there do appear to be natural discontinuities in the arrays of such measures which facilitate judgments.

In our study of sixty campus student organizations the customary classification of some types of organization, such as fraternities, was quite satisfactory, while for others, such as an ROTC honor society, a Journalism fraternity, and others, it was empirically superficial. The use of methods of clustering, such as the model discussed here, with data based on appropriately defined variables defining significant components of the social systems involved, may provide a useful methodology both for taxonomic analysis of organizations and for classification of individual organizations according to the best fit of their profiles.

Comparison of Social System Profiles

A heuristic comparison of the spaceship social system profile with profiles of eleven other miniature social systems is made on the pages preceding, in Tables 1 and 2 (adapted from Sells, 1966b). Though not empirically based, the comparisons do show the value of the type of analysis proposed. Although based on subjective judgment and on the unweighted and preliminary set of components, the results reveal widespread differences among the twelve social systems compared and raise questions that invite serious concern about the utility to studies of the spaceship problem of some of the most frequently suggested literature sources, as well as greater interest in others, often overlooked. Until adequate evaluation is made of the influences of variations in major system characteristics on behavior of organizations and their members, extreme caution is indicated to avoid superficial judgments in generalizing research results.

Concluding Comment

The scientific literature of the behavioral sciences has repeatedly reaffirmed the importance of the ecologic viewpoint, which is essentially expressed in the social system model presented in this paper (Sells, 1966a). Recognition that organizational functioning reflects the inter-dependence of organizations and their members with the total, physical, social, and cultural environment has been amply demonstrated. The emphasis on this principle throughout this symposium is a sign of progress in organizational theory.

Bibliography

Cronbach, L. J., & Gleser, G. C. Assessing similarity between profiles. *Psychol. Bull.*, 1953, 50, 456–473.

Findikyan, N., & Sells, S. B. Organization structure and similarity of campus student organizations. *Organization Behavior and Human Performance*, 1966, 1, 169–190.

Fisher, R. A. The "coefficient of racial likeness" and the future of craniotomy. *J. Roy. Anthrop. Inst.*, 1936, 66, 57–63.

Goffman, E. The characteristics of total institutions. In *Symposium on Preventive and Social Psychiatry*, Walter Reed Army Institute of Research, Walter Reed Army Medical Center, Washington, D. C., 1957.

Harrower, G. A study of the crania of the Hylam Chinese. *Biom.*, 1928, 20B, 245–293.

Hasluck, M. M., & Morant, G. M. Measurements of Macedonian men. *Biom.*, 1929, 21, 322–336.

Hemphill, J. K. *Group dimensions. A manual for their measurement.* Ohio Studies in Personnel, Res. Monog. No. 87, Bur. Bus. Res., Ohio State University, 1956.

Hodges, J. L. *Discriminatory Analysis.* USAF School of Aviation Medicine, Report No. 1, Project 21-49-004. Randolph Field, Texas, 1950.

Hooke, B. G. E., & Morant, G. M. The present state of our knowledge of British craniology in late prehistoric and historic times. *Biom.*, 1926, 18, 99–104.

Katz, D., & Kahn, R. L. *The Social Psychology of Organizations.* New York: John Wiley and Sons, Inc., 1966.

Morant, G. M. The use of biometric methods applied to craniology, being a critique of Professor Gordon Harrower's "A study of the Hokien and Tamil skull." *Biom.*, 1926, 18, 414–417.

Murdock, G. P., Ford, C. S., Hudson, A. E., Kennedy, R., Simmons, L. W., & Whiting, J. W. M. *Outline of Cultural Materials.* (4th rev. ed.) New Haven, Conn.: Human Relations Area Files, Inc., 1961.

Pearson, K. On the coefficient of racial likeness. *Biom.*, 1926, 18, 105–117.

Sawrey, W. L., Keller, L., & Conger, J. J. An objective method of grouping profiles by distance functions and its relation to factor analysis. *Educ. Psychol. Measmt.*, 1960, 20, 651–673.

Sells, S. B. (Ed.) *Symposium on Pattern Analysis.* USAF School of Aviation Medicine, Randolph Field, Texas. Special Monograph Report, 1955.

————. *Stimulus Determinants of Behavior.* New York: The Ronald Press, 1963. See Chapter 1.

Sells, S. B. Toward a taxonomy of organizations. Chap. 27 in Cooper, W. W., Leavitt, H. J., and Shelley, M. W. II, Eds., *New Perspectives in Organization Research.* New York: John Wiley & Sons, Inc., 1964. Pp. 515–532.

————. A model for the social system of the multiman, extended duration space ship. *Aerospace Medicine,* 1966a, 37, 1130–1135.

————. Ecology and the science of psychology. *Multivariate Behavioral Research,* 1966b, 1, 131–144.

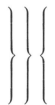

Choicepoints
in the
Classification of
Scientific Knowledge[1]

IRWIN ALTMAN
Naval Medical Research Institute
Bethesda, Maryland

This paper addresses some strategic issues and choicepoints in classification of knowledge in the behavioral sciences. Our interest is not to set forth the "best" classification path, but to highlight issues necessarily addressed in building taxonomies of knowledge. A second aim is more succorant. Though the behavioral sciences suffer from too little concern with systematizing the profusion of accumulating facts, our affliction is neither new nor unique. From Aristotle forward, philosophers, scientists, lawyers, and librarians have all had the burden of classifying seemingly unrelated, noncoherent volumes of facts. Most encouraging, many have successfully solved the problem. Therefore, let us also briefly explore such efforts to seek guidance and to tap their extensive wisdom, for strategic classification problems probably transcend disciplines.

Interest in synthesizing knowledge in the behavioral sciences has only recently grown and, even now, only a small minority see such work as equal in importance to empirical generation of new "facts." But the picture should rapidly change. In social psychological studies of small groups and interpersonal relationships (the area of greatest knowledge to the author), there are the seeds of mounting concern with integration of research information as reflected in systematic reviews of research, new textbooks and collections of readings, and so forth. Thus, the time may be ripe for making work in the classification of knowledge a

[1] From Bureau of Medicine and Surgery, Navy Department, Research Task MFO-22.01.03-1002, Subtask 1. The opinions and statements contained herein are the private ones of the writer and are not to be construed as official or reflecting the views of the Navy Department or the Naval Service at large.

respectable area of scholarly contribution and one worthy of support and reward. If so, it is important not to haphazardly scurry in all directions, but to capitalize on past and present experience in our own and in other disciplines.

Classification in the Behavioral Sciences

The behavioral sciences have not even remotely achieved the level of classification offered by Mendeleev in chemistry, Linneaus in zoology, or Dewey in library science. Furthermore, we have not yet engaged in the decades of sophisticated work that preceded such systems. But all is not dismal, for there is much ongoing work which bears on classification and synthesis. Let us quickly review such efforts, primarily in social psychology, which may assist in taxonomic development, for example, content analysis, behavior observation systems, factor analysis, propositional inventories, and *a priori* classification systems. After exploring some of their underlying properties, we will turn to disciplines having a longer history of concern with classification, for example, natural science and library science, and then attempt to induce strategic classification choicepoints and issues.

Content Analysis

The logic, strategy and tactics of content analysis is nicely described by Berelson (1952), Pool (1959), Auld and Murray (1955), and Marsden (1965). Although primarily used to generate data about communications, content analysis necessarily classifies behavioral events, and therefore has implications for synthesis of research information. Basically, it entails dividing communications into various sized units (such as words, sentences, and paragraphs), assigning units to categories or positions on some metric, and counting incidence of behavioral events. Marsden (1965) describes three content analysis methods or models: classical, pragmatic, and nonquantitative. The classical model stresses quantitative methods applied to manifest content of communication, with minimal inferences about communicator states. The pragmatic model is less restrictive and permits inferences about communicator implications. The nonquantitative model avoids sole use of frequency tabulations as an indicator of intensity, salience, and so forth, and searches for alternative metrics to assess communication content. Regardless of such differences, these techniques share many properties relevant to classification. For example, both the content analyst and the classification researcher always face the question as to size of behavior unit to observe. In addition, both must define antecedent and consequent context boundaries within which to classify behavior. Furthermore, they must determine what a "valid" indicator of the occurrence of an event is. Is it a frequency of one, an intensity of x? As a related question, is the appropriate unit of classification a behavioral event, or a relationship between situational and behavioral events? Content analysis has emphasized codifications of behavior; synthesis of research knowledge may require treatment of both behavioral events and relationships between behaviors and antecedent conditions. These and other issues will be addressed more fully later; they are raised here to highlight the fact that several problems of classification have already been touched on in the behavioral sciences.

Behavior Observation Systems

In the 1950's, a number of systems for coding ongoing small-group behavior were developed, the most well known being that of Bales (1950) (see Heyns and Lippitt (1954) and Altman (1966) for a review of these techniques). Unlike content analyses, behavior system coding is often done on the spot and uses style, tone, and other nonverbal, noncontent cues. They also usually code *all* behavior into some category and, in this sense, tend to be more exhaustive than content analyses. While by no means a firm differentiation, the question of exhaustiveness is an important one for classification of scientific knowledge, that is, the question of whether a system should be capable of codifying *all* research information in a field or should be very restrictive in scope.

Aside from such differences, the two approaches are quite similar. Both generate data by imposing descriptive dimensions on freely occurring behavior. Both focus on dependent variables (behavior) and generally omit thorough classification of antecedent factors such as group size and organizational structure. Within each approach, there is considerable variability in properties of exhaustiveness, size of behavior unit studied, number and sensitivity of categories and so forth. Both approaches also show wide latitude in the extent to which a strong theoretical base underlies the logic of a particular system, ranging from narrow, strictly empirical categorizations to broad, theoretically grounded approaches. These issues are of direct concern to the student of taxonomy.

Factor Analysis

Rather than using a predetermined observation structure to generate data, factor analysis performs statistical operations on already abstracted behavior events to indirectly identify behavioral uniformities. While exhaustively encompassing relevant classification dimensions within the body of treated data, there is no assurance of exhaustiveness of dimension description in the broader sense. Thus generalization may be restricted to the body of data processed by the technique. This is an area of decision to be faced by any student of classification — exhaustiveness and comprehensiveness of the taxonomy.

There have been several successful factor analytic studies in the small group field by Cattell (1948, 1953), Hemphill (1950, 1956), Borgatta (1955, 1956), and Carter (1954), in which dimensions such as individual prominence and achievement, group goal facilitation, sociability, role structure, and informal interaction, have been identified. It is important to note that in spite of differences in measurement method and procedure there is considerable communality in resultant dimensions in these studies, thereby widening the generality and possible utility of factor analytic work.

Factor analysis is potentially important for classification of scientific information as an empirical complement to *a priori* approaches and as an inductive check on measurement of relevant dimensions. It also can serve to identify new classification dimensions. While the generalizability of a single factor analysis may be questionable, overlapping studies tapping into the same area from different perspectives can minimize the problem (see Stogdill, 1959).

Propositional Inventories

There have been several recent so-called propositional inventories in the behavioral sciences, the most notable being those of Berelson and Steiner (1964) in general psychology, March and Simon (1958) in organization research, and Collins and Guetzkow (1964) in the small group field. In social psychology, Mann (1959) identified propositions relating performance and personality; Lott and Lott (1965) focused on group cohesion; DeLamater, McClintock, and Becker (1965) studied small group functioning. Unlike content and factor analysis, this approach directly attempts to integrate and organize research information through analysis of relationships between independent and dependent behavior variables. It emphasizes both, not behavior alone.

From a large bibliography of studies on decision-making in small groups, Collins and Guetzkow (1964) abstracted empirically tested hypotheses and sorted them into clusters of relationships. If findings from different studies were consistent, a proposition or principle was set forth. They also tried to develop linkages of propositions to produce more than a listing. March and Simon (1958) conducted similar analyses of organization research, starting from a conceptual framework of organizational functioning. Findings were organized around three general models: organization members as passive instruments, as bearers of attitudes and values, and as decision makers. Three types of integrative propositions were specified in each area: X-Y dependencies of either a functional or factorial type, qualitative descriptive generalizations of an "anatomical" type, and organization structure-function characteristics. What is interesting about this work is its initial identification of important areas of study and its recognition that a variety of integrative propositions can be made. March and Simon are atypical in using a general conceptual structure; most propositional inventory approaches seem to be primarily inductive.

Except for the March and Simon system, most inventories are restricted to existing knowledge and cannot readily encompass new information. It is also interesting that criteria for inclusion of studies –for example, good experimental design or adequate empirical data– are primarily methodological. Comprehensiveness of literature review and inclusion criteria, bases for drawing out findings from a study, unit of analysis of research information, and extent of support of a proposition, are often unclear. Perhaps existing work may best be characterized as "selective study of research relationships," rather than systematic and comprehensive organizations of literature. While only in its infancy, this approach has considerable promise for integration of research information.

Formal Classification Systems

Differentiating "formal" and propositional inventory approaches is probably artificial, though heuristically valuable. Formal classifications have detailed, prespecified theoretical or methodological frameworks within which research information is categorized. They possess one or more classification dimensions and categories. They have criteria for defining "acceptable" units of study, pre-established unit property descriptions, a rationale for dimensions and dimension categories, and an ordering principle among dimensions. In many respects, the March and Simon approach is a formal classification system. Our own work on small groups (McGrath and Altman, 1966) was a deliberate attempt to build a formal classification system based on operational definitions of variables rather than on conceptual content. The system was designed to be exhaustive — that is, capable of including existing and new small-group variables, and to allow prediction about relationships between as yet unstudied variables. Dimensions used to describe properties of small-group variables were: (1) *object* (member, group, or environment); (2) *mode* (static or dynamic properties of objects); (3) *descriptive-evaluative* judgments made about objects; (4) *source* of data (member, group, and experimenter); (5) *viewpoint* from which the data object was described (subjective, projective, and objective). The system was multidimensional and capable of including variables with any combination of values on these dimensions. It was used to code research relationships in a random sample of 250 small-group studies. From a resultant 12,000 empirical relationships, generalizations about the state of knowledge in the field were drawn. The system was evaluated through the testing of its basic principle for ordering relationships between variables, the more similar two variables were in operational properties (the five classification dimensions), the greater the likelihood of their being empirically associated. This ordering principle was largely confirmed, making the system potentially capable of predicting the probability of empirical association between variables, even as yet unstudied ones.

Indik (1963) offers a similar system for organizational behavior using seven classification panels of variables: organization structure, organization process and function, small-group structure, small-group process, individual attitudes and perceptions, individual behaviors, and organizational environment. While only limited attempts have been made to synthesize research information in the behavioral sciences, especially of the propositional inventory and formal classification variety, several critical decision issues to be faced by students of classification are apparent. One concerns the extent to which a system should have a strong theoretical underpinning. Another involves the nature and number of classificatory dimensions and their relationship. A further question deals with predictive versus solely descriptive approaches to taxonomy. Should systems be open-ended or closed, that is, capable of continuous expansion or closed and logically coherent within themselves? In addition, should they be exhaustive and capable of covering all subject matters or only built to handle a delimited area? To assist us in describing such issues, let us momentarily turn to classification attempts in other fields and then readdress these questions in more detail.

Classification in Library and Natural Sciences

Library Classification

Classification of knowledge has plagued and intrigued librarians for centuries and still exists as a problem today. A volume written in 1912, now in its third edition (Richardson, 1964), and a basic text (Mann, 1943) summarize working philosophies and dilemmas. Two themes pervade such writings. First, there is an inherent arbitrariness to classification of knowledge, and the secret is to find relevant dimensions for a particular use and a cross-referencing system to insure access to the knowledge. A second theme is that the process of classification is, at best, extremely imperfect, and the search for a wholly and permanently adequate system is likely to be futile. In an indirect way, Richardson highlights the difficulty of achieving a universally acceptable taxonomy by providing some one hundred pages of references covering centuries of work in library science, law, art, history, and so forth. One gets the impression that as users, historical contexts, and knowledge, changed there was a continuous evolution of classification theory and practice, a process not unlike the evaluation of scientific theories.

Mann (1943) summarizes the characteristics of an ideal library classification system (which have amazingly relevant implications for synthesis of research knowledge). An effective system should be: (1) *systematic*, or have an orderly progression from extremely general to extremely specific levels, (2) *comprehensive*, (3) *detailed*, at all levels of generality, (4) *explicit* and *unambiguous*, (5) *logical*, (6) *expansive* or capable of broadening and contracting. Consider now a few better known library systems, with an eye toward their underlying characteristics in terms of such criteria, and toward identifying important classification choicepoints.

The Dewey decimal classification system, first proposed in 1876, contained 42 pages of listing. The sixth edition of 1899 grew to 511 pages. By 1942 the 14th edition contained 1,927 pages, strong evidence that the system has undergone continual modification and expansion. Let this be a signal to those aiming for an eternally "perfect" system for synthesizing research knowledge. The Dewey system presents ten broad classes of knowledge such as philosophy, religion, social sciences, pure sciences, literature, and so forth. Within each are a number of *divisions;* for example, mathematics, astronomy, physics, chemistry, and so forth are under pure science. The main classes and divisions are content-oriented and peculiar to existing knowledge within each field. Beyond these the system is more multidimensional, using a series of *form divisions* common to all classes and divisions. These include theory, compendia, manuals and outlines, dictionaries and encyclopedias, periodicals, history, and so forth. These cut across superordinate levels and essentially yield a matrix of all possible combinations of classes and divisions. Within each of the above, further distinctions are developed by a successive decimal grouping procedure. The system has several important taxonomic characteristics. It is exhaustive and can include all existing and even future knowledge; it is open-ended and permits continued subdivision within classes; it is partly multidimensional; it can be employed at any of several levels of analysis by unfolding and collapsing subgroupings.

Two other well known approaches are the Cutter Expansive (Cutter, 1897) and Library of Congress systems. Cutter organized knowledge in terms of rational and logical linkages between categories and is less eclectic than Dewey. Thus, through use of an underlying "evolutionary" principle, books are ordered with respect to one another, for example, book arts follow the history of books from production to distribution to storage. The Library of Congress system was introduced in the 1890's and was designed to be comprehensive and to optimize ease of access rather than to achieve scholarly profundity. In this sense it is more akin to the Dewey than to the Cutter system.

The work of library classification is still advancing and goes far beyond the elementary ideas presented here. Space does not permit presentation of the work of Raganathan and others (1965), but the serious student of taxonomy would do well to explore research developments in library science and automatic indexing (see Stevens (1965) for a review of much of this work.)

Natural Sciences

Beginning with Aristotle's grouping of animals into families, our natural science colleagues have diligently labored through the centuries to organize vast accumulations of knowledge. The list of propounders of zoological and botanical taxonomies is too long to cite here (see Curtis and Guthrie, 1947). The system used today was first proposed by Linnaeus in 1758. It classified animal life according to structural characteristics, which in turn related to key functions of life. The taxonomy is more than a catalog or listing of information; it intends to represent a "family tree" and to identify probable evolutionary linkages among biological organisms. In this respect, it is more akin to the Cutter than to the Dewey or Library of Congress system. By proposing an underlying ordering principle, that is, evolutionary development, the Linnean taxonomy enables some degree of prediction as well as description. Organizing specimens in terms of how structural characteristics fall in evolutionary lines can lead to hypotheses about missing or lost species, which can then be subject to empirical verification. Such a characteristic is important to consider in any classification.

The Linnean system also has properties similar to some library approaches. For example, it proceeds from general to specific levels, with successively finer classifications including animal kingdoms, subkingdoms, phyla, class, families, genera, and species. It is also relatively exhaustive, since most species, existing or newly discovered, can be fitted into the scheme. Furthermore, it is open ended and points to new distinctions. It is also somewhat multidimensional, with basic dimensions relating to opposing structural characteristics such as being single cell or multicell, having gut cavity or no cavity, having radial symmetry versus bilateral symmetry or a vertebrate column versus no vertebrate column. While these dimensions are not necessarily orthogonal, they can be used in a combinatorial fashion to uniquely locate a specimen in a conceptually complex space, which is then provided with a nominal label of the species, genera, family, and so forth. As indicated previously, this multidimensional characteristic is implicit in the Dewey classification and highlights a critical choicepoint in taxonomy, that is, identification of the "correct'" and appropriate number of classification dimensions.

As with library and zoological classifications, the Mendeleev system for organizing knowledge about chemical elements was not an isolated historical event (Hopkins, 1937; Pauling, 1957). For at least 60 years prior, chemists toyed with systematic arrangements of elements according to triad and octave principles based on atomic weight. It was not until 1869 and then again in 1871 that Mendeleev proposed the periodic law. He assumed that properties of chemical elements are not arbitrary but depend on atomic structure and vary with atomic number in a systematic way. Through the use of atomic weight and atomic number, Mendeleev demonstrated that elements could be systematically arranged in a row by column table. Elements in different columns varied in metallic nature from inert through noble gases and metals. Progression down rows or periods yields communality of properties associated with atomic number. By so grouping elements, such known properties of color, distribution in nature, specific gravity, boiling point, hardness, malleability, ductility, and coefficient of expansion are systematically organized.

What features of the periodic table have import for classification? First, the table accounts for the preponderance of existing knowledge about chemical elements, making it descriptively complete. In addition, it relies on only a small number of generic dimensions (atomic weight and atomic number), which are in turn linked to a series of other properties in a reasonably direct fashion. Furthermore, it permits study at different levels of abstraction and detail, as do library and zoological classifications. Derivation of certain element operating characteristics, such as rules for compounding according to valence, are also possible. Most significant, the system permits prediction of element properties and likely existence of as yet undiscovered elements. This feature led to research culminating in the discovery of neon, krypton, and xenon. Furthermore, the organization was quite practical — a criterion easy to overlook by those concerned with basic theoretical problems. For example, in developing the electric light, Edison originally made use of carbon, which proved to be relatively inefficient. Through use of the periodic table it became clear that tantalum and tungsten would be more effective.

Lest we overly extol the simplicity and neatness of the periodic table, it should be noted that it has many irregularities and assymetries. There is one short period (row) with only two elements, two short periods with eight elements, two long periods of eighteen elements, and a very long period of thirty-two elements. Moreover, the column arrangement according to metallic properties and organization of certain rare elements is not completely consistent or orderly. Thus, while useful and praised for nearly a century, the periodic table has not overcome certain inconsistencies and flaws. This, coupled with the extensive prior history of attempts to build a chemical classification system can be too easily ignored by those attempting to use Mendeleev as a golden standard.

Useful library, zoological, and chemical classification systems have several common properties. All stemmed from fields which had a long history of study and which were ripe for synthesis and integration. For the most part, their students had a good idea of the population of subject matter and the appropriate units of study. While new books would always be written, new specimens discovered, and new elements identified, there was a large fund of history and experience available. Our situation in the behavioral sciences is very different. We are not yet in agreement about what the appropriate unit of study is and are not yet wholly confident about the reliability and validity of our findings.

Furthermore these other systems used in part or *in toto* a common set of dimensions to order subject matter, for instance, atomic number and atomic weight in chemistry, structural characteristics in zoology, and theory and method, in library classification. Users of these systems "knew" many important dimensions to use by virtue of a wealth of empirical knowledge and a history of attempts at classification and had "most" of the facts about their phenomena at hand. Our situation in the behavioral sciences is totally dissimilar. Replication of empirical findings is rare, and our data are often noncomparable from situation to situation. Moreover, the phenomena occur in situational contexts which are extraordinarily complicated and need description as much as behavior itself. And the potential dimensions for describing behavior are multitudinous, and there is little consensus as to which are important.

Thus, the other sciences had a good concept of their appropriate unit of study, elements or organisms, for example; of the structural and functional characteristics of those units, atomic structure or organs and their properties, for example; of the behavioral features, boiling point, compounding properties, and reproduction, for example. In the behavioral sciences, we have a wealth of information about the latter category, but have not yet established consensus on relevant units and their structural-functional properties, which makes the task of synthesis quite difficult. In many respects, we are in a historical position analogous to 100 to 200 years prior to Mendeleev and Linneaus. Obviously, we cannot easily achieve rapid solutions to such problems, yet we must begin systematically organizing our knowledge, for, unlike our predecessors, we must work with empirical facts that are now accruing at a geometrically increasing rate. Perhaps we can assist in the process by inducing and discussing several key choicepoints that the student of classification probably must face explicitly or implicitly.

Classification System Choicepoints

Unit of Classifications

Attention must be given to classifying three aspects of research knowledge: behavior, antecedents and general situational conditions, and relationships between behaviors and between behavior and situational conditions.

As indicated earlier, there has been much work on description of behavior via observation systems, factor analysis, and content analysis. The importance of an adequate behavior taxonomy needs no justification — it is intrinsic to the business of behavioral science. The problem is locating the "appropriate" level of behavior to classify — for example, muscle twitch, segmented social response, molar social behavior, and behavior at the group or organization level. Even in delimited areas in a field, such as small groups, there are a range of alternatives regarding size of social behavior unit to study. At one end of a molar-molecular continuum are observation systems which ignore all but temporal and stylistic aspects of behavior, for example, length of interaction, silences, and interruptions. Further along are approaches which focus on discrete social responses such as single sentences. Toward the molar end resides the work of Barker (1955, 1963), who argues that understanding social behavior requires simultaneous consideration of situational contexts and behavior description in "natural sized" units, which can vary in length from single words to lengthy interactions.

There is probably no universal answer to the unit size question except the obvious principle that the level of analysis be appropriate to the intent and purpose of the taxonomy. If study is of total organizational functioning, then it is probably unwise to overemphasize physiology of the nerve impulse. A working rule might be to take into account one or two levels of behavior above and below that which is of primary interest. Such a strategy is systems oriented, with the primary unit of study seen as composed of components or subsystems which are embedded in a larger system.

Inappropriate decisions about behavior unit molarity-molecularity can be debilitating, with overextension in either direction leading to a loss of focus and confused results. Had Mendeleev tried to organize chemical elements in terms of more molecular or more molar properties, the periodic table might not have been as lucid and useful, because issues and bases of classification may be different. This is the "forest and trees" problem. There are no known rules for selecting the "correct" level of analysis, but we must at least be sensitive to the problem and handle it as explicitly as possible.

A second "unitizing" matter involves antecedent and situational factors affecting behavior. Existing work on classification has primarily described behavior. There has been little interest in taxonomies of social and work situation characteristics, especially in social psychology (Altman 1966; Bennis, Schein, Berlew, & Steele, 1963; McGrath & Altman, 1966; Roby & Lanzetta, 1958). This has led to fragmented knowledge because there is little comparability of findings from situation to situation and task to task. Without a general taxonomy of situations, synthesis of research information is limited to relating behavioral events (however richly described and dimensionalized) to a nonsystematic *listing* of situational characteristics.

A third decision point about units of classification involves the research relationship. A system must contain statements of relationship of a behavior-behavior type or situation-behavior type. What form should they take and what criteria determine relationship validity and reliability? Our heritage has levied a "hard-headed" orientation on us, assigning meaning only to relationships achieving extreme levels of statistical probability. This may have led to an overly constricted basis of evaluation as to what a scientific "fact" is — too stringent in some cases, not sufficiently stringent in others. It has been demonstrated that the greater the conceptual "distance" between two variables (in terms of operational similarity), the less the likelihood of statistical association (McGrath and Altman, 1966). Thus, one can better predict individual performance from knowledge of individual problem-solving process than from personality, the latter being more remote from performance. The relationship between personality and performance is likely to be mediated by a set of intervening relationships which may attenuate direct personality-performance linkages (Couch, 1960). Thus, it may be fallacious to impose the same statistical requirement on all types of relationships. The student of classification may find it necessary to reassess the meaning of a "fact" in terms of such distance notions or through definitions which more directly specify amounts of contributory variance.

"Essential" and "Correct" Dimensions of Classification

This topic treats choicepoints relating to underlying conceptual structure, the nature and number of primary dimensions, and multidimensional and open-ended properties of classification systems.

General conceptual structure. The underlying logic of a system can vary from formal, syntactical, or structural to content, substantive, or subject matter oriented (McGrath & Altman, 1966). The difference between these approaches at the extreme is analogous to grammatical description of terms as active or passive voices, transitive or intransitive verbs, direct or indirect objects as opposed to description of the content of a sentence — "boys playing with dogs," "chairs being broken," or "conditions of weather." More closely related to research might be the classification of variables in a content-oriented fashion according to performance, group cohesion, or organizational well-being, or in more structural terms via operational definitions.

Formal classifications are more apt to provide a common generic language for codifying research information, with each entry relatable to every other one. They also increase the probability of having mutually distinct categories and being relatively exhaustive. However, such approaches tend to be rather abstract and general, and often do not make a sufficient number of important distinctions. They also can lead to communication difficulties because of their highly symbolic and abstract nature and can be hard to use in concrete, specific cases. Substantive or content-oriented approaches minimize these limitations, but have some of their own. Content classifications easily lead to semantic confusion. Researchers are notoriously prone to use the same verbal content label for operationally and conceptually different variables and different verbal labels for similar variables. Furthermore, strictly substantive classifications are ordinarily restricted to an existing body of knowledge. They are also compilations of nominally labelled categories which are generally unrelated to one another, and which require continual modification whenever new information is discovered. In this sense, they tend to be open-ended and can proliferate in Topsy-like fashion, reducing the possibility of systematic synthesis and integration.

Our solution for the small-group field (McGrath & Altman, 1966) was similar to what seems to have been the case in library science, zoology, and chemistry, namely a combined formal and substantive approach. We originally adopted a formal strategy, using several dimensions of data to classify variables — for example, data object, data source, objective-subjective data viewpoint, description-evaluation, and state-action properties. The system possessed exhaustiveness, thoroughness of definition, and interlocking of variables, and seemed capable of including existing and new variables. The basic ordering logic, that of operational concordance as a predictor of association between variables, was upheld. However, we discovered that the descriptive language, while systematic and organizing, was esoteric, abstract, and difficult to communicate. Reorganizing the system to retain important formal distinctions, but also to incorporate substantive categories, led to a more functional arrangement. This experience is probably not unique. The Dewey system lists specific *content* areas such as social science, mathematics, natural science, but also employs *formal* distinctions cutting across areas such as theory, method, and application. It may be that any classification approach should maintain close ties with the content of its field, along with a search for underlying formal properties.

The nature of classification dimensions. Identifying "important" dimensions is a formidable task. The following is a proposed set of generic classification dimensions, which may have potentially wide applicability to behavioral science phenomena, and for which specific categories or dimension values can be tailored to meet the needs of a particular field.

UNIT OF STUDY. Objects of different types constitute basic units of concern. They can be persons, groups, organizations, or animate and inanimate things (or whatever is of relevance to the specific field). Since behavior can involve an expenditure of some form of energy by one object toward another, it is necessary to distinguish between an operator object (X) and an operand object (X). They can be identical, as when a person thinks about or does something to himself. They can refer to different units, as when an organization takes action toward another organization, or toward some member of its own organization, and can involve combinations of inanimate and animate units, as when a group performs some task. The level of description on this dimension can range from molecular psychological processes to global organizational functioning. In our own work on classification, object distinctions included member, group, and environment, further subdivided to distinguish between the self and others, specific aspects of the environment, and so forth. This was found to be a most important dimension for synthesizing small-group research information, one that is likely to be critical in any taxonomy.

DYNAMIC-STATIC PROPERTIES OF UNITS. A static property describes some aspect of an object, as an entity, and provides a summary up to a specified point in time. It is cumulative in time — for example, a biographical, attitudinal, or personalilty property. An action or dynamic property treats an event or process that occurs during a bounded temporal interval — for example, group or member performance, communication, and interaction. The distinction between static and dynamic properties is roughly analogous to the grammatical distinction between the verb "to be" and the verb "to do," or the distinction between organ structure and organ function. We found this to be an important subordinate dimension of object characteristics.

ENERGY TRANSFORMATION PROCESSES. Operator-operand linkages involve energy expenditures of a physical or psychological type — for example, cognitive, social-emotional, perceptual, and motor. Energy processes can be peculiar to a given field of interest, but seem intrinsic to behavioral functioning.

INTENSITY. This dimension specifies a magnitude property of energy transformation processes as an operator deals with an operand — for example, degree of hostility, group cohesion, and shock intensity.

DISTRIBUTION IN TIME. One of the most neglected dimensions of social psychological and organizational phenomena relates to various temporal properties of behavioral events such as group or organization life history and experience, functional and temporal stage of development, rate of change of energy expenditure, continuity-discontinuity of operator-operand relationships, to name just a few. A good bit of confusion and noncomparability of many social psychological "facts" may be partly due to different temporal loci of studies, and the unrealistic attempt to cross-match information stemming from different chronological stages.

DISTRIBUTION IN SPACE. Expenditure of energy and operator-operand relationships can vary considerably in physical space loci, another aspect of social psychological functioning that has been ignored until recently. Such properties have played important parts in all other forms of classification, as exemplified by library groupings according to country and locale, zoological and chemical classification of distributions of elements, and organisms in nature.

ECOLOGICAL SETTING. This dimension includes time and space considerations discussed above, but also refers to the total environmental milieu within which the behavioral event or empirical fact is embedded. It can include the whole series of explicit and implicit control variables of an experiment. Barker (1955, 1963) has emphasized the importance of such a dimension for social psychology.

Number and weighting of dimensions. A particularly knotty classification problem concerns number and differential weighting of dimensions. These questions were probably easier to solve in chemistry and zoology at the time of Mendeleev and Linneaus than they are today in the behavioral sciences, in that a large body of knowledge existed and there was institutional consensus about what was important. General modes of solution available to us are empirical and theoretical analyses coupled with "sociological" consensus. Through the use of factor analysis and propositional inventories, attempts have been made empirically to induce key characteristics of organizational functioning and situations. To complement this work, whether it be strictly empirical or theoretical, reliance on independent results in the same area can be useful. For example, it was interesting that the McGrath-Altman system had considerable overlap with that proposed by Indik (1963) and by Foa (1958). While not a rigorous test, consensus may lend some credence to a dimension's importance by assessing whether distinctions in it "make a difference" in terms of incidence of association between variables, predictions, and so forth.

The student of taxonomy is in a dilemma regarding number and weighting of dimensions. Use of too few dimensions can result in underdifferentiation of the phenomena, with too many things labeled as similar. Use of too many dimensions can lead to an extraordinarily complex system (especially if all dimensions are weighted equally), with the resultant amount of information likely to overtax the absorption ability of users. Furthermore, the more dimensions the greater the likelihood that overly trivial distinctions will be present. The solution to this question is not simple, although the classical unfolding approach, proceeding from general to more detailed subordinations permits operation at any of several levels of abstraction. This approach, coupled with empirical tests of dimensional properties, may contribute to solution of the matter.

The multidimensionality of the system. This issue is partly related to the preceding issue and partly to that of system exhaustiveness and open-endedness. If one describes *all* phenomena in terms of a delimited number of dimensions, then the combination of dimension categories specifies the limits and scope of the system. For example, a three-dimensional system with three categories on each dimension yields a 3 x 3 x 3 classification space with 27 unique locations. This is an exhaustive system if each of the phenomena to be classified is located in one of the 27 cells. It is closed to the extent that the three dimensions are postulated as the only "important" ones. It is logically "tight" in that all phenomena are described in terms of the same language, and each classified event fits into only one location. Such a system permits specification of exact similarities and differences between phenomena. As indicated earlier, we attempted to build such a system for small group research. It is interesting to note that none of the classification approaches in library science, chemistry, or zoology are either wholly multidimensional or open-ended, but possess both properties to some extent. Perhaps this is a reflection of the difficulty or inappropriateness of developing a completely neat, exhaustive, and logical system.

Tests of the "Adequacy" of Classification Systems

The adequacy of a classification system is an important, though elusive issue. There is no definite method for dealing with the question and, in many respects, the problem is identical to that of evaluating a scientific theory. Deutsch (1966) has dealt with this question in detail and in a way that overlaps with the following. Fifteen evaluation characteristics for describing theories or taxonomies are proposed to include those relating to system generality, comprehensiveness and completeness, as in the number of categories, operating rules, phenomena encompassed, and so forth; system predictive capacity and properties; and system efficiency, originality and cost, as in accuracy, probability of leading to new studies, and a new taxonomy. Let us here consider key questions to be addressed by designers and users of taxonomies.

1. *Can variables, relationships, and phenomena be reliably located in the classification space?* Regardless of number and character of dimensions, there is an undeniable requirement that users agree on location of items in the taxonomy. Without such reliability, the system is chaotic. Obviously, statistical techniques exist to assess reliability, but attention should also be given to sociological, nonquantitative indicators of consensus. For example, when Mendeleev and Linnaeus offered their systems there were no statistical studies of reliability as we commonly know them. Rather, there undoubtedly were a series of implicit and explicit tests of fit, which were answered affirmatively and which indicated agreement among users.

2. *Can the classification system describe all known "facts?"* A taxonomy should encompass all that is known about the phenomena studied. Natural science and library schemas reasonably satisfy this requirement, partly as a function of their chronological maturity and long institutional history. Behavioral science classifications have not yet achieved the capability for comprehensive description.

This requirement also means that a variable or relationship is uniquely located in the classification space. Ideally, it also appears close to other similar items and distant from dissimilar ones in terms of dimensional properties and derivative properties. For instance, elements close to one another in the periodic table are not only similar on atomic weight and atomic number (the main ordering dimensions), but also in properties of color, temperature, hardness, and metallic nature. In short, things close together should be similar, and things far apart should be dissimilar.

This not only provides a basis for determining whether the main ordering principle was correct, but also stimulates the classification designer to use additional or different dimensions when the requirement is not met. Deutsch (1966) has referred to this as multiple relevance, generality (number of classes of phenomena included), and comprehensiveness of a system (number of distinguishable aspects of phenomena).

3. *Can new facts be incorporated into the classification system?* This is listed separately to emphasize that a taxonomy should be able to incorporate *new* information along with existing knowledge, as does a theory. To the extent that it becomes difficult to do so, revision is necessitated. Deutsch (1966) refers to this as "performance" capability. Undoubtedly, new facts and discoveries will always require system changes. If they are in subordinate areas, system viability can be preserved for a long period of time. However, it is likely that at some point new information will require major reorganization, as occurs for scientific theories.

4. *Can the system predict new "facts", phenomena, or relationships?* A sophisticated classification system should be more than a catalog of neatly arranged and accessible facts. It should also lay the groundwork for new theory and point to new areas of study. A taxonomy that does not possess predictive capability is restricted to currently known facts, has only limited potential for systematic future expansion, and is apt to be primarily an information storage and retrieval system. A predictive system will also stimulate research toward gaps in knowledge and areas of contradictory findings.

This capability seems to require an underlying ordering principle in the classification schema. For the periodic table, the ordering principle is related to atomic number and atomic weight; for zoological classification it involves concepts of evolutionary development. For the McGrath-Altman framework it is methodological and operational similarity between variables. Thus, to achieve predictive capacity one must go beyond specifying classification dimensions, and indicate how dimensional characteristics are combined. In our case, the taxonomy was based on the hypothesis that the greater the operational similarity of variables, the greater the likelihood of their being statistically associated. This basic ordering principle was evaluated by examining the relationship between operational concordance and frequency of statistical association. It is also capable of test by specifying probability of future associations between as yet unstudied variables.

A second aspect of this question relates to differential weighting of dimensions. Regardless of subject matter, there are an enormous number of dimensions that might be used. Obviously, dimensions that make a difference are needed. As additional distinctions begin contributing little new "variance", in the sense of factor analysis or regression analysis, they should be eliminated or given less weight. This is related to the system's functional and structural parsimony (Deutsch, 1966). In the small group field, we discovered that our basic ordering principle made more of a difference for some dimensions than for others, for example, regardless of other distinctions, when relationship data objects were similar, statistical association was high; when they were different, the probability of association was low. Type of judgment by a data source, as, for example, description versus evaluation, was not as important in sorting out empirical information.

Differentially weighting dimensions can be accomplished by specifying in advance, on the basis of theoretical concepts, differences in importance of various dimensions in the classification system and then conducting empirical evaluations. Or one can take an inductive approach and determine, on an interative basis, which distinctions make a difference and to what extent.

There is another aspect to the predictive capacity of a classification system that warrants attention. Until recently, behavioral science research has been largely bivariate, with study of relationships between variables taken two at a time and with little concern for more complex relationships or for sequential chains of relationships. For example, small-group researchers have studied relationships between individuals characteristics and group performance, group characteristics and group performance, interpersonal attraction and group performance. Interactions between these variables as determinants of group performance have been generally ignored and, more important, there has been little work on understanding sequential chains of relationships between them. An effective classification system should be capable of predicting and describing such intervening processes. It should provide a "total map" of all paths between any two points in the classification space. The test of such predictive properties can then come from comparison of forecasts of hypotheses with empirical findings — a process no different than theory evaluation. Deutsch (1966) refers to the predictive range, predictive accuracy, and fruitfulness of a system under this general heading.

5. *Is the system used and accepted by the scientific community?* This sociological criterion is an important one. A system unused by the community, however elegant, logical, or precise, does not serve its purpose. The Cutter library classification system is theoretically valuable, but it does not appear to serve the needs of the preponderance of library users. If its intent is widespread application, it has apparently failed. In our initial work on small-group synthesis, we developed a

reasonably tight, theoretically based system which, if carried to its ultimate, could be understood only by its authors! It was not readily communicable and probably would not have been widely used in its original form. We then proceeded to modify it in ways which would reasonably preserve the basic logic, but which would also be more communicable and usable. Interestingly, the result was probably a sounder system, although the basic reason for modification was solely pragmatic and functional.

Obviously, reasons for low usage of a system can be multitudinous, ranging from lack of understanding and complexity to inappropriate rejection. The proposer of a system must try to understand reasons for its nonacceptance and overcome them. In addition to such criteria Deutsch (1966) also introduces a concept of "cost effectiveness" in terms of such factors as training time, margin of advantage over older systems, and so forth.

6. *Does the system reproduce itself and lead to new distinctions?* The life of a classification system is probably some function of its capacity for internal change as new information is received, that is, its self-transcendence (Deutsch, 1966). A scientific theory must not only describe and predict. It must find flaws in its own structure and identify areas where, for example, too few distinctions are being made, and should permit identification of alternative directions. In our small group work, it gradually became clear that inadequate attention had been given to dimensions of "intensity" and "temporal stage." These distinctions were not intrinsic to the system, but its formal and operationally oriented approach made them salient when they were not being satisfied. In this sense, the system had some degree of internal creativity.

Concluding Remarks

To summarize some basic themes which were set forth in this paper, the problem of classification of scientific knowledge is not new. It has a long history in other sciences, which should be turned to and studied for guidance. In this paper an initial step was taken in this direction. It is clear from such work that the development of effective classification systems do not happen all at once; they have long and arduous histories.

Another theme is that the behavioral sciences have already begun dealing with problems of classification, although they are not always labeled a such. Factor analysis, content analysis, and propositional inventory approaches have important implications for classification of scientific knowledge. These need to be studied further with this in mind.

In addition, the logic, philosophy, and theory of classification overlap fields, whether they be sciences or otherwise. Study needs to be made of the spectrum of such efforts to understand common problems, strategies, and logic. Furthermore, there are a number of critical classification choicepoints which must be faced regardless of field of interest. These include strategies of classification, basic taxonomic units, appropriate weighting and number of dimensions, capability for complete description of existing phenomena, predictive capacity, to name just few core choicepoints. While it is not always possible to specify the correct paths out of such choicepoints, it is critical that the student of classification be aware of their presence and at least try to identify and consciously select alternatives.

As a final thought, it should be realized that there is no perfect classification system, nor is it likely that behavioral science has a sufficient history of experience to realize an early breakthrough in classification. Nevertheless, we must strive for rapid advances, else we shall be smothered by our facts.

Bibliography

Altman, I. Aspects of the criterion problem in small group research. I. Behavioral domains to be studied. *Acta Psychologica,* 1966, 25, 101–131.
———. Aspects of the criterion problem in small group research. II. The analysis of group tasks. *Acta Psychologica,* 1966, 25, 199–221.
Auld, F., & Murray, E. J. Content analysis studies of psychotherapy. *Psychological Bulletin,* 1955, 52, 377–395.
Bales, R. F. *Interaction process analysis: A method for the study of small groups.* Cambridge, Mass.: Addison-Wesley, 1950.
Barker, R. G. (Ed.) *The stream of behavior.* New York: Appleton-Century-Crofts, 1963.
Barker, R. G., & Wright, H. F. *Midwest and its children.* New York: Harper & Row, 1955.
Bennis, W. G., Schein, E. H., Berlew, D. E., & Steele, F. I. *Interpersonal dynamics: Essays and readings on human interaction.* Homewood, Ill.: Dorsey Press, 1964.
Berelson, B., & Steiner, G. A. *Human behavior: An inventory of scientific findings.* New York: Harcourt, Brace & World, 1964.
Berelson, B. *Content analysis in communications research.* Glencoe, Illinois: Free Press, 1952.
Borgatta, E. F., & Cottrell, L. S. On the classification of groups. *Sociometry,* 1955, 18, 665–678.
——— & Meyer, H. J. On the dimensions of group behavior. *Sociometry,* 1956, 19, 223–240.

Carter, L. F. Recording and evaluating the performance of individuals as members of small groups. *Personnel Psychology,* 1954, 7, 477–484.

Cattell, R. B. Concepts and methods in the measurement of group syntality. *Psychological Review,* 1948, 55, 48–63.

—— & Stice, G. F. *The psychodynamics of small groups.* Urbana, Illinois: University of Illinois, Laboratory for personality assessment and group behavior, 1953.

Cattell, R. B., & Wispe, L. G. The dimensions of syntality in small groups. *Journal of Social Psychology,* 1948, 28, 57–78.

Cattell, R. B., *et al.* The dimensions of syntality in small groups. *Human Relations,* 1953, 6, 331–356.

Collins, B., & Guetzkow, H. *A social psychology of group processes for decision making.* New York: John Wiley & Sons, 1964.

Couch, A. S. The psychological determinants of interpersonal behavior. Proceedings of the XIV International Congress of Applied Psychology. Copenhagen, Denmark: Munksgaard, 1961. Pp. 111–127.

Curtis, W. C., & Guthrie, M. J. *General zoology.* New York: John Wiley & Sons, (4th ed.) 1947.

Cutter, C. A. The expansive classification. Second International Library Conference. London, 1897, Transactions (1898), 84–88.

DeLamater, J., McClintock, C. G., & Becker, G. Conceptual orientations of contemporary small group theory. *Psychological Bulletin,* 1965, 64, (6), 402–413.

Deutsch, K. W. Communication codes for organizing information. *Behavioral Science,* 1966, 11, 1–18.

Foa, U. G. The contiguity principle in the structure of interpersonal relations. *Human Relations,* 1958, 11, 229–238.

Hemphill, J. K. *Group dimensions: A manual for their measurement.* Columbus, Ohio: Ohio State University, Bureau of Business Research, 1956. (Research Monograph No. 87)

—— & Coons, A. E. Leader behavior description. In *Leader behavior: Its description and measurement.* Columbus, Ohio: Ohio State University, Bureau of Business Research, 1956. (Research Monograph No. 88)

Hemphill, J. K., & Westie, C. M. The measurement of group dimensions. *Journal of Psychology,* 1950, 29, 325–342.

Heyns, R. W., & Lippitt, R. Systematic observational techniques. In G. Lindzey (Ed.). *Handbook of social psychology.* Cambridge, Mass.: Addison-Wesley, 1954. Pp. 370–404.

Hopkins, B. S. *General chemistry.* New York: Heath, 1937.

Indik, B. P. *The study of organizational and relevant small group and individual dimensions.* Technical Report 13, Contract Nonr-404(10). New Brunswick, N. J.: Rutgers — The State University, December, 1963.

Lott, A. J., & Lott, B. E. Group cohesiveness as interpersonal attraction: A review of relationships with antecedent and consequent variables. *Psychological Bulletin,* 1965, 64, (4), 259–310.

Mann, Margaret. *Introduction to cataloging and classification of books.* (2nd ed.) Chicago, Ill.: American Library Association, 1943.

Mann, R. D. A review of the relationships between personality and performance in small groups. *Psychological Bulletin*, 1959, 56, 241–270.

March, J. G., & Simon, H. A. *Organizations*. New York: John Wiley & Sons, 1958.

Marsden, G. Content analysis studies of therapeutic interviews: 1954 to 1964. *Psychological Bulletin*, 1965, 63, (5), 298–321.

McGrath, J. E., & Altman, I. *Small group research: Synthesis and critique of the field*. New York: Holt, Rinehart & Winston, 1966.

Pauling, L. *College chemistry*. San Francisco, Calif.: Freeman, 1957.

Pool, I. (Ed.) *Trends in content analysis*. Urbana, Ill.: University of Illinois Press, 1959.

Raganathan, S. R. The colon classifications. In Susan Artandi, Volume IV, Graduate School of Continuing Studies. New Brunswick, N. J.: Rutgers – The State University, 1965.

Richardson, E. C. *Classification* (3rd ed.) Hamden, Conn.: Shoe String Press, 1964.

Roby, T. B., & Lanzetta, J. E. Considerations in the analysis of group tasks. *Psychological Bulletin*, 1958, 55, (2), 88–101.

Stevens, Mary E. *Automatic indexing: A state-of-the-art report*. National Bureau of Standards, Monograph No. 91, March 1965.

Stogdill, R. M. *Individual behavior and group achievement*. New York: Oxford University Press, 1959.

PEOPLE, } GROUPS, AND } ORGANIZATIONS { **II**

**SOCIOCULTURAL ENVIRONMENTS,
ORGANIZATIONS, GROUPS,
AND INDIVIDUALS**

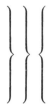

The Sociocultural Context of People, Groups, and Organizations[1]

DAVID POPENOE

Departments of Sociology and City Planning
Urban Studies Center
Rutgers — The State University

The mainstream of American sociological theory in this century has been primarily social psychological in orientation. It has dealt with the microsociological units of people and groups, and more recently, with large, formal organizations — the trinity which forms the subject matter of this symposium. Among the more fruitful theoretical approaches to these phenomena has been systems theory, particularly the social systems theories which have been especially useful in group and organizational analysis. Systems theory, in fact, is undoubtedly one of the most promising tools for integrating knowledge focused on people, groups, and organization, as several other papers in this symposium elaborate. Integration by this approach makes primary reference to the conceptual relationships between personality systems and various kinds of social systems (groups and organizations) going up the hierarchy of systems, and between personality systems and organismic systems going down the hierarchy, assuming the individual personality as a base point.

The focus of this paper, unlike most of the others in this symposium, is on the sociocultural context of organizations: the extension of the systems hierarchy *beyond* the several rungs on the ladder named people, groups, and organizations. Its major purpose is to make some contribution to the integration of the knowledge of this "macroworld" with the knowledge of the "microworld" as represented by the three foci of this symposium. Naturally, because of its utility, our orientation

[1] Particular thanks is due for the generous intellectual assistance of Harry C. Bredemeier in the development of ideas contained in this paper.

will be in terms of social systems theory. If the kinds of social systems theories which have proved useful in analyzing groups and organizations could be applied with very little adaption to the major units of the extraorganizational world, this would indeed be an important step toward an effective integration of social science knowledge.

The intent of this paper is to examine such applicability in very general terms by concentrating on two basic aspects of the extraorganizational world which make it somewhat different than the world of organized groups. The first is the distinction (continuum) between organized and unorganized social systems, the second, the distinction between social and cultural levels of analysis or between social systems and cultural systems. We shall try to show that at levels "hierarchically above" the formal organization, the basic factors of unorganized systematic interaction and the relations between the cultural and social levels of reality require modifications of the relatively "neat" social systems theories which have been developed around more organized, formal, smaller-scale, single purpose unities.

The concepts which are most often utilized to intellectually order the sociocultural world beyond the organization include community, society, nation, culture — or in earlier historical or less developed societies, clan and tribe. This paper will examine specifically the concept *community*, which has been analyzed recently in social systems terms by Warren (1963), Sanders (1966), Loomis (1960), and Mercer (1956); and the concept *society*, which has been examined recently in social systems terms by Parsons (1951, 1956, 1961, 1966), Levy (1952), and Loomis (1960), These two concepts cover the major aspects of the extraorganizational world and their specification and distinction is central to the purposes of this paper. One important aspect of these two concepts to be examined briefly in this paper is the assumption that they form part of a hierarchy of systems levels ranging from the group and organization through the community to the society.

Similarly, and even more elegantly, Miller (1955) and other "General Systems Theorists" (von Bertalanffy, 1955; Boulding, 1956) have suggested that the behavioral sciences can be integrated internally and with the other sciences "through a series of related definitions, assumptions, and postulates about all levels of systems from atomic particles through atoms, molecules, crystals, viruses, cells, organs, individuals, small groups, societies, planets, and galaxies." Miller (1965, a, b) has recently followed up this suggestion with a pioneering contribution to this area, and other behavioral scientists have made significant contribution, by drawing comparisons between certain social systems and biological and mechanical systems. This paper also will touch briefly on the validity of this kind of systems hierarchy and synthesis between biological and mechanical systems on the one hand, and sociocultural systems on the other.

In summary, the following kinds of questions are the stimulation behind this paper: What kind of system is a community, and how does it differ from a society as a system? Are communities and societies systems in the same sense and with the same properties as organized groups? Is there a hierarchically related set of social systems running individual, group, organization, community, and society, and possibly below the individual into the biological and physical world and beyond the society into the world of the larger universe?

Some Basic Concepts of General Sociocultural Theory

It is essential to this discussion that the reader have some knowledge of the concepts which are central to the analysis of the sociocultural order. What follows, therefore, is a brief conceptual map of this order. These concepts rely heavily (as does this entire paper) on the contributions of P. A. Sorokin, particularly his *Society, Culture and Personality* (1962), but they are not too dissimilar from the concepts employed by several other recent general social systems and "socal action" theorists such as T. Parsons (1961).

The world is made up of three fundamental classes of phenomena: the inorganic, the organic, and the superorganic. The presence of life superimposed upon inorganic phenomena (the subject matter of the physical sciences) distinguishes the organic phenomena (the subject matter of the biological sciences); the presence of mind or thought in its developed form, superimposed upon organic phenomena, distinguishes the superorganic phenomena (the subject matter of the social sciences). Superorganic phenomena (or what shall hereafter be referred to by the more common term sociocultural phenomena), in their developed form, are found exclusively in the realm of interacting human beings and the products of their interaction. (We shall not take up here the important distinctions between man and the higher forms of animal life.)

All empirically rooted sociocultural phenomena are made up of three major components:

Meanings-values-norms. Cultural symbols.

Biophysical vehicles (or media, conductors) through which immaterial meanings-values-norms are objectified, and made manifest.

Conscious human beings (and groups) that create, operate, and use the biophysical conductors in the process of their interactional activities.

These components can be conceptualized as composing three levels or aspects of culture:

Ideological. The totality of cultural symbols — meanings-values-norms — possessed by individuals and groups.

Behavioral. The totality of the meaningful actions of individuals and groups, through which cultural symbols are manifested and realized.

Material. The totality of all other vehicles, conductors, and so forth.

Viewed from the point of view of the systematic interconnection of these various components and levels, the following three "action-systems" become prominent:

Personality (or personality system). An organization of ideological and behavioral culture with reference to an individual person.

Society (or social system). A totality of interacting personalities with their sociocultural relations and processes.

Culture (or cultural system). A totality of cultural symbols possessed by the interacting persons together with the totality of cultural vehicles. (Some would exclude the behavioral level from such a concept.)

It is important to point out that none of these units can exist concretely without the other two; they are dimensions of the same inseparable reality. A personality cannot exist without society and culture, a society requires interacting personalities and a culture, and there is no living culture without personalities and a society. For pedagogical and analytic purposes, however, they may be and quite obviously are studied separately, as will be developed below. For example, the same "mental phenomenon" (that is, sociocultural phenomenon) can be variously viewed as an aspect of an individual personality, a social structure in a social system, or a unit of a cultural system.

This completes the brief summary conceptual map of the sociocultural world.

Groups and Organizations: Toward a Clarification of Concepts

Before proceeding to discuss the extraorganizational world, we shall briefly discuss the social units which are the specific focus of this symposium — people, groups, and organizations. In his introductory paper, Indik has suggested a rather elaborate breakdown of this triumverate into their constituent structures and processes. The problem with this classification lies in its starting point. The concepts "group" and "organization" have been derived from two recent streams of social research — one focusing on small, informal "groups" and the other focusing on large, formal "organizations." The question is, to what degree are the differences between these two concepts so fundamental as realistically to constitute a major division in a classification scheme?

Though this scheme may be useful in integrating the work of two research foci, it does not seem that the distinction between a group and an organization is fundamental enough to be the basis for such an elaborate scheme of general classification of social phenomena.

Among other things, the terms group and organization are inadequately defined. Indik states that a group is a "set of two or more individuals who have some systematic relation to each other and who have some common goal and some common basis for their association with each other." On the other hand, "an organization is a set of two or more interrelated groups having a common status and control hierarchy and devoted primarily to the attainment of specific goals." By these definitions a group and organization are essentially similar. They both have individuals in systematic relation to each other, and they both have common goals. Even their size does not have to differ much: a group can consist of two persons, and an organization can consist of a set of two groups — or four persons. It is suggested by the definitions that an organization but not a group has a "status and control hierarchy," but in actual fact almost all groups have such hierarchies, though they may differ greatly in complexity. It is also suggested that a group is a primary unit of an organization, but not *vice versa* — that is, an organization is hierarchically above a group. While this is true in most cases, it is not uncommon to find small organizations unified into a loose (informal) group of some type. It is also not clear to what extent an organization can be defined as "a set of two or more groups," that is can we really call the group the primary unit of an organization?

Because of the great similarities between groups and organizations, as suggested by those definitions, it is no accident that the structures and process listed for both systems by Indik in his paper are essentially identical.

If one were to take the more common distinction between a group and an organization, based on size (number of interacting members) and the degree to which it is "formally" established, similar difficulties arise. Though size has important effects on group structure and process, it is by no means the most significant independent variable. In addition, many small groups are formally initiated (for example, a family), and many large groups may be informally initiated. The word "formal," of course, is somewhat ambiguous, in that it may refer to a high level of (formal) organization, or it may have to do with whether the group was initiated intentionally and purposefully or unintentionally and spontaneously (informally). The "formality" of an organization seems indeed an important characteristic; the way in which an organization was initiated seems a secondary characteristic.

We could go on to discuss other common differentiating factors, for example, face-to-face interaction, primary-secondary relations, short and long life spans, and so forth. Suffice it to say that all of these factors (together with the ones mentioned above) are significant aspects of social groupings, but that the dichotomy "group-organization" tends to mask the great diversity which exists among the whole spectrum of social groups, and tends to be based on differentiating factors which themselves may not be the most significant ones.

This discussion is not meant to single out Indik as an exception; his point of view is characteristic of most small-group theorists and many organization theorists (see Sorokin, 1966). The discussion is meant to point up that *primary* differentiating factors among organized groups are normative and not formal; they must refer to content and not form as will be developed in the next section.

Sorokin's Taxonomy of Groups

The following is an outline of a general scheme for the classification of groups, developed by Pitirim A. Sorokin (1962), that has been almost completely overlooked in the literature. It is intended not only to suggest a positive alternative to the scheme discussed above, but also and primarily as a basis for the discussion of the extra-organizational world which follows. Specifically, it introduces the analytic distinction between causal-functional interaction or unity and meaningful-symbolic interaction or unity. It must be noted at the outset that this taxonomy, like many others, focuses primarily on social groupings at the level of the organization concept. It may not be satisfactory at present to integrate small-group theory with organization theory. It is felt, however, that such integration would be immeasurably enhanced by the development and utilization of an adequate taxonomy for the more powerful and differentiated groups, and that it is entirely possible that this same taxonomy could be extended to the intraorganizational informal groups. In any event, since the primary focus of this paper is extraorganizational, the matter will not be taken up here.

Sorokin suggests that the forms of interconnection of sociocultural phenomena range from a mere spatial or time adjacency, through indirect and then direct causal-functional unities, to systems (such as all organized groups) which are interconnected with both causal-functional and meaningful ties. "Causal-functional ties" refers to "simply a relatively constant and tangible empirical interdependence of A and B in their coexistence of sequence or concomitant variation" (Sorokin, 1966), whereas "meaningful ties" refers at the cultural level to logical or aesthetic consistency or complimentarity. Concrete "groups" which manifest these various forms of interconnection range from pure sociocultural congeries (or agglomerations) at the one extreme, which are not systems in the usual sense of the term, to organized groups at the other extreme, which are systems. These distinctions do not always assume great importance in the world of organized group analysis; they are of great importance in considering the environment of such groups, however, as is discussed further below.

The *fundamentum divisionis* for the classification of all social groups according to Sorokin is the intensity or closeness of causal-functional interdependency among its members or units, and secondly, and even more important, the character of the group's component meanings. It is the component of meanings which gives a group individuality (based on its causal-functional unity). Furthermore, Sorokin distinguishes between those groups which are unified by a single set of meanings, and those which are unified by two or more sets of meanings. The first groups are called "unibonded," the second "multibonded."

The further question immediately must be raised, however: What set of meaning-values-norms can be regarded as unibonding? Almost any meaning may be such a value for a few individuals over a short period of time (as is the case in many transitory small groups). If we look for meanings which have guided lasting groups, however, the matter can be approached by examining basic human needs or by examining logical classes of meaning-values: scientific, aesthetic, economic, moral, and so on. Sorokin rejects the first approach on the grounds that not enough is known about basic human needs, and the second on the ground that such a classification does not entirely correspond to actual groups and thus may result in a classification of meanings and not of groups. From an historicosociological point of view, Sorokin therefore uses the observational approach and determines what groups in the human population have actually been the powerful and permanent groups. He finds some unibonded groups organized around biological values — age, sex and race — and the remainder around sociocultural indicators of value — kinship, territorial proximity, language (nationality), the state, occupational, economic, religious, political, and a category which includes scientific, philosophical, aesthetic, educational, recreational, ethical, and other "ideological" values.

Persons linked by two or more of these unibonded ties constitute a multibonded group. In each society there is an enormous number and diversity of such groups, of course, but the most important historically, according to Sorokin, have been the family, clan, tribe, nation, caste, feudal estate, and social class.

Only when the fundamental "normative" component of the group is known, says Sorokin, and in the case of multibonded groups, the number and characteristics of the bonds, is it most useful to proceed to the "secondary" characteristics which define the nature of groups. Of the latter, Sorokin emphasizes size, degree of organization, type of government (for example, centralized as opposed to decentralized), type of stratification, having short or long life span, degree of solidarity, degree of cultural integration, and the mix of various cultural components (persons, vehicles and meanings). Some of these secondary characteristics are further discussed below.

The Dimension of Organization

We are now in a position to concentrate on a discussion of two basic problems which are relatively unimportant in a consideration of small groups and formal organizations, but which assume prominence when considering groups like communities and societies. The first of these is the continuum between organized and unorganized groups; the second is the distinction between the social level and the cultural level of systems analysis. The first of these points is taken up here; the second is dealt with in a later section.

Most social systems theory has been developed around relatively organized groups. If a social system is defined merely as "a set of units with relationships among them" (von Bertalanffy, 1955), or more simply "two or more units in interaction" (Parsons, 1953), then our problem does not arise. However, these definitions apply to *all* systems, not necessarily only to social systems. Definitions which apply more specifically to social systems are "the interaction of a plurality of individual actors whose relations to each other are mutually oriented through the definition and mediation of a pattern of structured and shared symbols and expectations" (Loomis, 1960) or "the activities, interactions, and sentiments of the group members, together with the mutual relations of these elements with one another during the time the group is active, constitute what we shall call a social system" (Homans, 1950). Note that the added ingredient in the last two definitions is what Sorokin calls meaningfull interaction (added to causal-functional interaction).

More specifically, Loomis (1960) lists nine elements that constitute a social system: belief (knowledge), sentiment, end, goal or objective, norm, status role (position), rank, power, sanction, and facility. Parsons (1956) and Bredemeier (1966) discuss four functions of social systems: goal-attainment (or decision-making), adaptation, integration, and tension management (or pattern-maintenance). The point is that such concepts primarily apply to organized groups and not to *all* sociocultural systems or realities. To clarify it, let us turn to Sorokin's distinction between organized and unorganized groups.

Sorokin (1962, Chapters 4 and 8) suggests the following characteristics of organized groups (that is, the unibonded and multibonded groups mentioned above):

1. Law norms (official and unofficial) regulating conduct, relationships of group members.
2. Official laws and government.
3. Division of all forms of conduct and relationship into obligatory, recommended, and prohibited.
4. Precise definition of rights-duties, functions and role, social status and position of every member.
5. Social differentiation and stratification.
6. Economic order.
7. Name or symbol of the group.

By Sorokin's definition, therefore,

. . . a social group, as a totality of interacting individuals, is organized when its central set of meanings and values, as the reason for their interaction, is somewhat consistent within itself and assumes the form of the law-norms precisely defining all the relevant actions-reactions of the interacting individuals in their relationship toward one another, the outsiders, and the world at large; and when these norms are effective, obligatory, and, if need be, enforced, in the conduct of the interacting persons. (Sorokin, 1962, p. 70)

The other characteristics mentioned above follow from the centrality of the basic normative structure.

At the other extreme, an *un*organized group is amorphous in all of the above respects:

. . . the rights, duties, possessions, functions, roles, social status and position of its members are undetermined and undefined either in broad outline or meticulous detail; so are its categories of the lawful, recommended, and prohibited forms of conduct and relationship; so are its official law and government, structure of social differentiation and stratification, economic order, and so on. Consequently, all remains uncrystallized. The whole system of social relationships and values is confused and vague. Members do not know who is ruler and who is to be ruled; what are the rights and duties of each; what is the proper form of social relationship between them; what actions and conduct are recommended, lawful and prohibited for each party. (Sorokin, 1962, p. 91)

All of the so-called organized groups, of course, vary somewhat in terms of the characteristics outlined above. Similarly, it is widely recognized that the relatively unorganized groups such as publics, crowds, mobs and categories of individuals (for example, sex) do not possess most of these characteristics. It is not so clearly understood, however, that such supraorganizational systems as communities and societies may also vary greatly on these dimensions and in many cases tend toward the pole of unorganization. To the degree that they are unorganized, the applicability to them of social systems theories which use concepts developed in the course of studying organized groups is diminished.

An additional set of properties (Sorokin, 1962, Chapter 2), which applies to organized groups and less so to relatively unorganized groups (and which is built into much of contemporary social systems theory) is the following:

1. Individuality. Distinguishing the group from the outside environment.
2. General and differential interdepedence and conductivity. The tangible interdependence of all important parts upon one another, of the parts upon the whole, and the whole upon the parts.
3. Continuity of the group individuality despite changes in component vehicles and members.
4. Self-directing (immanent) change and life-career, maintaining a margin of autonomy from external forces of change.
5. Selectivity, in the sense that it takes in only certain elements from the outside world and rejects or leaves outside of itself other elements.
6. Limited variability. Limited possibility of variation.

It should be recognized that these properties are central ingredients of most social systems theories, and yet they are not at all elements of pure social congeries or agglomerations, of which there are many in the sociocultural world, and in general they become less realistic to the degree that a social group is unorganized. In summary, a central problem in the application of social systems theory at the extra-organization level is to make sure that the social systems concepts developed around organized group studies are not transferred without modification to relatively unorganized groups.

Society and Community: A Conceptual Clarification

Before proceeding to the culture–social systems distinction, let us stop to apply the social system organization dimension to the community — society concepts, and thus state the problem more concretely.

This discussion may be framed in terms of a question: Are there any major "organized groups" at a level in the systems hierarchy above that of most organized groups (as usually conceived) such that the familiar organized groups could be treated as subsystems of them in the formal sense — or rather, is the extraorganizational world an amorphous "environment" or "situation" — or is it something in between? First, let us consider the *state* (in our system, the Federal government together with state and local governments). The state is considered by Sorokin as a unibonded group, and as such, it might be considered on the same hierarchical level as other "formal organizations." It is quite special, however, in that it acts as a kind of clearing house for all other groups. The question of the state is raised here not to pursue the matter but rather to clarify it for a discussion of the concepts nation, society and particularly community. The state is treated as a special case of an organization which is roughly on the same level in the hierarchy as other unibonded organizations.

The *nation* represents a somewhat different matter, however. Most social systems analysts who attempt to apply a social systems framework to "society" are in fact applying it to a powerful and organized multibonded social group which in modern times has displaced (from power) the family, the clan, and the tribe. The nation, in Sorokin's terms, is a coalescence of territorial, state, and language bonds. The nation seems to qualify as an organized group because of the strength of this triple bond, and because the state component is a highly organized unit. However, this picture changes drastically if either of the three bonds is removed from the nation. In such cases, and they are common both historically and today, there is much less validity in considering the nation as an organized group.

In short, the United States of America realistically can be considered as an organized social system to which most constituent organizations are hirarchically subsidiary. Thus the United States to some degree has a common culture, common goals, common psychological traits, etc., and most of the numerous characteristics and properties of organized groups. It should not be inferred from this, however, that one can subsume under the concept "U. S. A." *all* of the important aspects of culture, social organization, and personality which are characteristic of the population living in the area known as the U. S. A. All such phenomena may be subsumed under the concept *society*, which signifies the total sociocultural order of a population living in a given territory.

We now come to the concept *community*, which is undoubtedly one of the most ambiguous terms in the social sciences. It is used to mean at least five different things:

1. A localized population agglomeration either without further

specification or with regard to all the sociocultural aspects of that population. In this sense it is the local equivalent of the term society as defined above.

2. As an unibonded territorial group, where only the territorial bond of the local population is considered.

3. As a specific type of multibonded group which has a territorial bond as one of its components. An example is the ideal-typical small, isolated community utilized in rural sociological studies.

4. As a synonym for solidarity — "sense of community."

5. As referring to the "territoriality" aspect of all sociocultural systems, that is, their anchorage and relations in space.

We shall temporarily reject the last two definitions for present purposes because they refer to characteristics which are applicable to all human groups, and are not themselves definitions of group types. This leaves the first three definitions. If we regard a community as the local equivalent of a society at the national level (definition one), the next question we can raise is this: Is there a local equivalent of the nation? If so, then we have a powerful, organized and multibonded group at the local level (definition three) to which organizations may be subsystems in the formal sense. This, in turn, would make an important difference for the selection of theoretical materials for purposes of extra-organizational analysis. Our answer is that we do not have in most cases such a local equivalent of the nation in modern, Western society.

If one examines the localized population agglomerations across the country, and particularly the more prevalent and significant urban areas, one finds that the only bonds which hold them together are territorial (definition two) and state citizenship. The other bonds are quite weak — occupational, economic, religious, political, racial, kinship, for example, and language. The differences become more important at this level than at the national level. The state-citizenship bond is, of course, much more important at the national than local level, and the territorial is one of the weakest and unorganized of all bonds in contemporary times.

Not only are most community aggregations in our society relatively unorganized in the sense defined above, they also lack a position of hierarchical *control* over the constituent organizations because of their generally weak *sociocultural power* (the term power has been used above in several places), a concept which is related to, but not identical with, the concept of organization.

Sorokin (1962, pp. 168–169) defines a powerful social group as one which "exerts a powerful causal-meaningful influence upon individuals, upon other groups, and upon the course of sociocultural phenomena generally." He lists five criteria for determining such "power":

1. Size of group membership.
2. Totality of meanings-values-norms at the disposal of the group (qualitative aspect of the members).
3. Totality of the vehicles possessed by the group for influencing the individuals, groups, and sociocultural universe.
4. Solidarity of the group.
5. Technical perfection of its structural-functional organization (subdivision of numbers two and three).

Most contemporary territorial groups (such as metropolitan areas) fall down on the majority of these points, particularly the last three.

For most intents and purposes, therefore, there do not exist in modern times many localized, powerful, and organized groups hierarchically superordinate, but similar in structural properties, to the so-called formal organization. Most so-called local communities are not social systems in the sense of rather highly organized social groups. They *are* social systems, of course, in the sense of a group of people with some measure of causal-functional interdependence and a somewhat smaller measure of meaningful interdependence.

In summary, let us use "community" and "society" as highly general and to some extent substitutable concepts which refer to population agglomerations which have some measure of causal-functional and/or meaningful interdependence. In actual practice, the term "community" is applied to localized population agglomerations where the space-time ratio is such that causal-functional interaction becomes more significant. The term "society," on the other hand, usually refers to much larger population agglomerations, where often the meaningful tie becomes of greatest importance, (to be explained below). More concretely, on the one hand, we have local "ecological complexes" such as the New York metropolitan area, which are primarily distinguished by causal-functional ties; on the other hand, there is the Kurdish society, which cuts across several nations in the Middle East and consists primarily of symbolic-meaningful ties. Both of these are *social systems* only in the minimal sense of the term.

Furthermore, community and society as concepts must be distinguished from the more powerful and organized multibonded groups at each level — on the one hand, the powerful and highly organized contemporary nation-state, and on the other, the rather weak, localized, political–and social–territorial groups.

The Analytic Dimension of Culture Systems

At both the community and society levels of analysis — that is, the analysis of whole population agglomerations rather than merely organized groups — the dimension of cultural interaction in the sense of cultural systems becomes important. In the study of organizations (organized groups), meanings-values-norms are looked at not primarily for their own sake but rather as properties of interacting individuals or as the *raison d'etre* of their interaction and their groups. The normative component that is of primary interest in organized group study, for example, is that which gives the group its identity and degree of organization. One could have a complete set of such normative components for every organization in a community aggregation and still be a long way from having adequate data about the total culture of that community. The cultural map of a community and the social organization map are in fact two quite different things.

In a cultural focus one is primarily interested in meanings-values-norms for their own sake — *their* interaction and integration into systems or congeries as they are objectified through overt actions and other vehicles in the empirical universe. Norms at the purely ideological level can be (meaningfully) integrated and not integrated in various degrees, and they combine into various subsystems (subcultures) and systems. Sorokin's bases of vast cultural systems, for example, are language, science, philosophy, religion, the fine arts, and the derivative systems of applied technology, economics, and politics. It should be obvious that a focus on this level of reality reveals many characteristics and relationships of the sociocultural universe which cannot be clearly discerned at the purely social organizational level, and it almost goes without saying that this larger culture is a highly important part of the environment of individuals and groups.

In addition to the specific cultural system that is an organized group's reason for being, each group and its members possess several cultural systems neutral and contradictory to the main system as well as a multitude of cultural congeries. These extragroup cultural systems are necessary for the individual and group member to function in dealing with the many aspects of reality that go well beyond the specific normative specialization of the group. Alternatively, the major cultural systems are not confined to a single group or even set of groups. For these reasons, the maps of cultural systems and of social systems do not perfectly coincide and in fact refer to different unities having different boundaries.

This important distinction between the social and cultural levels of reality has long been held by many social and cultural anthropoloists. In addition to the early contribution of Sorokin, it has been put forth recently in an important article by Kroeber and Parsons (1958). The orientation is held by a growing number of sociologists, particularly those concerned by sociocultural "wholes" and with historical and contemporary sociocultural change (see Levine, 1966).

The point of this discussion is that social systems theory is not the same as cultural systems theory. The analysis of organizations (social systems) focuses on a circumscribed world in which the primary ideological component is the normative structure which "organizes" the organization. Social systems theories built around such organizations therefore do not have to deal with cultural systems, *per se*. A focus at the extraorganizational community and society levels, however, requires a consideration of cultural systems such as language, science, philosophy, religion, and so forth, for a basic understanding of these sociocultural worlds.

The Theoretical Analysis of Communities and Societies

This section attempts to pull together the important points made above in discussing the theoretical problems and approaches to the analysis of communities and societies.

Let us start by considering the sociocultural context of organized groups as simply and concretely an aggregation of groups in a particular area, to which the terms population, agglomeration, society, or community may be and often are applied interchangeably and with equal utility. If our aggregation were an isolated Greek or Medieval city-state, the terms community and society would be synonymous. Because of transportation and communication technologies in modern times, however, we must distinguish between localized aggregations of groups (ecologically organized around daily interaction patterns) and national-societal level aggregations of groups (which consist of a composite of such localized agglomerations). Naturally there are no hard and fast dinstinctions between these agglomerations, and indeed there are various agglomerations ranging in size between them, for example, regions of various types. At the two extremes, however, we can use the nonspecific concepts of community and society to refer to all aspects of the sociocultural order at each level.

In principle, and at a high level of abstraction, the analytic approach to *both* of these macrosociological phenomena is the same, and differs in the same respects from the analytic approach to organized groups. The primary considerations are the following.

1. Each contains a wide variety of relatively unorganized systems of interaction: crowds, publics, mobs, markets, ecological com-

plexes, and primarily causal-functional relationships among a wide variety of different factors. To disregard all of these and to focus on these units only as organized systems is to misconstrue many of the interactional ties which bind these units together with some degree of cohesion (that is, which cause the clustering of human activities).

2. Each has as a major component of its sociocultural order a set of ideological (culture) elements which interact as culture systems and which have an analytical reality independent from social systems level components. These elements are organized differently from, and cannot be reduced to, the sum total of the normative or ideological components of each of the organized groups in the given agglomeration.

In view of these similarities, one must ask the next questions: What are the differences between the community and society foci? Why focus on one rather than the other? Rather than utilizing community and society as organized groups standing in hierarchical relationships to one another, they are better treated as analytic levels of analysis, the use of which is dependent primarily on the degree of generalization desired about sociocultural phenomena, and to some extent on the *kind* of sociocultural relationship or phenomenon which is the primary interest of the analysis.

First, at the societal level, the nation-state can be utilized as a major, concrete organized group, the normative structure of which is "American society" or "American culture." Most of contemporary American macrosociology together with economics and political science, are organized to focus on the nation-state as the basic unit. An example of such a focus in contemporary sociology is the concentration on American social institutions of one type or another, such as religion, the family, economics, and so forth. Very often the term social institution is used to mean an analytic category of unibonded (single-function) organizations rather than as a concrete sociocultural reality *per se* (as for example a specific cultural system).

At a level higher than the nation-state, and the most meaningful environment of the nation-state in addition to other nation-states, are the cultural systems of Western civilization with reference to which the "lower level" norms of the American nation-state are defined — that is, the systems of philosophy, religion, fine arts, and so forth. The level of cultural systems, as indicated above, does not seem susceptible to treatment as an organized group — and in fact consists of meaningful (logical-aesthetic) interaction and integration to the exclusion of the causal-functional type. In its pure form this kind of sociocultural material can be and is excluded from the circumscribed world of organized group analysis (even when focusing on the nation-state as an organized group).

At a level "lower" than the nation-state, the familiar organized groups become relevant. These in a sense may be regarded as primary units of the nation-state — that is, their normative structure is defined primarily with reference to the norms of the nation-state.

The analytic utility of a community focus is much more difficult to establish. First, there is an important sense in which local communities within societies differ from one another, and hence must be comparatively studied. If the differences are extensive, as for example in the case of the traditional rural-urban distinction, the communities must be studied in their every aspect — that is, as holistic microsocieties. Similarly, local communities are very often regarded as microcosms of the parent society (particularly by social and cultural anthropologists), similar to the larger society in most important respects. In this case, which is primarily dictated by the practical consideration of data collection and so forth, the holistic microsociety view of the local community is also the relevant one. In both of these cases, however, it is important not to confuse microsocieties with micro-nation-states. The equivalent of the nation-state does not exist at the local level. Even the local government is but a weak creature of the "state," which in turn is somewhat autonomous from the national political-state. And the microcosmic cultural community does not always correspond, even, with this weak local-political unit. In the above foci, therefore, the local community must be studied in all its diversity but without even the simplifying conception of the nation-state, which is available at the societal level.

A second focus of community studies is on the local territorial group considered not as a powerful multibonded group like the nation-state, but rather as a group roughly on the same analytic level as other organized groups. An example of this focus is the work on community power structure. This focus on the *territorial bond* of organization of the local aggregation should not be confused with all sociocultural aspects of the aggregation, on the one hand, or with the concept of territoriality on the other.

The concept of *territoriality* is the heart of the third focus of community studies (see Hawley, 1950). By territoriality is meant the way in which sociocultural reality is "anchored" and patterned in space — the concrete spatial enactment or manifestation of social and cultural systems (which operate for the most part *through* personality systems). Territoriality can be studied with reference to any sociocultural phenomenon from an individual to a nation-state. Each level of generalization brings a slightly different set of territorial relationships into focus. The community aggregation level, however, is the point from which the general territoriality phenomenon most usefully can be brought into focus. This is why the concept of territoriality is so often linked with the concept of community.

A final aspect of community studies which distinguishes them from society studies is than contemporary circumstances community aggregations are always units of (in the most general sense) society aggregations, and this fact always looms large in importance. The analogous phenomenon at the societal level, of course, is the relation of the society to the world of societies.

For purposes of this discussion, the important point about each of these community studies foci is that none of them is concerned with the community as a major, specific, and concrete organized system in a hierarchy of major systems. Community, in any of the above senses, has few of the properties and characteristics of an organized group. In most cases it will have no central decision-making capacity which it can call its own; it will have very imprecise definitions of rights and duties, functions and roles, social status and position; it will have low solidarity, little individuality, little margin of autonomy from external sources of change, great possibility of variation, and so on. Individual groups within the community aggregate may indeed have most of these properties, but the community itself as a group generally does not.

Conclusion

This paper has suggested that a social systems theory which is built around the specific properties and hierarchical and analytical levels of organized groups will take some modification to be applicable to socio-cultural units such as communities and societies. Specifically our discussion has been focused around the organized-disorganized nature of social groups (social systems) and the reality of cultural systems as distinct from social system (group) realities. Because of both these dimensions, the organized group does not relate to its environment in a subsystem relationship similar to that pertaining to a subsystem relationship within an organization.

First, the environment of an organization contains a wide variety of unorganized groups or congeries as well as partially organized social unities. To overlook these is to do much greater damage to the reality of the community and societal order than is the case in the related "simplification" of intraorganizational phenomena as typified by most of social systems analysis. Second, for certain purposes the organized group can be regarded as an organized subsystem of an organized higher system — the nation-state, but this should not blind one to the cultural realities of the sociocultural context of organizations which are not subsumed under the nation-state concept, nor should it be assumed that there is an equivalent to the nation-state at the community level of which organized groups might be sub-systems. Third, the analysis of culture systems, which is so important a part of the reality of the sociocultural environment, does not seem subject to very useful analysis by the kind of conceptual apparatus developed for social systems, particularly those concepts which make reference to the properties of organized groups.

In short, the organized group on which most social systems analysis is focused and which bears the closest analogy in the sociocultural world to organic and mechanical systems is undoubtedly one of the most important phenomena of the sociocultural world — but it is by no means the only phenomenon. One usefully may be blind to sociocultural diversity in the lower-order social unities, but not so usefully in the higher-order communities and societies.

Finally, it seems relevant to conclude with some observations about general systems theory of the type promulgated by Miller, *et al.* All systems do indeed share a common pattern, by definition. A system is a set of interdependent units. In this sense a mechanism, an organism, a personality, a group, a nation-state, and so forth, are all systems. Indeed, almost everything in life is related systematically to the degree that it is related at all. This insight is critically important in all the sciences. Beyond this, however, it is equally as important to be aware of the *qualitative* differences among system types. Just as mechanical and organic systems are qualitatively different from each other, so these two systems are qualitatively different from sociocultural systems. It is ironic that sociology, at least, has struggled over the last century to be relieved of physical and biological reductionism, only to be thrust back in that direction in modern times through the work of "living systems" theorists, on the one hand, and "cybernetic systems" theorists, on the other.

A concentration of this paper has been that there are further important distinctions to be drawn within the sociocultural world itself, particularly that between Sorokin's causal-functional interaction and meaningful interaction. The latter represents a systematic form, as expressed in purely ideological cultural systems, in which interdependence takes logical and aesthetic patterns (and can be discerned primarily with rational and intuitive modes of cognition). Thus it is fundamentally different from the causal-functional interdependence (which is discerned through the rational and empirical modes of cognition), which the sociocultural world shares with the biological and physical worlds.

It is our deeply held belief that the systematic approaches or orientations hold the greatest promise for the fullest understanding of the sociocultural world, as well as the natural world — and particularly for the integration of knowledge about these worlds. Systems approaches are mostly little more than orientations, however — orientations which force us to perceive interdependent wholes. They are not short-cuts to knowledge — probably quite the contrary — and their utilization for forcing qualitatively different aspects of reality into preconceived molds, and thus losing important distinctions, represents in our judgment a grave misuse.

Bibliography

Boulding, K. E. General systems theory — The skeleton of science. *Management Science*, 2, 1956, 197–208.

Bredemeier, H. C. Transactional analysis and the societal system. Unpublished draft, Rutgers — The State University, 1966.

Hawley, A. *Human Ecology*. New York: Ronald Press, 1950.

Homans, G. C. *The Human Group*. New York: Harcourt Brace, 1950.

Kroeber, A. L., & Parsons, T. The concepts of culture and of social system. *American Sociological Review*, 1958, 23, 582–583.

Levine, D. N. Cultural integration. Unpublished draft, University of Chicago, 1966.

Levy, M. J. *The structure of society*. Princeton: Princeton University Press, 1952.

Loomis, C. P. *Social systems: Essays on their persistence and change*. Princeton: D. Van Nostrand, 1960.

Mercer, B. E. *The American community*. New York: Random House, 1956.

Miller, J. G. Living systems: Basic concepts. *Behavioral Science*, 1965a, 10, 193–237.

———. Living systems: Structures and process. *Behavioral Science*, 1965b, 10, 380–411.

———. Toward a general theory for the behavioral sciences. *American Psychologist*, 1955, 10, 513–531.

Parsons, T., & Smelser, N. J. *Economy and society*. Glencoe: The Free Press, 1956.

Parsons, T., Bales, R. F., & Shils, E. A. *Working papers in the theory of action*. Glencoe: The Free Press, 1953.

Parsons, T. *The social system*. Glencoe: The Free Press, 1951.

———. An outline of the social system. In Parsons, T., Shils, E. A., Naegele, K. D., & Pitts, J. R. (Eds.), *Theories of society*. New York: Free Press of Glencoe, 1961.

———. *Societies*. Englewood Cliffs, N. J.: Prentice-Hall, 1966.

Sanders, I. T. *The community: An introduction to a social system.* (2nd ed.) New York: Ronald Press, 1966.

Sorokin, P. A. *Society, culture and personality: Their structure and dynamics.* New York: Cooper Square Publishers, 1962.

———. *Sociological theories of today.* New York: Harper & Row, 1966.

von Bertalanffy, L. General systems theory. *Main currents in modern thought,* 1955, 71, 75–87.

Warren, R. L. *The community in America.* Chicago: Rand McNally, 1963.

Organizational Dimensions and Their Interrelationships: A Theory of Compliance[1, 2]

AMITAI ETZIONI
Department of Sociology
Columbia University

Introduction

The importance of organizations as a distinct social phenomenon hardly needs to be demonstrated. Most members of modern societies are born in, educated by, work for, pray or play in, and are buried by organizations. In social science literature, though, it is not fully accepted that organizations constitute a distinct analytic category. Even less a matter of consensus is the question of which analytic categorization is to be used in studying this distinct phenomenon. In this paper, we first briefly indicate why we take a nonreductionist position; we then present one analytic categorization of organizations which grew out of a secondary analysis of a large number of organizational studies. We conclude by reporting two new studies, conducted after this analytic categorization and the related propositions were published; the studies seem to lend it a measure of support.

A Nonreductionist, Analytic Position

We suggest that social science data, or data about human behavior, are most productively approached with the assumption that the units of analysis relate to each other like a set of Chinese nesting boxes. That

[1] This contribution is a by-product of the author's work under Grant No. (WA)CRD 280-6-175 from the Department of Health, Education, and Welfare.

[2] In this paper, the author draws on his own *A Comparative Analysis of Complex Organizations* (New York: The Free Press, 1961). By far the best statement of this approach in the psychological literature is presented by Edgar H. Schein, *Organizational Psychology* (Englewood, N. J.: Prentice-Hall, 1965), pp. 44–47. The author is indebted to Prof. Bernard Indik for a stimulating discussion prior to the drafting of this paper and to Sarajane Heidt for comments on an earlier draft.

is, while there are some universal building stones which appear in all
the units, units differ in that emergent properties which appear in some
do not appear in others, and in that some units provide contexts for
others — that is, they set constraints on the variability of attributes and
relations in those units that are in context. Finally, and most important,
statements about the relations among the variables which characterize
one unit cannot be translated into statements about other units without
a significant, unaccounted for, residue remaining. Nonreductionists use
various lists of the units. We use roles as universal building stones and
small groups, complex organizations, collectivities, and societies as our
main units.

In defending a nonreductionist position in favor of a distinct sub-
theory for the study of complex organization, one that focuses on their
emergent properties, three kinds of reductionisms are eliminated. The
most commonly discussed is that of psychological reductionism, which
views all statements as reducible to propositions about personality or
an undifferentiated "behavior." The second one recognizes a social
level in addition to a psychological one, but sees no need for analytic
gradations within this level. The third, cultural reductionism, recognizes a socio-cultural level but refuses to grant psychological attributes
an independent analytic status. Like the second, it usually does not
see a need for gradations in the social level itself.

Our position is that both a social level as distinct from a psychological one and gradations within this level can be defended by one
set of arguments; empirically, we suggest, the propositions advanced
below, which explain *part* of the variance of behavior in organizations
in terms of organizational variables, cannot be accounted for in terms
of nonorganizational variables. Pragmatically, it seems productive to
make these distinctions because they lead to new understandings of
the phenomenon under study. Logically, we recognize a distinction
between subunits, units, and supraunits that can be universally applied.
We apply it here to organizations (as the unit), small groups (as subunits), and collectivities and societies (as supraunits).[3]

Our approach is analytic in the sense that we join those that hold
that social science may be advanced by promoting theories as sets of
variables that are systematically related, and that statements about these
relations should be submitted systematically to empirical validation.

A Methodological Aside

While there is no logical association between the subject matter
of each social science discipline and one research technique, there

---

[3] For additional discussion of this point by the author, see Chapter 3 in his *The Active
Society: A Theory of Societal and Political Processes* (New York: The Free Press,
1968).

clearly are historical associations. Experiments are more likely to be conducted by psychologists than by anthropologists, an historian would be more likely to be consulted for document analysis than a sociologist, and so on. These techniques can also be ranked in terms of their degree of precision and degree of inclusiveness. While some techniques lend themselves more readily to inclusiveness (or coverage), others are more specifically precise. While many scholars ultimately aim to be both precise and inclusive, it must be noted that many make a choice to sacrifice to some degree one quality for the other. It further seems that the average experimental psychologist ranks higher on precision but lower on inclusiveness than, let us say, an average anthropologist. Many a psychologist is willing to invest much more of his time and research budget in improving his research tools and measurements than many a sociologist; often, less research energy is left to invest in coverage. The following discussion is to be viewed as the opposite kind of endeavor — as an attempt to cull, by the use of relatively primitive tools, some highly inclusive generalizations. Those accustomed to a more carefully measured but also more meager diet will have to be tolerant with the "loose" and "sweeping" statements that follow. This is particularly the case as the findings are based largely on secondary analysis of numerous studies which vary much in their reliability, definitions of concepts, and quality of data.

The Basic Findings: A Positive Association between Power and Involvement

Why an Analytic Classification?

Earlier organization theories focused largely on what organizations have in common. Weber, for instance, specified six attributes he expected all organizations to have.[4] March and Simon (1958) inventoried hundreds of propositions in a book entitled *Organizations*, but never specified to which organizations these propositions apply, implying that they apply universally. But even a cursory examination of these theoretical statements shows that they hold for some organizations but not for others. To take one example, Weber expected all organizations to be monocratic; he was using the image of German bureaucracies, specifically those of the state, the army, and the church. But universities and hospitals are not monocratic; the decisions concerning the activities most directly related to their goals — teaching, research, and therapy — are not ranked in a monocratic hierarchy. We suggest, hence, that organizations should be *defined* by one attribute — social

---

[4] Weber, M. *Essays in sociology.* New York: Oxford Univ. Press, 1946, pp. 196–204.

units that pursue specialized goals[5] — to set organizations apart from other social units, such as families, friendship groups, collectivities, and societies. On all other attributes, organizations are best assumed to vary unless proven otherwise.

If this is granted, the question becomes one of whether or not there is a variable which can order, in an analytic fashion, the large variety of organizations which exist. That is, we seek a variable that is part of a theory and will provide for an exhaustive classification. Secondly, we need a productive classification, one in which organizations that are classified as belonging in one "box" in terms of the classifying variable will also "bunch" on one or more other dimensions. After having tried several variables, we found that the kind of compliance relations that prevail in an organization provides such a variable. We turn now to present the basic concepts used, the resulting classification, and the bunching on the other variables.

The Centrality of Compliance

We suggest that organizations differ systematically in the means they use to control their participants and in the orientations their participants have toward them, and that these differences provide a ground for an analytic classification. Organizations are an "artificial" unit because they are relatively more deliberately designed, structured, and restructured than other social units. Families, friendship groups, collectivities, and societies change or develop; only organizations can be reorganized. Organizations have subunits deliberately set up in order to collect information systematically about the performance of the unit and to revise its policies, rules, and structure on the basis of this information. Other social units have no such subunits, or — like modern societies — have them only to the degree that they have organizations (for example, state administration). This is not to suggest that organizations have no informal, expressive, unguided aspects. But they are much more artificial than other social units.

Because of this artificiality, organizations have to rely more on formal controls and deliberate reward of conforming performances and punishment of deviating ones, in contrast to the informal sanctioning which is built into the natural relationships of the family and friendship groups. In organizations, attempts are made to keep performances in patterns that are highly unnatural, at least in terms of the norms of other social units in which the members of organizations are socialized and

---

[5] This definition follows Talcott Parsons, "Suggestions for a Sociological Approach to the Theory of Organizations," *Administrative Science Quarterly*, Vol. 1 (1956), pp. 63–85, 225–239.

possibly in terms of native personality needs.[6] Thus, for instance, for an organization official to treat all clients "universalistically" — disregarding their color, status, family, or friendship relations to him — is not "natural" and is a behavior that, if it is to survive, needs systematically to be reinforced, and that reinforcement must be organized — hence, the centrality of compliance for organizations.

To analyze further these structures and establish a basis for comparison, one should take into account (a) differences in the kinds of sanctions various organizations rely upon, (b) the orientation the participants have to an organization as they enter it, and (c) the effects these two factors have on each other. We turn now to explore these two factors and their relationship in some detail.

Organizational Sanctioning and Power

The capacity to sanction is much affected by an actor's power. *Power* is an actor's ability to induce another actor to carry out his directives or other norms he supports. Many objections have been raised against this concept; they can only be treated here briefly. First, it is a probablistic concept, in that an actor has power over another if the other will tend to follow his directives but not necessarily have to do so in each instance. Secondly, it is not based on *post hoc* observations, as one can make a prediction, on the basis of analysis of the means available to two or more actors and their internal characteristics and mechanisms, about how likely one will be to have power over the other(s), before any power is actually applied. Thirdly, assets and power are not to be confused. Power is made out of assets (the possessions an actor has), but, as assets may be put to other usages than the generation of power (for example, they may be saved or consumed), no one-to-one association between assets and power is to be assumed or expected. Assets, though, are to be treated as power potentials. Finally, power is a sector-specific concept in that to have power in one sector of human behavior — for instance, in economic matters — does not automatically mean having power in others, though there is a halo effect and a possibility for conversion of power in one sector into another.

The power we deal with here is that of organizations, and we are concerned only with its application in sanctioning behavior as far as conduct in the organization is concerned. By stating that the power is of an organizational variety, we mean that it is available to some participants to control the others to conform to the *organizational* rules and instructions. The use of the same means to advance the personal

---

[6] If there are such needs is a much debated point which cannot be explored here. It will be argued in our forthcoming *The Active Society, op. cit.*

goals and wishes of the power wielders triggers processes which lead
to its cancellation. Further, persons who leave the organization do not
take its power with them, and new ones that join get it, if recruited in
accord with the "proper" organizational rules.

Power, analytically, can be exhaustively classified according to the
means of control applied. If they are symbolic, such as gestures and
signals, we refer to the power as *normative*. If they are material objects,
or cash used to obtain them, we refer to the power as *remunerative*. If
they are physical means which entail contact with the body of those
subjected to power, such as inflicting pain, deformity, or death, we
refer to *coercive* power. Threats and promises are classified according
to the kinds of transactions which are threatened or promised; a promise
to pay is remunerative, a threat to slap is coercive.

Three marginal comments are necessary. (a) Any concrete power
may be either exclusively one of the three kinds or various combinations
thereof. (b) Coercion is not synonymous with non-voluntary behavior.
All behavior induced by power is involuntary, even if it is induced by
the threat of excommunication which is symbolic and, hence, normative.
Coercive power refers here only to control by the use of physical means,
sometimes referred to as means of violence. (c) While some power
can be generated through threats and promises, without actually involving sanctions, there must be a certain frequency of actual sanctioning
for power to be effective; otherwise, the credibility of threats and promises is expected to decline.

Our main finding regarding organization power is that *most
organizations most of the time tend to specialize in their reliance on
one kind of power in the control of their lower participants*. While
organizations often mix their means of control and draw on two or all
three kinds, most of them rely more heavily on one of the three kinds.
In turn, while there are differences in the power mix used to control
various subgroupings of the participants in any one organization, there
is a typical pattern for all lower participants in most organizations.
We choose to focus on the lower participants because they constitute
the largest majority of the participants and because differences in
control of these, we shall see, provide a highly productive comparative
base in terms of corollary differences. Thus, for instances, prisons rely
relatively more heavily on coercion (including confinement) of their
inmates than do factories to control their workers, not to mention
churches to control their worshipers. Factories rely relatively heavily
on remunerative power as compared to prisons and churches, and
churches rely largely on the power of symbols, that is, normative power.

The reason that organizational control structures tend to specialize
in applying one kind of power seems to be that the various kinds are

contradictory; when applied jointly, they neutralize each other. A study which compared the application of normative power by itself to one where it was given similar status to utilitarian power showed the purer application to be more effective (Merton, 1946). Organizations which give two kinds of power a similar status tend to segregate their application internally, or are not effective (Etzioni, 1961).

These statements are not without methodological difficulties. Instances of use of various kinds of power are not easy to count and are difficult to weigh. Only very few of the numerous studies of the various organizations we analysed have direct, validated, and quantitative measures of the power mix used. We, hence, had to make do with various approximations. Here is an example of a *relatively* good indicator, taken from a study of a factory and used to show the highly remunerative control used.

TABLE 1. "Method of Recognition" Preferred by Workers and Supervisors*

Method of Recognition	Rank Order	
	Workers Like	Supervisors Find Effective
Recommend pay increase	1	1
Train employees for better jobs	2	6
Recommend promotions	3	3
Give more responsibility	4	4
Praise sincerely and thoroughly	5	5
Give more interesting work	6	9
Tell superiors	7	7
Give privileges	8	8
Give pat on the back	9	2
Make notes of it in ratings and reports	10	10

* Source: F. Mann and J. Dent, *Appraisals of Supervisors* (Ann Arbor: Survey Research Center, University of Michigan, 1954), p. 25.

We would have preferred the question to have been phrased differently; "methods of recognition" has human relations and psychological connotations and may well evoke normative notions in the supervisors' minds (and may explain, in part, why the workers see the methods used as more "remunerative" than the supervisors).[7] We would like to know more about the frequency distributions, because the intervals between the rungs are, in all likelihood, uneven and there may be subgroups of supervisors or workers that are highly atypical which would affect the interpretation of the scale. We would also like to have directly comparable data for other organizations. All these data are not avail-

---

[7] The supervisors ranked remunerative methods first but normative ones as second and third, while the workers' first three are remunerative. F. Mann and J. Dent, *Appraisals of Supervisors* (Ann Arbor: Survey Research Center, University of Michigan, 1954).

able. Hence, our secondary analysis, which draws on this and other such studies, is, as we said earlier, necessarily one of first approximations.

To the degree that such data and analysis can be relied upon, we conclude, on the basis of such studies, the following ranking of organizations:

TABLE 2. A Compliance Classification*

Organizations in each category are listed according to the relative weight of the predominant compliance pattern in their compliance structure. Those giving the predominant pattern greatest weight are listed first.

1. *Predominantly coercive*
    Concentration camps
    Prisons (most)
    Correctional "institutions" (large majority)
    Custodial mental hospitals
    Prisoner of war camps
    Relocation centers
    Coercive unions

    Place in category undetermined: Forced-labor camps

2. *Predominantly utilitarian (remunerative)*
    Blue-collar industries and blue-collar divisions in other industries
    White-collar industries and white-collar divisions in other industries (normative compliance is a secondary pattern)
    Business unions (normative compliance is a secondary pattern)
    Farmers' organizations (normative compliance is a secondary pattern)
    Peacetime military organizations (coercive compliance is a secondary pattern)

3. *Predominantly normative*
    Religious organizations (including churches, orders, monasteries, convents)
    Ideological political organizations
    General hospitals
    Colleges and universities
    Social unions
    Voluntary associations
        a. Fraternal associations (high social compliance)
        b. Fund-raising and action associations (high social plus secondary emphasis on pure normative compliance)
    Schools (coercion in varying degrees is the secondary pattern)
    Therapeutic mental hospitals (coercion is the secondary pattern)
    Professional organizations (including research organizations, law firms, newspapers, planning firms, etc.; utilitarian compliance is the secondary pattern)

    Place in category undetermined: "Core" organizations of social movements.

4. *Dual structures*
    Normative-coercive: Combat units
    Utilitarian-normative: Majority of unions
    Utilitarian-coercive: Some early industries, some farms, company towns, and ships

* Source: Amitai Etzioni, *A Comparative Analysis of Complex Organizations* (New York: The Free Press, 1961), pp. 66–67.

Dual organizations refer to those whose power is an exception to the rule; no one kind of power prevails, but two seem to be given about equal status (we found no organizations where all three had equal status).

One other complication must be introduced. It is not self-evident who the lower participants of an organization are. There is some disagreement if, for instance, the students are "in" a university, as participants, or "out," as clients. Indeed, it has even been suggested that the customers of a firm are to be considered part of the organization (March and Simon, 1958, p. 89). For reasons we discussed elsewhere in detail (Etzioni, 1961, pp. 16–27), we assessed participation on three main dimensions: involvement, subordination, and performance requirements. We use a simple scoring of *low, medium,* and *high* and include as participants all those who score medium or high on at least one of these dimensions. Customers of a supermarket score low on all three and, hence, are not participants by this definition. Students score medium to high on at least two and, therefore, are "in." Members of voluntary associations may be in or out, depending on the sociological reality of their participation, as assessed on these dimensions. If they are formally members, but do little with or for the association, have little involvement in its affairs, and largely disregard its "orders," they are not participants by our account.

Participants' Involvement in Organization

Our second main finding is that *most of the lower participants of most organizations have an involvement in their organization which is "typical" to their kind of organization.* For instance, most inmates of most prisons are more hostile toward their prisons than are most workers toward most factories. We define *involvement* as a cathectic-evaluative orientation of an actor, which is characterized in terms of intensity and direction. The intensity ranges from high to low; the direction is either positive or negative. The distribution of involvement of all participants of all organizations seems to have a curvilinear shape. At the one end are the intensely negatively involved, while at the other end are the positively intensive; in the middle are those which are either positively or negatively involved but with less intensity.

Data about the involvement of lower participants in organizations are much more available than data on power applied to them and are easier to quantify, as no three-way mixes are involved. There is one hitch, though; from the viewpoint of the lower participants, each organization has several facets, and their involvement in them varies. The orientation toward organizational goals, for instance, is often different from that toward the supervisors, and the latter is different from the orientation to the organizational control mix.

There are two ways to proceed from here: either to compare the involvement of the participants of various organizations as regarding the same facet (for example, inmates', workers', and students' involvements in the goals of their respective organizations), or to build indices of involvement for each organization encompassing the basic facets and compare the index scores. In a previous report, we attempted some of each (Etzioni, 1961, pp. 16–22), but much of the comparison remains to be done. As far as our secondary analysis allows us to tell, using either one of these procedures, organizations can be ranked, according to the modal involvements of the lower participants, as being relatively more or less intensively involved and the modal involvement being positive or negative.

Power and Involvement

Our third finding is that *there is an association between the kind of power mix typically used by an organization and the modal involvement of its lower participants.* Highly coercive mixes tend to be met with intensive negative involvement, normative mixes with intense positive involvement, and remunerative mixes with less intense positive or negative involvement, depending on the mix. This statement, we claim, holds not just for the "crude" associations of the three basic mixes, but also for "finer" ones. Thus, in the contemporary United States, the control mix of white collar workers seems, on the average, somewhat less remunerative and somewhat more normative than the mix of unskilled blue-collar workers, though both are predominantly remunerative. In line with our basic proposition, there is some evidence that unskilled blue-collar workers are *somewhat* more negative (or less positive) in their modal involvement. Or, most colleges are more "purely" normative in their controls than most high schools, and — we suggest — modal student involvement is more intensely positive in colleges, though it is positive in both and the power mix is predominantly normative in both the average college and high school. Similarly, correctional institutions are somewhat less coercive than prisons, and inmate negative involvement seems somewhat less intense.

Next, the basic statement seems to hold (though with some lag, which must be expected for obvious reasons) for changes over time. That is, when an organization changes its power mix, let us say a "custodial" (that is, highly coercive) prison becomes relatively "therapeutic" (that is, more normative), we expect (and there are some reports of changes in inmates 'orientations toward) less intensely negative involvements.

The power-involvement association seems to have one main exception: when coercion is *very* high, negative involvement does not rise but reverses itself. There is some evidence that men in concentration camps did not focus their hostility on the organization but on each other (Bettelheim, 1943).

When we seek to refer to the power mix and involvement mode jointly, we refer to the *compliance* structure of an organization. Structures, which, in line with the prevailing associations, have power mixes and involvement modes which complement each other, may be referred to as "congruent structures." "Noncongruent" compliance structures — having, for example, normative control and negative involvement — are to be expected and are found, because the kind of power mix an organization uses is affected by factors other than the kind of involvement the participants exhibit, and the kind of involvement the participants exhibit is affected by factors other than the power mix the organization applies. For instance, for an organization to employ coercion, it needs a societal license which may be extended, limited, or revoked. To rely heavily on remunerative power, an organization requires a suitable income, which is not always available. The participants' involvement is affected by their previous socialization experience with other organizations and with the one under study.

When the power employed and the involvement exhibited are noncongruent, we expect a high level of intraorganizational strain and pressure for one of the "sides" to adjust. When environmental factors unlock, the compliance structures are expected to move toward one of the congruent types. Thus, if intensely hostile inmates are treated by a new prison staff (social workers, psychiatrists) with normative means, either they will change their orientation to a more positive one — or the staff will tend to turn toward more coercive controls, within limits of the environmental tolerance.

We view the kind of power mix an organization typically employs and the modal involvement of its lower participants as two variables which affect each other, but not one as the cause and the other as an effect. An organization may be under pressure to rely on a relatively coercive mix because of the intense hostility of the lower participants; or friendly lower participants may be antagonized because a coercive mix is employed. While the two factors affect each other, each is affected by other factors, and hence, they vary independently and no one-to-one relationship is expected. For instance, in the study quoted earlier, the workers' attitudes were less positive than would be expected on the basis of the supervisors' controls (at least if one accepts their reporting of their methods of control as accurate).

The Correlates of Compliance

The fourth finding seems to us to be by far the most important one, to justify many of the preceding definitional exercises and methodological concessions, and to contain a set of many specific findings: we suggest that *organizations which differ in their power mix and in the modal involvement of their lower participants will also differ on a score of other dimensions,* which amounts to saying that these two dimensions make for wholly different social units. (If this statement is valid, it also lends support to our earlier claim for the fruitfulness of the classification used). We characterize these first in *Gestalt* terms. In order not to complicate the discussion unnecessarily, we focus on three archetypes — prisons, factories, and churches — leaving out finer gradations of power mixes and involvement modes, and limiting ourselves here to congruent types.

Organizations where coercion is relatively heavily relied upon and the modal involvement is intensely negative — traditional prisons, for instance — tend rigidly to be divided into two castes, with little expressive contact between them and considerable inter-caste tension and open conflict. Mobility from one caste to the other, in effect, does not exist. While one caste controls the other, like an occupation army, it does not, as a rule, provide leadership for the other. The two castes do not make a social whole, though they function within the limits of one organization. Their values are at least in part antithetical. Various "ameliorations" are found — for example, there are often some "collaborators" with the guards among the inmates, and there often is some "corruption of authority" on the side of some guards who are less coercive than most of the others. But, by and large, the archetype of two hostile camps, one subjugating the other, holds for most relations.

Organizations where normative power is relatively heavily relied upon and the modal involvement is intensely positive — in an effective church, for instance — will tend to be well integrated into one community, with many expressive contacts across the ranks, comparatively little inter-rank tension, and mainly latent conflict. Mobility up the ranks is comparatively common. There is a relatively high degree of value consensus among the lower and higher participants. Much leadership "flows" down the organizational structure. There are some contrary factors, such as conflicts among leaders (for instance, lay and religious ones) and conflicts among strict versus moderate normative interpretations. But, by and large, the archetype of one community functioning in one organization prevails in most relations.

Organizations that rely heavily on remunerative power are "in the middle." The participants in such organizations are often divided into three or more "classes," differing in socioeconomic background, education, and consumption habits. Workers, supervisors, and management are the main ones (Dalton, 1947). While most of the mobility is within each "class," there is cross-class upward mobility. The relationships among the classes vary considerably from factory to factory, but, on the average, there is less of an expressive split than in coercive organizations and much more instrumental cooperation, but much less of an expressive community than in churches, though both kinds of organizations rank about the same on instrumental matters (a kind of activity which is marginal for churches but central for factories). Workers tend to have leaders of their own but also to accept some leadership from supervisors.

Now, these basic differences in the general character of organizations which differ in their compliance structures can be "dimensionalized" along a large variety of specific dimensions, such as degree of consensus across the ranks, amount of cross-rank communication and frequency of communication blocks, status of lower participants' leaders, and so forth. We found that in some instances the relationship between the nature of the compliance structure and such a dimension is linear; that is, there is a straight positive association between the dimension, let us say the level of cross-rank consensus, and place on the power mix and involvement continuum. In other cases, the relationship is curvilinear, with the dimension — for instance, organizational scope (the degree to which the organization penetrates into various life spheres of the participants) — higher at the two ends of the compliance continuum than in the middle. For all variables studied, though, one association or another with the basic classifying variables — power mix and involvement mode — was found (Etzioni, 1961).

Some Validation in Primary Research

Since the basic classification and some of its correlates were published in 1961, a number of studies were made testing the basic classification and its basic correlates or adding to the correlates (Jones, 1965; Leeds, 1964; Levinson and Schiller, 1966). In one study, relying on a statistical analysis of a large number organizations, no association was found between our compliance classification and the organizational goals (Haas, Hall & Johnson, 1966). The same study attempts to correlate organization goals with another organization classification, that by Blau and Scott (1962), which classifies organizations according to their main clientele, but also found no association. While there are some questions about the quality of the data used in this study, the negative finding weakens our proposition. On the other hand, all the other studies support or extend it. The most important of these is a study of the power used by the Chinese Communist party to control the peasantry and the orientation of the peasantry to this party and the means of control it employs (Skinner, 1965). The importance of the study is that it is dynamic: it shows in detail how, as the party changed its control again and again, the peasants' involvement changed very much in the way the preceding analysis would lead one to expect.

Zelda Gamson (1966) compared the faculty of two departments of a state college. She found that faculty members of one department who are less normative in their ways of handling students than those of another, on one dimension, are also different — in the same direction — on several others.

TABLE 3. Mean Percentage of Faculty Time Spent on Teaching Duties, Curriculum Planning, and Counseling Students,* Spring, 1961–Spring, 1963**

	Spring 1961		Fall 1961		Spring 1962		Fall 1962		Spring 1963	
	NS	SS	NS	SS	NS	SS	NS	SS	NS	SS
Teaching duties*** (Classes, grading, preparation)	83%	68%	74%	60%	79%	68%	65%	65%	71%	72%
Curriculum planning	6	8	9	9	6	4	11	6	9	8
Counseling (Individual students or organizations)	3	12	7	14	5	11	7	9	8	5
N	9	12	10	13	10	14	12	11	11	10

* Does not include research.

** Source: Zelda Gamson, "Utilitarian and Normative Orientations Toward Education," *Sociology of Education*, Vol. 39, No. 1 (Winter 1966), p. 66.

*** P of differences between NS and SS in spring, 1961 and fall, 1961 $<.05$. After 1961, differences are not statistically significant.

NS stands for the less normative Natural Science department, and SS for the more normative Social Science department. The faculties of the two departments also differed in their conceptions and expectations of students, educational objectives, norms regarding student-faculty relations, and conceptions of their effects on the students. No data on student involvement are reported.

Joseph Julian studied the compliance structures of five hospitals — a university hospital, a medium-size general voluntary hospital, a large general voluntary hospital, a tuberculosis sanatorium, and a veterans' hospital — all located within the metropolitan area of a large western city. The hospitals were ranked according to the degree to which their control mixes were "purely" normative or included a coercive element. The involvement of 183 patients was studied and found to be in line with the basic proposition — that is, more positive in the normative hospitals than in the normative-coercive ones. Then, the type of hospital was associated with the amount of inter-rank communication blocks, with the following finding.

. . . more reported communication blocks occurred in the normative-coercive hospitals than in the normative hospitals. Blockage occurred with regard to contact involving primarily instrumental activity in both an upward and downward direction. Furthermore, it was shown that the amount of control as well as the type of control is related to the nature and degree of communication blocks. (Julian, 1966, p. 389)

There is nothing conclusive about the data available either from the secondary or primary analysis. It seems safe to conclude, however, that a basic analytic classification of organizations seems to appear in varying ways in a large variety of data. Additional research will have to ascertain more precisely what it looks like, what its dimensions are, and probably revise our conception of it. It seems, though, quite certain that there is "something out there" and that we have some notions of its basic contours. Secondly, these organizational variables illustrate what is meant by emergent properties, of which organizational characteristics are a sub-set. While it may still be argued that such statements about organizational variables "really" reflect states of personality, the burden of proof is on those who can provide evidence to this effect.

Bibliography

Bettelheim, B. Individual and mass behavior in extreme situations. *Journal of Abnormal and Social Psychology*, 1943, 38, 417–452.

Blau, P., & Scott, W. R. *Formal organizations*. San Francisco, California: Chandler Publishing Company, 1962.

Dalton, M. Worker response and social background. *Journal of Political Economics*, 1947, 55, 323–332.

Etzioni, A. *A comparative analysis of complex organizations*. New York: The Free Press, 1961.

————. *The active society: A theory of societal and political processes.* New York: The Free Press, 1968. Chapter 3.

Gamson, Zelda. Utilitarian and normative orientations toward education. *Sociology of Education*, 1966, 39 (1), 46–73.

Haas, J. E., Hall, R. H., & Johnson, N. J. Toward an empirically derived taxonomy of organizations. In R. V. Bowers (Ed.), *Studies on behavior in organizations*. Athens, Ga.: University of Georgia Press, 1966.

Julian, J. Compliance patterns and communication blocks in complex organizations. *American Sociological Review*, 1966, 31 (3), 382–389.

Jones, G. N. Strategies and tactics of planned organizational change. *Human organization*, 1965, 24, 192–200.

Leeds, Ruth. The absorption of protest. In W. W. Cooper, H. J. Leavitt, & M. W. Shelly, II (Eds.), *New perspectives in organization research*. New York: John Wiley & Sons, 1964. Pp. 115–135.

Levinson, P., & Schiller, J. Role analysis of the indigenous nonprofessional. *Social Work* (1966), 11 (3), 95–101.

Mann, F., & Dent, J. *Appraisals of supervisors.* Ann Arbor: Survey Research Center, University of Michigan, 1954. P. 25.

March, J. G., & Simon, H. *Organizations.* New York: John Wiley & Sons, 1958.

Merton, R. K. *Mass persuasion: The social psychology of a war bond drive.* New York: Harper Brothers, 1946.

Parsons, T. Suggestions for a sociological approach to the theory of organizations. *Administrative Science Quarterly*, 1956, 1, 63–85, 225–239.

Schein, E. H. *Organizational psychology.* Englewood Cliffs, N. J.: Prentice-Hall, 1965.

Skinner, G. W. Compliance and leadership in rural Communist China, a cyclical theory. Prepared for delivery at the 1965 Annual Meeting of the American Political Science Association, Washington, D. C., September 8–11, 1965.

Weber, M. *Essays in sociology.* New York: Oxford University Press, 1946. Pp. 196–204.

A General Systems Approach to Social Taxonomy

F. K. BERRIEN

Psychology Department
Rutgers — The State University

I should like in this paper to approach the problems that confront us from the standpoint of general systems theory — although the use of the term *theory* may be somewhat premature and cavalier. Once having sketched the main outlines of the assumptions and definitions, I would like to focus on groups and then return to a closer examination of the panels and variables that Indik has provided.

Perhaps a little historical background would be helpful. The impetus, if not the origin, of general systems theory (GST) came from von Bertalanffy (1955) — a theoretical biologist, who was subsequently joined by Boulding (1956) — an economist, J. G. Miller (1955) — a psychologist and psychiatrist, Ashby (1958) — a bacteriologist, Rapoport (1956) — a mathematician, and a growing number of persons of diverse formal training and professional affiliation. The development of GST has profited from concurrent theoretical advances in cybernetics, information theory, game theory, and graph and network theory in mathematics, to name but a few of the sources from which stimulation has been drawn and to which GST has made some contribution.

Perhaps the main thrust of GST has been in the direction of finding analogies and isomorphisms between electronic, chemomechanical, and biological systems. The conceptual links with psychological and social psychological phenomena are certainly more ambiguous and are only now beginning to appear. Miller's 1955 article elucidated some 19 propositions having relevance to biological, psychological and societal systems. He was forced then, as he has in more recent publications (1965), to employ much anecdotal and rather less experimentally derived data to show the relevance of psychological phenomena to GST.

GST has simply not had the time to stimulate experimental tests, although the theory is rich in stimulus value.

The effect of GST is to provide a counterbalance to the complexities of terminology and conceptualization that characterize all social science and, to a lesser extent, the semiexact physical sciences. While striving for simplistic conceptions, GST recognizes the requirements for specialized limited terms and concepts within disciplines, but asserts that these specialized concepts are enriched in meaning as they are related to a more general class of concepts.

To this end I should like to draw your attention to the numerous points of similarity between those variables that Indik ascribes to organizations, on the one hand, and to groups, on the other. It is this similarity which gives me the knife-edge wedge to introduce the possibility of a classification at a more general level. Specifically I should like to propose that there may be a way of conceiving most, if not all, of these variables as the common features of any system without specific regard to groups, organizations, individuals, or communities.

In offering this possibility I am well aware that my notions are at least audacious, perhaps unfruitful, and surely in need of further development. However, I am encouraged to present the ideas, because I think by some such approach Indik's encyclopedic list or any other may be further organized in a way that will generate hypotheses about the rules which govern the relationships between and among the variables. On this point he has been almost silent. I am encouraged also by the knowledge that what follows bears some correspondence with the concepts offered by Katz and Kahn (1966) and Sells (1966), and in one sense may merely be extrapolations or higher level abstractions of what has already been offered. I shall have to start with a set of rather pedantic definitions.

Definitions

A system is a set of *components* surrounded by a *boundary* which accepts *inputs* from some other system and discharges *outputs* into another system. By components we mean essentially other smaller systems. Thus human beings are systems who are components of groups, and groups are the components of organizations, and organizations are components of still larger segments that compose a community.

I should like to emphasize that the definition of a system just proposed is one that is not limited to human beings, groups, or organizations. Professor Andre Lwoff of the Pasteur Institute, Paris, and a Nobel laureate in physiology began his Nobel lecture with these words (1965):

An organism is an integrated system of interdependent structures and functions. An organism is constituted of cells and a cell consists of molecules which work in harmony. Each molecule must know what the others are doing. Each one must be capable of receiving messages and must be sufficiently disciplined to obey. You are familiar with the laws of control regulation. You know how our ideas have developed and how the most harmonious and sound of them have been fused into a conceptual whole which is the very foundation of biology and confers on it its unity.

If one were to reread this statement, substituting for *organism*, organization for *cell*, group, for *molecule*, person, the statement would still have the ring of truth. In other words, if one takes a general systems view the language of the biologist is not foreign to the social psychologist when either is talking about the fundamental processes in each field. Furthermore, the later sentences in the quotation reflect Lwoff's conviction that a set of theoretical statements may also be considered as a functional system.

Let me now return to the so far undefined terms in the basic definition.

The *boundary* of a system is a bit more difficult to define. In general terms it is the screen or filter through which inputs must pass to enter the system and outputs must pass to be discharged. Miller (1965) has used the term to mean an energy transducer. Light waves are transformed into nerve impulses by the boundary retina. Beef protein molecules are transformed by the digestive processes into human protein molecules before they are assimilated by human cells. Hemphill (1956) had as one of his group dimensions "permeability," by which he meant the ease with which new persons could enter or leave a group. The perceptual system of an individual is selective, screening in and screening out some stimuli. Organizations are also selective. Spectator behavior acceptable at an athletic contest is frowned upon in a church. Examples could be multiplied which illustrate the proposition that all systems running from cells at least through societies accept certain inputs and reject others, and it is the boundary that does the selecting.

The boundary of a system is not necessarily a specific line like the rind of a melon, although in some cases it may be. Instead, the boundary is best defined as a filtering-transducer function. The full range of possible social behaviors of which an individual is capable is constrained by the role behavior he adopts. For him, the roles he plays are his boundary and this may change depending upon the human social system in which he finds himself.

In this connection I am reminded of William James' delightful statement in which he described the dilemmas of the individual. "I am often confronted," he said,

. . . by the necessity of standing by one of my empirical selves (roles) and relinquishing the rest. Not that I would not, if I could, be both handsome and fat and well dressed, and a great athlete and make a million a year, be a wit, a *bon vivant* and a lady killer, as well as a philosopher; a philanthropist, statesman, warrior and African explorer, as well as a tone poet and saint. But the thing is simply impossible. The millionaire's work would run counter to the saint's; the *bon vivant* and philanthropist would trip each other up; the philosopher and lady-killer could not well keep house in the same tenement of clay. Such different characters may conceivably at the outset of life be alike *possible* to a man. But to make any of them actual, the rest must more or less be suppressed. (James, 1890)

The roles we select are only some among many.

The boundary of a group consists of the social mores, norms, ethics, customs, and obligations to which the individual must conform as the price of inclusion. Initiation ceremonies for fraternal groups, admission standards for colleges, professions of faith for religious organizations, certain élan or a "good" address for social clubs, adherence to an informal and unofficial production level for work groups are examples of the boundaries through which one must pass to be included in functioning group systems.

Under some circumstances the boundary may not select properly. Microbes and viruses in addition to appropriate nutrients, after all, do penetrate biological systems and cause mischief. However, as Walter Cannon and others before him emphasized, the healthy biological systems immediately react to neutralize, combat, or expel the noxious intruders. In like fashion, the norms and mores of a group may not always *prevent* a group member from behaving in ways at variance with those norms, but if he does, the group treats him in various ways that have the effect of neutralizing and insulating his influence, or in extreme instances, physically excluding him from the group's territory (Schachter, 1951; Merei, 1949). The norms, like the semipermeable walls of a cell, screen inputs according to criteria intrinsic in the components of the social or biological system itself. Should the boundary fail in its function, the rest of the system mobilizes its defenses, protecting itself from destruction. Yet even these defenses may be overwhelmed and the system — either social or biological — may disintegrate.

We have spoken of *inputs*. I should like to make a distinction between two kinds of inputs; maintenance and signal. These are also screened by the boundary. Maintenance inputs are those which sustain the system. A computer requires electrical power before it will do any work. Food, air, water are needed merely to sustain living biological systems. The sleekest of airplanes or autos require fuel before they will move. What about social systems?

Let me propose, following Homans (1950), Newcomb (1950), Katz and Kahn (1966), Thibaut and Kelley (1959), and a host of others, that a social system requires a minimum level of social interactions which feed back to provide what I shall call group-needs satisfactions (GNS). By this I mean that a group is held together once the social interaction has started by the satisfactions its members experience as a consequence of group membership. How far down the phylogenetic scale this may extend we don't at present know, but the burgeoning studies of social behavior among infrahuman species suggest social bonds can be found among insects if not lower. We set it as a proposition that no human group will *voluntarily* hold together unless its members find a minimal level of satisfaction from their interpersonal interactions. Moreover as we shall see later, there are several other auxiliary sources of GNS. This does not exclude the possibility of coerced groups such as a chain gang of prisoners, or a disgruntled work group under economic pressures accepting employment at high wages. It does say that as these coercive conditions diminish, GNS must increase merely to make possible the system's responsiveness to signal inputs, that is, to do something other than just exist. The external sources of maintenance for a social system are different for different types of systems. A work group in an organization would receive maintenance from what Fleishman and Harris (1962) call considerations emitted by supervisors. A committee of a church, a fraternal club, or a university would receive maintenance partly from whatever prestige accrues to the members from being appointed and from the good regard with which its output is held by the larger organization. Or, if one wishes to consider a total church, a business enterprise, a university, a hospital or a charity like the Red Cross, its external sources of maintenance come from its public reputation as perceived by its components.

Signal inputs to a system are those messages or stimuli which trigger the internal processes of the system to perform those functions of which it is capable. This definition requires us to make explicit an assumption which lies behind much of what has already been said, namely that the structure of a system, the attributes of its materials and components are a determiner of its functions. A telephone system will not do the work of a cake mixer. Or one person with his repertory of skills may not do the work of another with a different skill pattern. A bank cannot manufacture automobiles. Each of these systems is built differently and consequently performs differently. Moreover the signal inputs acceptable to each is different because of the difference in the system's structure. A savings deposit mailed to the automobile manufacturer would cause some consternation, exceeded perhaps only by the disturbances in a bank that received an order for a car. I have used extreme examples only to make evident the fundamental principle that *each kind of system, whether sense organ or organization, will accept only certain kinds of signals as process starters and the processes themselves depend upon the structure of the system.*

It is necessary to add a footnote regarding the structure-function relationship. A given structure may perform a finite number of functions. That is, a hammer may drive nails, serve as a doorstop, a weight in a balance scales, etc. But no function can occur without some structure.

The outputs of a system like the inputs may be distinguished as two kinds: the outputs for which the system was designed, and wastes or entropy. The first of these we label *formal achievement* (FA) when speaking of groups or organizations, but other descriptive terms apply to other systems. However, to understand what we mean by formal achievement, we must deal with two more assumptions. First, throughout the presentation so far we have assumed that all the systems with which we deal are *open* rather than *closed*, that is, the systems are nested in such a way that they receive inputs from, and discharge outputs to, collateral systems, subsystems and suprasystems. Moreover, each of the supra-, sub-, or collateral systems with which a particular system is related possesses the properties we have been describing. This being the case, our second assumption is that *some of a system's output must be acceptable to some other system as an input.* We have already said that inputs are filtered; hence, for a collection of systems to function as a supra-system, it is necessary that the FA produced by the components be of limited, special kind. Moreover, since a given structure can perform several functions and thus produce several different outputs, it is the "receiving" system which selects the outputs useful and acceptable to itself. Those outputs which are not useful to some other system or to the system for its own use are wastes. But even the outputs rejected by one system may in some cases be useful to another. Those not used by any system add to entropy.

All of us in this audience have at one time or another written an article or two — perhaps even a book — that we thought was an output of merit, but the first editor to whom it was sent did not think so. So you try another, or several editors. Perhaps you revise, rewrite to make it more acceptable. In extreme cases you file the piece, and it becomes waste so far as the publication systems are concerned. This is no more than the familiar trial-and-error principle, but what I am suggesting is that all systems in relating to other systems go through such a process and thereby constrain the full range of possible outputs to only those acceptable to some other systems. It is furthermore by this process of producing and selecting appropriate outputs that small systems collaborate to form larger systems, whether they are individuals forming a group, groups forming organizations, or organizations forming a community.

Now it is possible that what is considered waste by all other systems may not be waste to the system which produced it. A sugar mill produces sugar for commercial sale, but it also produces bagasse — the dried refuse of the sugar cane — that in years past was discarded. It is now burned in the furnaces that propel the mill itself. Or the rejected manuscript may nevertheless have served to increase your own intellectual grasp and clarified your thinking.

I have gone into these prosaic illustrations to make an additional point, namely, that *portions of the outputs considered waste by some supra-system may feedback into the system to help as maintenance inputs.* A group may take pride in its formal achievements and this may contribute to its GNS even though the consumer of the group's FA may consider such pride irrelevant. As a consumer, I am not interested in whether or not the milk I drink is produced by contented cows! I am interested in having it delivered on time in the appropriate quantity and free of contamination. The labor union whose FA is the protection and enhancement of its members' wages, working conditions, and rights — sometimes at considerable cost to its members, or the winning football team — are illustrations of the proposition that formal achievement may in some cases be a contributor to the maintenance of the system.

We have introduced another concept which needs some attention — feedback. This merely refers to the arrangement found in nearly all stable systems for controlling the input rate as a function of the output. This audience requires no detailed elaboration of the concept, which has been a powerful tool in the design of numerous chemical, electronic, or mechanical systems. Ecologists, biologists, and physiologists are currently searching for the "natural" feedback channels in their various systems, which go a long way toward understanding how a system is able to survive within larger systems that themselves vary both with respect to the input resources and output demands. Social psychologists, like the engineers, however, work with man-made systems, but unlike the engineers we have been less interested and skillful either in deliberately building feedback channels or in discovering precisely what they are in social systems. We have talked about adaptation and equilibrium without a clear understanding of how the system was adapting, or what was in equilibrium. But in mechanical, electronic, and biological systems equilibrium is the consequence of feedback.

A Systems Model

I should therefore like to offer a model of a general social system, which I believe may be applicable to organizations, groups, and the social psychological aspects of individuals. With this I believe it is possible to conceive of adaptation as the consequence of feedback from output to input on both the maintenance and signal side. Figure 1 gives an oversimplified diagrammatic presentation, and like all such simplified maps it cannot possibly portray all that is implied.

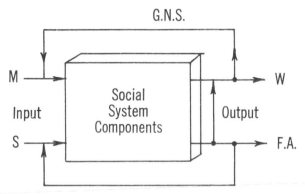

It will be noted first that we have not specified the components of the system nor the nature of the relations between the components. This is a black box. In servo or cybernetic theory a black box is any set of components whose interconnections are either unknown or for purposes of analysis are temporarily set aside. We can say parenthetically that all the relationships between the components (or between systems) can be described as some combination of mathematical relations. That is, their inputs and outputs either add to, subtract from, or compare (equal to, greater than, less than) with each other. Furthermore, and this is more important, the relationships between the components may change from time to time and the detailed description of all the existing relationships among the components is called the *state* of the system. A system of N components with R possible relations may have any one of $(R)^{N(N-1)}$ possible states at any particular point in time. With as few as four components and five possible relationships the number of states is $(5)^{12}$. This is a very large number. Since the relation between components may be modified at the next moment in time, a different but not completely new state becomes possible. Some aspects of a state are relatively stable and others are easily changed merely as a consequence of processing inputs. Evidence for this lies in the fatigue of systems as a consequence of work: the phenomena of learning and forgetting, of growth and decay. The difficulties in describing all possible states of the components at any point in time is therefore formidable and furthermore, the complete description of any single state may have only transitory and temporary validity.

Before going on to the problem of adaptation, I would like to digress by pointing out that this analysis helps to understand why so many of our studies of social systems fail on replication. The several programmatic studies of organizational outcomes as a function of various styles of leadership conducted by our colleagues in Michigan, Ohio, California, and elsewhere have provided less precise generalizations than many of us had expected. A possible reason for these somewhat disappointing results lies in the varying states of the systems from place to place and time to time.

Furthermore, the process and structural variables which Indik has listed for the components of organizations, groups, and persons make for any one of these panels a matrix of states which is finite but extremely large and enormously difficult to manage. I shall have more to say about this problem toward the end of this paper.

Adaptation in Social Systems

Let us return to problem of adaptation, in the light of the model simplified in Figure 1. We have earlier assumed that a certain level of maintenance is necessary before a noncoerced social system can respond to signal inputs. I should like to build a proposition on that assumption, namely that the amount of formal achievement of a social system is some function of the amount of maintenance input. The most parsi-

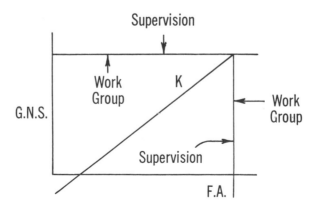

monious function to assume is that of a straight line, until empirical data provide a basis for some other relationship.

We may chart this proposition very simply as it might apply to a work group in an industrial organization. Figure 2 illustrates a situation in which the work group functions in such a way as to increase its GNS, but this level is balanced by the supervision or suprasystem, which serves as a damper or suppressor on GNS.[1] At the same time the suprasystem's principal pressures are toward increasing the FA while the work group provides a balancing resistance to these FA pressures. In such a system, both outputs are controlled by a balancing of conditions. The *upper* limit of FA is determined by the physiological capacities of the workers, their norms, and methods of operation. The *lower* limit of FA is established by the suprasystem, which demands a minimal level of output on pain of reprimand, or in extreme cases, separation from the suprasystem. The *lower limit* of GNS is in the hands of the work group itself, which will disband when satisfactions reach some unacceptable level. Finally the *upper* GNS limit is controlled by the supra-system which imposes restraints on what it construes as too much socializing, coffee time, or other interpersonal interaction not contributing directly to FA.

Although we have used a typical work group to illustrate the adaptation principle, it can be applied to organizations such as a church, an academic department, social clubs, political parties, or even temporary systems such as *ad hoc* committees (M. B. Miles, 1963) Such a model borrows heavily from two sources: first, Lewin's concept (1947) of driving and resisting forces whose confrontation results in a dynamic equilibrium, and second, Walter Cannon's propositions (1945) concerning homeostasis, in which he held that any disturbance to a system will be met by some mechanism which will dampen or oppose the disturbance. The point of resolution between levels of GNS and FA that we propose should fall along or close to the line K if the system is to be considered adaptive. The greater the departures from K brought about either by an excess of GNS or FA represent conditions of reduced adaptability. For example, groups in which there is a great deal of sociability and frequent parties, but which are low in productivity because supervision is either lax or incompetent, are groups that we would expect to be poorly adaptive to emergencies or fluctuations in signal inputs. These are the socializing goldbrickers in industry. Contrariwise, groups in which the pressure for FA is excessive and GNS

---

[1] This is not a contradiction to the earlier assertion that some maintenance may come from supervision. Here we are asserting that the external control over all maintenance comes from supervision or the agent of the supra-system.

is low would likewise be considered by this model as poorly adaptive. These are the disgruntled, complaining, grievance-sensitive employees who may nevertheless be productive to the limits coerced by their supervisors, yet relatively unresponsive to changes in routines, work methods, or assignments.

A biological system which is poorly nourished, living on the bare edge of subsistence, is not one which can accept a major shift in its signal inputs either positive or negative. We are arguing that the same holds true for social systems. In like fashion biologic and social systems which are excessively "fat" (great maintenance inputs) are likewise lethargic to shifts in stimuli which would provoke "leaner" systems to outputs useful for some other systems. The crux of the adaptation concept is that some system variable (body temperature, blood composition, metabolic rate, GNS) is maintained relatively constant in the face of external variations. Such constancies are possible only by appropriate system changes in other variables. It is paradoxical that suprasystem variations excite changes that result in some constancy.

Some Further Deductions

The model has heuristic utility. Suppose that the subsystem fails to limit the eastward movement of FA or a decrement in GNS. In either case, point A will fall to the east of line K. Similarly, should the subsystem relax its normal control functions, point A will fall to the west of line K. Thus the model provides an automatic indicator of the source of imbalance and is a diagnostic aid in determining where corrective measures might be taken. Major departures from K become symptoms of some maladaptation in the internal relations of the total system when one or the other or both sets of constraints are defective.

Figure 2 shows K with a slope of 1. This is purely hypothetical and is not meant to be fixed. Any other positive slope may be characteristic of a set of groups. The specific slope for a given case is a function (linear or log) of the scaling of the two measures which has not been specified. However, it is likely that the intercept of K, when GNS is zero, will be some positive value of FA. Exogenous conditions (economic pressures) sometimes compel individuals to be productive even when GNS is at low or zero levels. Prison camp groups working under the pain of punishment or death would be examples.

The resolution of forces at point A cannot be considered a sudden or immediate consequence which comes about quickly. For those groups which have existed for some time, point A is "norm determined," that is, the norms of both the subsystem and suprasystem play an important part in bringing about the resolution of their respective needs. It should be clear from our earlier discussion of norms that these, in turn, may vary from one group or organization to another. Within one firm having a given reputation, kind of work, and personal policy, the resolution at point A may be quite different than in another kind of firm. The Michigan studies, for example, of a large insurance company revealed that in work groups having "employee-centered" supervisors the norms were such as to lead employees to expect a moderately high degree of personal consideration. This finding was not confirmed by the same team of investigators when studying railroad section gangs (Katz Maccoby, Gurin, & Floor, 1951, pp. 33–34). The railroad workers, whether in high-productive or low-productive gangs, evidently were operating within norms that did not require supervisors to give them as much consideration as was true of the office workers. Both studies, however, are silent on the question of adaptability.

The model further leads one to expect that if some exogenous or other suprasystem conditions operate in such a manner as to force FA westward to some low value, without simultaneously reducing GNS the subsystem will tend to counteract the FA movement. Such a condition would be a reversal of the usual direction in which the forces operate and would constitute a case in which an out-of-the-ordinary adjustment is required. This is essentially what has happened in those organizations in which their FA becomes irrelevant or no longer useful to the suprasystem. Consider the National Foundation for Infantile Paralysis. After the vaccines were discovered and distributed to large masses of the population, the original mission of the Foundation was largely accomplished. The suprasystem thereafter had no use for the FA of the Foundation. But it did not disband. It modified its name and found a new target for its FA. This has been the history of several other similar organizations. Garden clubs often evolve out of organizations originally formed to protest a real estate developer's failure to complete his portion of a contract. If an organization accomplishes its mission (suprasystem no longer requires its FA), the organization will disintegrate unless it finds another FA that is acceptable. In terms of the model, if the suprasystem forces augment — rather than counteract — the subsystem forces, the subsystem is in grave danger of collapsing.

Adaptation is that process whereby survival is ensured. The model suggests how this is accomplished in various ways by social systems.

Limited Empirical Support

Is there any empirical evidence to support such a model as we have presented? I can report that some exists, but it is both indirect and inconclusive. For example, taking measures of GNS in an industrial plant four months before and about a week after an announcement that the plant would be permanently closed showed no marked drop in GNS

(Berrien and Angoff, 1960). In another situation GNS was extremely low. Here slight changes in work routines created major disturbances in FA and further depressed GNS (Indik and Tyler 1961). Like Miller, I must candidly state that much of the supporting data come from case studies and anecdotal reports which do not meet the highest standards of empiricism. Moreover such data as do exist have to be reinterpreted into systems terminology. One reason for this state of affairs lies in the fact that general systems approaches are simply too recent to have generated the necessary experimental tests. The case studies in which one can find support for the model are those reported by Zalesnick, Christensen, and Roethlisberger (1958), Ronken and Lawrence (1952), Roethlisberger and Dickson (1939), and Barnes (1960).

A second reason for the paucity of empirical support stems from the fact that the requisite research designs involve frequently, or better yet, continuously measured observations over an extended period on bona fide systems. Most of the social experiments conducted in laboratories are on groups with no group history and a short life using cross-sectional rather than longitudinal measures. The variables are generally taken on comparable groups before and after some experimental manipulation. It is therefore not surprising that a theory which attempts to address the essence of *process* should at this point have little quantitative data on which to rely. The justification for presenting it in its empirical nakedness now is the justification for any theory — the possibility that it may stimulate research to prove its naivete. We need a major change in the kind of data we collect.

Our understanding in any field proceeds by a marriage of theory and the right kind of data. As Boulding (1966) has so lucidly pointed out, Malthus' vision of an underemployment equilibrium had to wait a hundred years before the requisite national economic statistics were available to permit Keynes to revive and elaborate the Malthusian theory. I fervently hope that the general systems approach to social systems will not have to wait that long. Parenthetically, we have had one Ph.D. dissertation by J. E. Durkin (1966) on two-person groups in which continuous measures were taken, and I can report that the methodological problems are difficult but not entirely insurmountable.

Model Applied to the Taxonomy of Variables

Perhaps another way of testing the usefulness of the GST approach is to discover whether it helps better to understand panels of variables such as Indik has presented. He has already made the distinction between structure and process which is a central distinction in the general systems approach. However, if we look at the variables which are included as process, some of these can be considered inputs either from collateral systems, subsystems, or suprasystems, and others are attributes of states. For example, Panel Two, B, entitled *Control,* under this is "The average amount of influence exerted by members in the organization." This is a collateral relationship, either positive or negative, between collateral systems equal in the hierarchy. However, the third variable, listed as a control, is "The descrepancy between the actual distribution of influence and the *desired* distribution in the organization." This carries with it a feedback implication between the system output and the demands of some other suprasystem — that is to say, some standard of what is desirable exists somewhere inside or outside the system against which the existing distribution of influence must be compared. If the distribution is too limited or too widespread, presumably a correction is indicated and such a process is the essence of feedback.

This example further leads us to ask where among the variables is there a specification of organizational or group outputs? Organizations and groups exist to do something and one cannot set standards of what is a desirable distribution of influence or any other variable without also a specification of the ends to be achieved. In Panel Five A, Indik lists motivational variables for individuals such as the need for achievement, affiliation, power, and so forth, but one wonders whether groups and organizations exist solely to satisfy these individual needs or whether the larger systems also have "needs." If we accept the general systems proposition that a system must produce outputs acceptable to its subsystems and suprasystems, then it becomes clear that (a) some specification of the acceptable output(s) ought to be included as an indispensable variable and (b) feedback comparisons ought to be indicated between various levels within an organization as well as between the individual, group, and organization levels. Panel Six emphasizes the outputs of individuals working within organizations, but as I read them, one would have some difficulty in assessing those organizational outputs that required the combined efforts of numerous people. General systems theory holds that systems at any level of complexity produce outputs unique to the respective levels. That is, one automobile plant may produce starters and alternators, another frames, and another wheels, but the final assembly plant produces automobiles ready to operate. This final product is not merely a disordered collection of its parts. The parts are articulated in a particular design. It is this feature that I don't find in either the organization or group panels and one which would be required by GST.

One implication in the panels as so far developed is that the group or organizational output is the sum of the individuals' outputs. In some situations, this may be the most obvious group output and is often the easiest to measure. However upon closer examination, at least in many industrial settings, the standards of performance held by supervisors include other less obvious features that are difficult to define separately. In many investigations of group effectiveness a rating labeled "overall performance" has become the catch-all for these undefined subtleties. The logic of the systems theory forces us to look for these subtleties, if we accept the proposition that the outputs are in some identifiable way different from inputs, as a consequence of the components doing something with those inputs.

Moreover, the general systems orientation also forces one to be explicit about what it is that is the focus of observation. It is manifestly unfeasible in any study of an organization to encompass all the measures that Indik has listed. What system do we want to look at? Indik includes supervision in the Organizational Function Panel as a heading with four variables: initiating structure, considerations, leadership style, and supervisory skill mix. These can be considered as variables separated between maintenance and signal inputs, from a suprasystem to subsystems. As such, these are not based on a view of the organization as a whole or as a black box, but instead they refer to the relations between two levels within the organization, each of which is a black box. General systems offers no objection to examining the internal workings of a black box, but it does require that we be specific about which system is temporarily considered such. One of the difficulties with the variables within some of the panels, as now constituted, is that they are not consistent in this respect. Some are suprasystem inputs to components of the organization, others are relations like "influence" between collateral components. The first set of relations tends to emphasize signal inputs while the collateral relations in an adaptive system tend to be of a maintenance sort.

One could go through other panels and variables in this manner assigning them a place within the general systems framework, but to do so here would be both boring and require greater patience than one can expect of a charitable audience. I can report that the exercise has been carried to a point where I feel confident that GST can encompass the full range of phenomena although some minor adjustments and additions may be required in Indik's definitions.

In what I have said there is an underlying theme. I have talked about relationships between system inputs and outputs. A taxonomy implies to me not just labelled pigeonholes for phenomena. There needs to be some ordering of the phenomena as Altman has already indicated. The ordering which Indik's panels provide is an excellent start as was also that provided by McGrath and Altman (1966) earlier.

I have the feeling, without having done all the spadework necessary, that if we were to use the general systems framework, which has proven so useful in other fields, we could devise a functional taxonomy, arranging group, organizational, and individual variables in a way that would lead to discovering how the variables are functionally related.

We need more than a dictionary of variables, useful and indispensable as dictionaries are. We need, I submit, a grammar, a set of preliminary rules to tell us how the relevant variables probably fit together. General systems theory is one such set of tentative rules which has the potential virtue of linking our science with other sciences in a way that will encourage those enormous, powerful generalizations which bring conceptual unity to common sense diversity; that make mature sense out of what William James called the child's big, booming, buzzing, confused view of the world.

Summary

In line with the General Systems approach to social groups, I have tried to present the essentials of a systems theory in terms which frankly simplify, perhaps oversimplify, many complex details. This however is the function of any theory — to find the unformities in any phenomena that at first blush seem unrelated. I next sketched a model of adaptive groups in terms of the input, output, feedback concepts which found their first expression in electromechanical systems but which appear to be useful to an understanding of social systems. Finally the last part of the paper is an effort to organize the variables and panels which Indik previously presented into the rubrics of general systems theory, hopefully in a way that will suggest testable hypotheses concerning the manner in which one set of variables may relate to another.

Bibliography

Ashby, W. R. General systems theory as new discipline. *General Systems,* 1958, **3**, 3–17.

Bales, R. F. The equilibrium problem in small groups. In T. Parsons, R. F. Bales, & E. A. Shils (Eds.), *Working papers in the theory of action.* Glencoe: Free Press, 1953. Pp. 111–161.

Barnes, L. B. *Organizational systems and engineering groups.* Boston: Harvard University Graduate School of Business Administration, 1960.

Berrien, F. K., & Angoff, W. H. *Homeostatis theory of small groups IV: Light manufacturing personnel.* Technical Report No. 6, Contract Nonr-404(10), 1960. New Brunswick, N. J.: Rutgers — The State University.

Boulding, K. E. General systems theory — The skeleton of science. *Management Science,* 1956, 2, 197–208.

————. *The impact of social science.* New Brunswick, N. J.: Rutgers University Press, 1966. Chap. 1.

Cannon, W. B. *The way of an investigator.* New York: W. W. Norton, 1945.

Durkin, J. *Groups in loops.* New Brunswick, N. J.: Rutgers — The State University. Ph.D. dissertation, 1966.

Fleishman, E. A., & Harris, E. F. Patterns of leadership behavior related to employee grievances and turnover. *Personnel Psychology,* 1962, 15, 45–53.

Hemphill, J. K. *Group dimensions: A manual for their measurement.* Columbus, Ohio: Ohio State University, Business Research Monographs No. 87, 1956.

Homans, G. C. *The human group.* New York: Harcourt Brace & Company, 1950.

Indik, B. P., & Tyler, J. M. A technique for the longitudinal study of group stability and its application to group homeostasis. Technical Report 9, Contract Nonr-404(10), 1961. New Brunswick, N. J.: Rutgers — The State University.

James, W. *Psychology,* Vol. 1. New York: Henry Holt & Company, 1890. Pp. 309ff.

Katz, D., & Kahn, R. L. *The social psychology of organizations.* New York: John Wiley & Sons, 1966.

Katz, D., Maccoby, N., Gurin, G., & Floor, L. G. *Productivity, supervision and morale among railroad workers.* Ann Arbor: Survey Research Center, University of Michigan, 1951.

Lewin, K. Frontiers in group dynamics. *Human Relations,* 1947, 1, 2–38.

Lwoff, A. Nobel lecture (1965). Stockholm, Sweden: The Nobel Foundation, Copyright © 1966.

McGrath, J. E., & Altman, I. *Small groups research: Synthesis and critique of the field.* New York: Holt, Rinehart & Winston, 1966.

Merei, F. Group leadership and institutionalization. *Human Relations,* 1949, 2, 23–39.

Miles, M. B. On temporary systems. In M. B. Miles (Ed.), *Innovation in education.* New York: Teachers College Press, 1964.

Miller, J. G. Toward a general theory for the behavior sciences. *American Psychologist,* 1955, 10, 513–531.

————. Living systems: basic concepts. *Behavioral Science,* 1965, 10, 193–237; 380–411.

Newcomb, T. M. *Social psychology.* New York: Dryden, 1950.

Rapoport, A. The diffusion problem in mass behavior. *General Systems,* 1956, 1, 48–55.

Roethlisberger, F. J., & Dickson, W. J. *Management and the worker.* Boston: Harvard University Press, 1939.

Ronken, H. O., & Lawrence, P. R. *Administering change: A case study of human relations in a factory.* Boston: Harvard Graduate School of Business Administration, 1952.

Schachter, S. Deviation, rejection and communication. *Journal of Abnormal and Social Psychology*, 1951, 46, 190–207.

Sells, S. B. Ecology and the science of psychology. *Multivariate Behavioral Research*, 1966, 1, 131–144.

Thibaut, J. W., & Kelley, H. H. *The social psychology of groups.* New York: John Wiley & Sons, 1959. Chapter 9.

von Bertalanffy, L. General systems theory. *Main Currents in Modern Thought,* 1955, 71, 75–87.

Zaleznik, A., Christensen, C. R., & Roethlisberger, F. J. *The motivation, production, and satisfaction of workers: A prediction study.* Boston: Harvard University Graduate School of Business Administration, 1958.

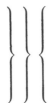

Integrating Small Behavioral Units Into Large Formal Organizations

ROBERT T. GOLEMBIEWSKI

Political Science Department
University of Georgia

Like all of man's efforts, this paper has its own belief system. Explicitly, three components are most central in that system. First, a mature small-group analysis certainly will resemble the spiritual singer's wheels-within-wheels, each a-moverin' in ways diverse yet subtly interacting. Second, that maturity has been but unevenly achieved. Virtually all observers agree on these two points (Thibaut & Kelley, 1959; Golembiewski, 1962; Hopkins, 1964; and McGrath & Altman, 1966). Third, various applied uses of group theory and methods heighten the urgency of the required research effort. Opinions tend to polarize on this third point, but to a common end. Many proponents and most opponents of such applications share the basic common quality of being short-suited in a research sense.

Given these three beliefs-cum-evidence, the present overriding goal stresses the interacting development of "basic" and "applied" approaches to the small group in large organizations. Specifically, this paper articulates various aspects of both the ideals of, and the achievement in, small group research and applications.

A Benchmark Relational Map: A Partial Small-Group Theoretical "Wheel"

This paper follows dual tracks, often simultaneously. It proceeds from the relatively certain to the relatively hypothetical, and from microphenomena to macrophenomena. Specifically, the basic benchmark will be a model of the relationships of selected "input" dimensions of the small group (Golembiewski, 1965b), as these variables hypothetically interact through "linkage" variables with two "outcome" variables of particular relevance to the student of large, formal organizations. These outcome variables are participant satisfaction and productivity. Figure 1, on pages 130 and 131, following, portrays these benchmark relations. Solid lines depict dominant relations in nature; broken lines indicate relations that have only sometimes been observed.

The model in Figure 1 is patently spare, particularly in the case of the linkage variables. This analysis will make several attempts to be specific about probable occupants of that class of variables. Paradoxically, we know quite a bit more about practical ways of linking small groups into large organizations than we do about conceptually describing the dimensions which are affected by the processes set in motion (Bennett, 1955). Consider the sole linkage variable in Figure 1. High structural integration is more likely to co-exist with a "general" versus a "directive" style of supervision. Generally, at least in western countries, general supervision seems more compatible with the personality predispositions of more people in more organizations (Golembiewski, 1965a, pp. 179-97). Specifically, however, we know little about the properties of tasks, phases of work, and so forth, that must qualify the generalization above. For example, Bass (1965, p. 38) observes that a highly productive firm differed from a less successful one in that it employed younger workers, fewer ex-miners who were more likely to be suspicious of management, better-trained employees, and workers who lived closer to their jobs.

The convenience of relying on our benchmark model is great despite its conceptual and relational lacunae, but some of the costs of convenience must be acknowledged. Thus the relatively complex rationale underlying the model will not be repeated here, and some necessary qualifications consequently will go unremarked. In addition, Figure 1 certainly provides only elementary structure for the mass of research on small groups (Altman, 1966). The need for analytical structure is acute, moreover. By way of cleverly spotlighting the literature's emphasis on a locus rather than on a delimited class of phenomena, much small group research might better be called "small room" research. More centrally, the relational model in Figure 1 applies only to specific operational definitions of the selected dimensions (Golembiewski, 1965b, pp. 89-90). These operational definitions are not central for present purposes, but research designs could not tolerate the present casualness.

Costing out convenience as above, however, does not imply lack of substantial confidence in our benchmark "wheel." Quite the opposite is the case, in fact. Four evidential elements, particularly, support this confidence. First, the model of relations is consistent with a very large body of research. Second, the model permits reconciling a number of

INPUT VARIABLES

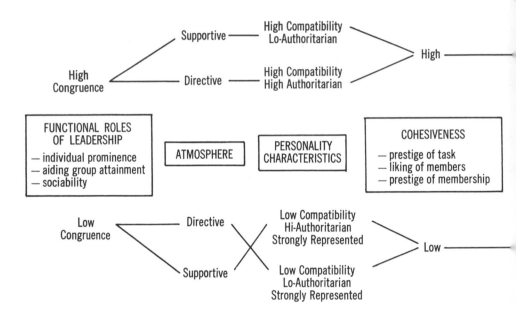

Figure 1

LINKAGE VARIABLES   **OUTCOME VARIABLES**

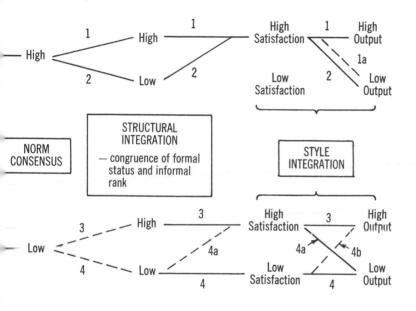

dilemmas posed by apparently conflicting research findings. For example, the finding that high cohesiveness covaries with low output as well as with high output caused many researchers to refine their operating models (Seashore, 1954). Indeed, too many students to suit Dubin (1965, pp 44–45) have still not adjusted their phenomenological maps to even this early contradiction in research findings. Figure 1 accounts for the contradiction in several ways, as by positing structural integration as an intervening variable. Consequently, Figure 1 reinforces those who refined their models, and it also guides those who have not. Third, the model is guiding some research that promises healthy payoffs. Fourth, as will be demonstrated, the model links nicely with a number of phenomenal subsystems that help account for significant variance in nature.

This brief catalog provides formidable evidence that Figure 1 diversely feeds on and fosters scientific research. The model is consistent with considerable existing research; it helps reconcile apparently contradictory research; it supports useful research designs; and it can be extended in reasonable ways to other phenomenal areas. In these multiple senses, then, the model reflects the dialectic of the processes of scientific research leading to the eventual development of deductive theories of wide scope and great power.

Selected Extensions of the Benchmark Relational Map: Preliminary Outlines of Four Interacting "Wheels"

Here, as elsewhere, the test-of-value of a construct is what one can do with it. Directly, then, four specific senses in which Figure 1 is on the side of the angels in scientific analysis will occupy the bulk of this paper.

Personality in Groups and Organizations: Conceptual Map and Accumulating Research on Birth Order

Personality correlates have long been poorly treated in small-group analysis and, despite the rising flood of research, matters have remained largely the same. The point may be reinforced epigrammatically. The effects of group composition are spotlighted dramatically in some studies (Schutz, 1958; Tuckman, 1964), but these effects of personality variations on behavior and group properties are neglected in most work.

Personality correlates will be tied into Figure 1 via sibling order, which has long been considered an important factor in explaining behavior. Many rationales supporting the effects of sibling order on behavior could be sketched. In straightforward terms, for example, the oldest sibling often faces substantial pressures from family and friends to develop quickly into a "little adult" with all-around capabilities. The first-born, that is, experiences pressures to become an "early generalist." Later-born siblings reasonably may decide to compete in depth rather than in breadth. This reasonable decision by later siblings often will be reinforced, as parents and adults tire of their attempts to make later siblings into the perfect human beings the adults never quite became. We may hazard some general parallels with the literature on child development. Thus McArthur described first-borns as hard-working, serious, and adult-oriented. A second-born sibling, in contrast, had "the opportunity to learn from a member of his own age group, instead of learning everything from adults" (McArthur, 1956, p. 53). The greater symmetry between teacher and learner apparently has some direct behavioral covariants. Second-born siblings were peer-oriented, easygoing, and friendly.

One research finding is the focus here for developing the relevance of birth order to small-group analysis. Thus Schachter has demonstrated that under anxiety first-born female siblings sought interpersonal comfort; they were affiliative (Schachter, 1959). Later-born siblings tended to become "loners" under the same condition. Evidence supporting both tendencies exists, although the literature hardly is a monolith. Thus contributions to the literature alternate between refining Schachter's leading contribution (Dohrenwend and Dohrenwend, 1966) and criticizing it (Smart, 1963). Similarly, some researchers report that sibling-order effects are quite general (Alexander, 1966; and Dember, 1964), while others insist on the need to specify intervening variables such as the sociocultural contexts that influence child-rearing practices (Glass, Horwitz, Firestone, and Grinker, 1963).

The complexity and unevenness of existing research on sibling order can only be sampled here, but that sampling has direct relevance for the study of small groups. For example, Capra and Dittes (1962) report that alcoholics tend to be later-born siblings in a proportion much greater than that indicated by chance. Although a statistical artifact (Smart, 1963) may explain the association, alcoholism does suggest a withdrawal from interpersonal relations consistent with Schachter's original finding. Similarly, first-born siblings among emotionally disturbed veterans were more likely to seek to establish relationships with the world, in the sense that they entered psychotherapy more frequently and persevered in it longer than later-born siblings (Moment & Zaleznik, 1963, p. 147). This findings suggests the greater desire of first-born siblings to establish some interpersonal relationship, if only a therapeutic one. The finding also suggests the first-born siblings' greater acceptance of authoritative figures. Relatedly, some evidence supports the implied proposition that later-born siblings will

function more effectively in "alone" situations. Thus U. S. Air Force
fighter pilot aces in the Korean War included an over-representation
of later-born siblings (Schachter, 1959).

Research also has begun specifically to tie in birth-order interactions to the benchmark model in Figure 1. Thus Moment and
Zaleznick (1963, p. 149) isolated some interesting and predictable
covariations between an individual's ordinal position in his family of
siblings and his performance in small groups. Their focus was on
behaviors classifiable as functional roles of leadership. "Stars" — those
with high and congruent ranks on several functional roles — were first-
born subjects in nearly three of four cases. Similarly, underchosen were
later-born siblings in a proportion far greater than chance.

TABLE 1. Performance of Functional Roles in
Small Groups and Birth Order

Rank Derived from Socio-metric Choices Received on Two Functional Roles		Functional Role Typologies	Sibling Position Percentages**	
Ideas*	Congeniality*		First Born	Later Born
High	High	Star	73	27
High	Low	Technical Specialist	40	60
Low	High	Social Specialist	25	75
Low	Low	Underchosen	36	64

* For specific operational definitions, consult Moment and Zaleznik (1963), pp.
32–37.
** The data are from Moment and Zaleznik, pp. 36, 149. The expected percentages
are 45 per cent — first-born, 55 per cent — later-born.

Some reactions to Moment and Zaleznik's data in Table 1 may be
detailed. First, the relation of birth order and rank on functional roles
withstood several tests of internal coherence. For example, "stars"
scored highest on "belongingness preference" (Moment & Zaleznik, p.
72), consistent with the presumed greater affiliative tendencies of first-
born siblings.

Second, the findings suggest adaptations to authority that could be
crucial to performance in both social and formal organizations. For
instance, Moment and Zaleznik's "stars" gave more father-son rather
than uncle-nephew responses to a Thematic-Apperception picture, in
which either was possible, than did the social specialists. They say:

The father-son relationship is one of authority in which distance but
respect is generally expected. In contrast, the uncle-nephew relationship . . .
is more egalitarian and marked by warmth and affection. Presumably, the
Social Specialists found it less threatening to place their stories in settings

where authority is avoided and emotional closeness is fostered. It is also possible that, unlike the Stars, the Social Specialists found exercising authority, with its implied use of aggression and control, anxiety provoking. Instead, their preferred mode of influencing others was through establishing bonds of affection.

Summary

Birth order may be one heretofore neglected predictor of behavior in small groups. Generally, birth order may help explain affiliative differences between group members. Derivatively, differences between the cohesiveness of groups may be similarly understood and predicted, for, as Figure 1 shows, that variable taps personal liking of group members. Specifically, birth order ties into differences in performing functional roles in groups. Congruence on the functional roles of leadership, of course, has been shown to be a powerful predictor of group performance (Heinicke and Bales, 1953).

Properties of Tasks and Structures in Organizations: Alternative Formal Frameworks for Group Dynamics

If anything, the study of the formal tasks performed by group members and of the institutional contexts within which groups operate has been given even less priority than the impact of personality characteristics on group processes. One thinks of only a few exceptions to the general neglect of the institutional environment within which the work of small groups is performed. The research by Charles Walker and his colleagues on the Yale Technology Project has perhaps been most insistent on understanding the impact of the "immediate job" (Guest, 1962; Turner & Miclette, 1962; Walker & Guest, 1952).

A similar story of neglect of task attributes characterizes both experimental and natural-state research. Few experimental demonstrations zero-in on task effects (Calvin, Hoffman, & Harden, 1957; Gibb, 1949). Nor does our point hold only for the laboratory. Rare indeed (Turner & Lawrence, 1965; Abruzzi, 1956) is the piece of research concerned in depth with task properties. Even such well-managed studies as that of Mann, Indik and Vroom (1963), and Vroom and Mann (1960), illustratively, shrug off task as a variable. These researchers noted some consistent differences in their data between two kinds of workers, explaining (Mann, Indik, and Vroom, 1963, p. 5) only that: "The men on the night shift had to depend on each other — were highly interdependent — in the way in which they did much of their work; the men on the day shift were not."

There is, furthermore, a neglect in linking tasks with organizational structure. In an effort to fill this neglect let us consider two alternative structures tying together three activities that yield some product or service, as follows.

A	B
Orthodox Model	Unorthodox Model
1. Departmentalizes around individual functions or processes.	1. Departmentalizes around autonomous flows of work, as far as possible.
2. Emphasizes vertical, or superior-subordinate, relations.	2. Attempts to integrate horizontal relations of individuals contributing to the same flow of work with the demands of vertical hierarchy.
3. Usually prescribes a narrow span of control.	3. Can permit a very wide span of control.

Figure 2 presents the two models in simplified graphics. Note particularly that the orthodox model requires a large "managerial unit;" the unorthodox model permits a much smaller basic unit. Worthy (1959, pp. 92–93) defines a "managerial unit" as being "no smaller than that portion of the organization falling within the jurisdiction of an individual who controls enough elements of the total process to make effective decisions regarding the total process."

These conceptual simplicities generate a complex, extensive, and significant hypothetical network. To illustrate the point, consider only this relational fragment torn from Figure 1:

Input Variable	Outcome Variable
High Cohesiveness	High Productivity
	Low Productivity

A more specific linkage is needed. For — as Dubin, et al. complain (1965, pp. 44–45) — neither theory nor practice can be satisfied very long with the finding that high cohesiveness will be associated with high or low output.

Figure 2 helps demonstrate how the traditional model encourages high cohesiveness low output sequences. First, the larger Managerial Unit A is, the more likely it is that tensions will develop between its subunits S_A, S_B, and S_C. And these tensions will tend to make subunit identifications correspondingly more salient (Dalton, 1959; Sayles, 1964).

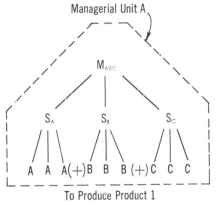

Figure 2A. Orthodox model for organizing work

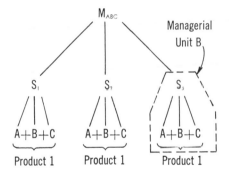

Figure 2B. Unorthodox model for organizing work

Figure 2. Two Alternative Formal Organization Structures

Second, while high cohesiveness is not likely to develop in the total managerial unit in an A structure, its development in the subunits must be viewed with managerial concern. In sum, the orthodox structure in a sense forfeits the social power implicit in high cohesiveness. That is, high cohesiveness in a subunit in an A structure is likely to be applied to the more effective reduction of output which any one subunit can itself bring off. In this second sense, employees use their cohesiveness to gain satisfaction by successfully thwarting management (Adams, 1953).

Reasonably, B structures make better use of the potential inherent in high cohesiveness. Achieving cohesiveness in Managerial Unit B, to develop some support for this summary conclusion, is both relatively easy *and* managerially useful. The members of any subunit, for example, will have many reasons for developing cohesiveness. Thus they are mutually responsible for an entire flow of work, and their performance is easily and nonarbitrarily comparable with that of other subunits. And the high cohesiveness of any subunit can be directly applied to increase the effectiveness of its flow of work, for any one subunit can independently increase output. The facility of measuring performance inhibits any one subunit form from lowering output (Herbst, 1962; Melman, 1958).

Reality is more complex than the argument above, patently, but the state of relatively controlled research on structural effects does not permit much greater specificity. Consider Worthy's (1950, p. 172) generalization that ". . . mere size is unquestionably one of the most important factors in determining the quality of employee relationships: the smaller the unit the higher the morale and vice versa." Despite general acceptance of Worthy's proposition, research has provided only qualified support. Thus, lower-level executives in small firms reported greater satisfaction than their counterparts in larger organizations. At higher levels, however, executives in large firms oppositely reported greater need fulfillment than executives in smaller firms (Porter, 1963). If an explanation for this finding seems clear enough, ambiguity increases as attempts are made to become more specific. For example, Porter and Lawler (1964) found that higher job satisfaction in organizations of less than 5000 employees was more likely in "flat" structures. However, employees in organizations with more than 5000 employees disturb the pattern. In these larger firms, employees in "flat" structures did not report more job satisfaction than employees in "tall" structures. Sheer company size seemed an important variable in determining the degree to which executives felt their needs were fulfilled at work.

What these complex present data clearly indicate is uncertain, beyond underscoring the need for further research. Thus Triandis (1966, p. 78) proposes a dual linkage between organizational structure and satisfaction outcomes, via the concept of "congruence." Perhaps. Alternatively, the heart of the matter may be that neither size nor organizational flatness is as important as the size of the managerial units. Indeed, some research (Baumgartel and Sobol, 1959) strongly supports this proposition. And analytical extrapolations seem fairly convincing on the point that whenever a choice exists, smaller managerial units are managerially preferable (Golembiewski, 1965a, esp. chap. 7; Golembiewski, 1967). Substantial operational difficulties complicate testing the suggested relation. Finding such different managerial units producing comparable work, or creating them in the laboratory, is a challenge that must be met before true comparative analysis is possible, however.

In the absence of a tried-and-true comprehensive theoretical network of structural effects, then, the linkages of small-group and task properties with various behavioral outcomes will be demonstrated here by taking some liberties with Sayles' (1958) insightful but reportorial study of industrial work groups. The four types of "groups" isolated by Sayles — his specific focus was on union bargaining activities — can be described in tabular form. Table 2 does the job. The characteristics of groups and of their work are selected from Sayles' fuller account.

TABLE 2. Task and Structural Properties

Strategic Groups
1. Relatively high skill, "better" but not "best" jobs.
2. Mono-processual, but central in a flow of work.
3. Individual operations, difficult to time-study.
4. High mobility, some variety in task.
5. High consensus about leadership roles. (p. 19).*
6. "Ranked substantially above Erratic and Apathetic Groups" in general performance (p. 19).

Conservative Groups
1. Highest skill, "monopoly of critical, scarce skills" (p. 34).
2. Individual operations, many in scattered locations.
3. Great "latent strength" makes prolonged struggles with management rare.
4. Often "takes time for a consensus to develop," sometimes beyond the point of timely action, but their skills and power usually "are unquestioned" (p. 36).
5. Evaluated most highly by management as "satisfactory" employees.

Erratic Groups
1. Relatively low skill.
2. Mono-processual, but not central in a flow of work.
3. Easy for time-study.
4. Short assembly lines.
5. Followed highly autocratic leadership (p. 14).
6. Considered "most dangerous," experienced behavioral swings, reactions often inappropriate to stimuli.

Apathetic Groups

Type I: Low skill, dangerous, dirty, long assembly lines, short-term employees. Type II: Multi-processual crews in large departments, with sharp differences in status and earnings within crews, and tension between crews.	1. Low power. 2. Low group cohesion (p. 9). 3. Not troublesome, but also not "highest" on "consistent productivity and 'cooperativeness'" (p. 8). 4. Lack "clearly identified or accepted leadership" (p. 12).

* Page references are to Dalton, 1959.

Hopefully, the conveniences of tabular treatment far outweigh the sim-
plifications required. In addition, Table 2 assigns each of the types of
groups to ranges along high/low continua of several input variables
and linkage variables.

The interactions of task and structure with group cohesiveness
in Sayles' data seem both clear and reasonable, at a discursive level.
Thus Sayles himself concludes (p. 5) that "the organization of work
contributes significantly to the behavior of work groups." For example,
Erratic groups were constrained by three properties of their work: its
low skill, its noncentrality, and its amenability to time-study. But
Erratic groups also possessed counterbalancing advantages that facilitated cohesiveness: monoprocessual departmentation and physical
proximity in short assembly lines. Consistently, neither of these commonalities characterized Apathetic groups, whose designation says it all.
Reasonably, also, Erratic groups could best exploit their advantages by
following "autocratic leadership" intended (if not necessary) to overcome the organizational and social weaknesses implied by task and
structure. Hence also the extreme "conversions" that are said to characterize Erratic groups, as informal leaders and/or normative consensus
change. Further, the probability that the autocratic style does not well
serve preferences of many (most) members of Erratic groups explains
their wide "issue scope" and their varying influence with formal authorities. For example, the scapegoating common under an autocratic style
suggests the emotional press under which nonauthoritarian group members live, and it also illustrates their tendency to react to threat by
turning their aggression against one another (Lewin, Lippitt, and
White, 1939). Under such conditions, "issue scope" and group cohesiveness must be highly variable.

Similar constructions also could tie task and structural properties
of the other three types of groups to the model of relations in Figure 1,
but let us in summary tether the argument. We take as very probable
the proposition that both task and structural properties significantly
interact with group properties. The analysis-by-construction has significant weaknesses, but it nonetheless implies a clear mandate. That
is, the neglect of the interactions of group properties and task/structure
implies significant unaccounted variance in predicting real-world outcomes.

The Worlds of Technology: Critical Phenomena in an Applied Theory

Few students of the small group in organizations have carefully
studied the interaction between technological conditions, the worker's
consciousness, and his behavior. Roughly, research has fixated on ways

in which supervisors might change their own behavior so as to induce higher productivity and employee satisfaction. Little attention has been given to the technological constraints that inhibit a supervisor from changing his behavior even if he desperately wanted to do so.

The neglect of differences in technology implies high costs. Summarily, the magnitude of the disappointment-potential of applications of small-group findings to large organizations *in the absence of concern with technology* may be suggested in terms of two descriptive variants, a firm's prevailing strategy for growth and a firm's place on a continuum of technological development. Obviously, the implicit nominal definition of "technology" is vague. But our purpose is illustration, not definition.

Chandler (1962) has drawn compelling attention to the intimate interaction of different organization strategies and the structural arrangements appropriate for them. He focuses on four strategies for growth. These strategies, corresponding roughly to historical sequences in a firm's development, are (1962, pp. 13–17): growth by *increasing output* on a narrow product line *at a central site;* growth by *adding field units* for increasing output on a narrow product line; growth by *adding functions for* a narrow product line; and growth by *diversification* of product lines. Chandler confirmed the structural variations associated with these strategies for growth by an historical analysis of several of our present industrial and commercial giants, such as General Motors. His argument applies with equal force to government agencies (Baum, 1901; Penniman, 1961).

Overall, large organizations require different and increasingly sophisticated structural arrangements as they move from a stress on growth by increasing volume at a central site to an emphasis on growth by diversification. For example, the traditional "line-staff" model suffices in organizations that have begun growing by adding field units. But that model generates exquisite problems in a diversified organization (Golembiewski, 1967). Organizations growing by diversification generally have had to create smaller managerial units while the traditional line-staff model evolves where the units are larger. As these structural arrangements change, so also appropriate managerial practices may change. Thus a "directive style of supervision" stands a much greater chance of success in the latter than in the former structure. Directly, then, neglecting growth strategies may lead to inadequate theoretical statements and particularly to awkward practical applications.

The neglect of technology can be shown more specifically to have important consequences for group processes in organizations. Dubin (1965) has raised the issue forcefully, relying on Woodward (1958), and we shall concentrate on his argument. Woodward distinguishes three technological types of firms. These are: firms that handle goods *in small batches or in small units,* as in the assembly of a locomotive or custom tailoring; firms that handle goods *in large batches or in mass-produced units,* as in automobile assembly; and firms that utilize *continuous-process* production, as in some petroleum refineries. These gross distinctions generate others. Dubin generally classifies "unit" systems of production as "worker-centered." He explains that relatively "high levels of skills may be required at the worker level" and that "control functions reside in the hands of the worker" as a consequence of the extended involvement of the employee with the product. Oppositely, "process" systems of production are "supervisory-centered." The great potential loss due to error encourages the concentration of inspection and control functions in the managerial ranks (pp. 14–15), with employees becoming "relatively incidental and instrumental to these preoccupations" (p. 24) of management with inspection and control. Moreover, Dubin, et al. (1965, p. 19) see process systems of production as becoming more and more important.

These technologically derived considerations suggested to Dubin a challenge to much of the behavioral gospel about effective managerial techniques. For example, Dubin notes that the research program at the University of Michigan dealing with clerical and railroad workers strongly associated high output with "general supervision," "worker autonomy," and so on (Likert, 1961). And Dubin notes that a study of supervisory practices in eight British factories in the electrical industry (Argyle, Gardner, and Cioffi, 1957 and 1958) did not replicate the Michigan findings. The probable way of reconciling these findings seems clear to Dubin. The British factories "would all probably be classified as employing large-batch or quasi-mass production," he notes (p. 29). In contrast, the Michigan researchers drew their conclusions from railroad and clerical workers, both of whom were involved in unit systems of production. The contrasting findings consequently might imply that "the responsibility of individual workers may be maximal" in unit production. The correlate was patent (p. 29): ". . . workers in unit production technologies will produce most when given only general supervision. This relation is to be attributed to the technology rather than to a general principle that all work situations demand maximum autonomy for workers." Dubin reaches similar conclusions by similar analyses of Fleishmann's well known studies of supervisory "structure" and "consideration" (Fleishmann & Harris, 1962; Fleishmann & Peters, 1962). He also extends similar if sketchier analyses to supervisory "sensitivity" (Nagle, 1954; Cleven & Fiedler, 1956), as well as to "participation" (pp. 39–42).

No one can respond with certainty to Dubin's argument, except to agree that technological differences are associated with a variety of organizational differences that may have significant behavioral correlates. This is the case with the span of control, for example. Spans of control seem to differ with technological types, but preliminary studies do not always agree on the direction of the change (Woodward, 1958; Burack, 1966; Parisi, 1966).

Three additional notes hopefully will speed the required attention to technological differences. First, the job of nominal and operational definition of "technological states" has barely begun. The job will not be a simple one, by all indications. Thus Burack (1966) includes mechanization as one of his five differentiating "primary factors," and Bright's (1958) scale includes 17 "levels of mechanization."

Second, Dubin focuses on only two levels of the hierarchy, the employee and the first-line supervisor. Thus operators in a process system of production "may become incidental and instrumental" to the control activities of "management," but intra-"management" relations do not obviously fall in the same category. That is, what Dubin says may be applicable to *first-line supervisory relations* much more than to *interpersonal and interlevel relations* in organizations regardless of the system of production. The difference is no mere play on words.

Third, Dubin's summary emphasis is not consistent with all relevant research (for example, see Argyris, 1964). Consider data supplied by Mann (1965). Mann was interested in these three aspects of supervisory competence (p. 83): *technical competence,* or the supervisor's abilities to operate and maintain the equipment for which he is responsible; *administrative competence,* or the supervisor's abilities to plan, schedule, assign and monitor work performance; and *human relations competence,* or the supervisor's abilities to get people to work well together, to give recognition, to level interpersonally, and so forth.

Mann's research is complex, but several simplified highlights may be noted. First, technological differences do not necessarily determine skill-mixes that employees consider desirable in supervisors. In two plants whose technologies differed, if apparently not markedly (p. 84), "satisfaction with supervisor" correlated most highly with the supervisor's rated human relations competence, and significantly more so than with technical competence. When a wider technological continuum is considered, however, different relations may be obtained. Mann observes (p. 96) that men in "more highly automated plants . . . can distinguish most clearly between their foremen's technical and human relations skills. . . . In older plants . . . there is little chance to demonstrate any but human relations skills. . . ."

Second, in a study of hospital personnel, Mann noted a tendency for "desirable" mixes of supervisory skills to vary by levels of the organization. Most of these employees seemed to be engaged in unit production. Hence technological differences alone do not account for variance in desirable supervisory skills. Third, even within a very narrow technological range, "phase differences" might influence the mix of supervisory skills considered desirable by employees. Consider the change-over to automatic data processing in an accounting department, including the four years from introduction to stable state. Mann (p. 91) observed summarily that: "In general, there seemed to be an initial shift in emphasis from human relations to technical and administrative skill, and back again to human relations skills at the end of the transition period." The "end of the transition period", of course, found the department involved in what apparently was a process system of production. This suggests a more subtle interaction of technology and behavior than Dubin implied.

No conclusive reaction to Mann's findings is possible, then, but we can be definite nonetheless. Whatever the precise nature of the interactions of technology, group properties, and outcome variables, those interactions will be complex.

Group Methods in Organization Change and Development: Another Case of Practice Leading Theory

The need-to-know that differentiates man from anthropoids supplies press enough to cope with the three problem areas considered above, but practice severely increases that urgency. The group "is there," not only as some scientific Everest that some few deem a great challenge, but also as a veritable mother-lode of social control in organizations. And the rush for the sociopsychological "Klondike" clearly has begun. Empirical and value issues associated with group theory and its applications thus assume increasingly awesome proportions.

Furthermore, the applications of group-training methods to organization change and development of interest here — those using "sensitivity groups" in various ways — share important commonalities. We stress two commonalities by way of background and one by way of theoretical substance. First, a great perceived need exists for what the approach promises to do. That is, organizations do not permit realization of what a significant proportion of their members feel are real needs. Second, the sensitivity lab approach is kaleidoscopically diversified in what it is and how people respond to it. Thus the group approach has been used for: intrapersonal and therapeutic learning (Bugental & Tannenbaum, 1965); learning that is interpersonal and substantially oriented toward group processes (Frank, 1964); or learning that is

TABLE 1. Four Value-Loaded Dimensions Relevant in Laboratory Approaches to Organization Change and Development

MetaValues* of Lab Training	Proximate Goals of Lab Training	Desirable Means for Lab Training	Organization Values** Consistent with Lab Training
1. An attitude of inquiry, reflecting (among others): a. A "hypothetical" b. Experimentalism.	1. Increased insight, self-knowledge.	1. Emphasis on "here-and-now."	1. Full and free communication.
2. "Expanded consciousness and sense of choice."	2. Sharpened diagnostic skills at (ideally) all of these levels: a. individual; b. group; c. organization; d. society.	2. Emphasis on the individual act rather than on the "total person" acting.	2. Reliance on open consensus in managing conflict, as opposed to using coercion or compromise
3. The value system of democracy, having as two core elements: a. A spirit of collaboration; b. Open resolution of conflict via a problem-solving orientation.	3. Awareness of, and skill-practice in creating, conditions of effective functioning at (ideally) all levels.	3. Emphasis on feedback that is nonevaluative in that it reports the impact on the self behavior, rather than on the feedback that is judgmental or interpretive.	3. Influence based on competence rather than on personal whim or on formal power.
4. An emphasis on mutual "helping relationships" as the best way to express man's interdependency with man.	4. Testing self-concepts and skills in interpersonal situations.	4. Emphasis on "unfreezing" behaviors the trainee feels are undesirable, and on practice of replacement behaviors, and "refreezing" new behaviors.	4. Expression of emotional and task-oriented behavior.
	5. Increased capacity to be open, to accept feelings of self and others, to risk interpersonally in rewarding ways.	5. Emphasis on "trust in leveling," on psychological safety of the trainee.	5. Acceptance of conflict between the individual and his organization, to be coped with willingly, openly, and rationally.
		6. Emphasis on creating and maintaining an "organic community."	

* Adapted from Schein and Bennis, pp. 30–35 (1965); and Bradford, Gibb, and Benne, pp. 10–12 (1964).
** From Slater and Bennis (1964).

structured in such ways as the "grid laboratory" (Blake & Mouton, 1964). Reactions are similarly varied. "Outside" critics have zealously attacked "sensitivity training" and/or its organizational applications (Odiorne, 1963; Gomberg, 1966). And "insiders" have contested vigorously over numerous empirical and value questions of applied behavioral analysis (Lakin, 1966), as well as over the range of applicability of "laboratory methods."

Third, applications of group methods to organization change and development share a basic commonality that may be expressed in terms of Figure 1. That is, in general, lab work seems to me to involve the development among the trainees of a group with high cohesiveness. This high cohesive group then becomes the control system which develops and strives to maintain high normative consensus while managing tension and providing emotional support. This normative consensus is complex, as Table 1 on the preceding page suggests, showing four ways of classifying value-loaded features of laboratory approaches to organization change and development. Disagreements among laboratory trainers might exist about the details in Table 3, but denial of any of the values or value-related techniques seems unlikely. In any case, some such normative consensus among a core group of "freed-up individuals" facilitates and supports efforts to engage broader segments of an organization in a program of change.

Within the context of these three commonalities, several important points of agreement are beginning to emerge from experience with lab programs of organizational change. They deserve brief listing here.

Agreement I. The value system of most organizations (Argyris, 1962) and indeed of society (Schein & Bennis, 1965, pp. 291 ff.) often must be modified or changed to permit individual growth and productivity.

Agreement II. Organizational applications of the lab approach stress the organic versus the mechanistic nature of organizations (Shepard, 1965). Thus a common emphasis will be upon assembling the competencies necessary to do the job (Leavitt, 1964), on team management (Blake & Mouton, 1964), or on problem-solving (Blake, Shepard, & Mouton, 1964). Generally, this point of agreement reflects disenchantment with traditional organization structure. Attention is directed to organizing around flows of work or around projects.

Agreement III. Relatedly, points of organizational fragmentation are a strategic point for applications of the lab approach. The fragmentation may set department versus department, line versus staff, headquarters versus the field, or labor versus management. Various lab designs can help clarify the bases of tension and can set the stage for reducing it (Blake, Mouton, & Sloma, 1965). For example, desired changes in attitudes and behaviors resulted from an effort to state and to work through simultaneously some of the very complex interactions within one firm between headquarters and a field sales force; between several departments within headquarters; and between several hierarchical levels (Golembiewski and Blumberg, in press).

Agreement IV. Applications of the lab approach stress the ideal of a change program simultaneously affecting behavior, task, and structure. Thus one of the most reliable findings about the efficacy of sensitivity training is that the organization to which the trainee returns will prove a major determinant of the degree of success in "back-home" applications (Miles, 1965).

Considered together, these points of agreement suggest that research on the small group in organizations does not complement applications of group methods to organization change and development, and vice versa. In essential senses, their weaknesses compound one another.

Let us drive the point home in terms of three particulars. First, we lack appropriate empirical theory to guide group dynamics approaches to organization change. Epigrammatically, the classroom reflects a complexity that more than matches the capacity of existing theory (Miles, 1964, p. 473). So much more ill-equipped are applications in incredibly more complex formal organizations.

Second, and relatedly, the lack of theory is tied to the inadequate volume of research dealing with applications of the lab approach to organization change. Thus Schein and Bennis (1965, p. 323) note:

Discouragingly, but not unexpectedly, the research effort seems weakest in these situations where the risks are highest and the tasks are most complex. We are referring to the uses of laboratory training in inducing change in organizations. In some organizational change programs, a great deal of attention is being paid to research, but not enough research is yet being done.

The brief history of laboratory applications to organization change helps explain the state of research. The exigencies of action also have ruined many a beautiful experimental design. But explanations of course do nothing to change the existing state.

In contrast, the situation concerning theory and research about the application of laboratory methods to individual learning is much more in hand. Thus much is known about who is likely to learn what in which laboratory designs (Luke & Seashore, 1966). And certainly there is no doubt about the considerable power of laboratory experiences to change attitudes (Argyris, 1966) or to change behavior (Schein & Bennis, 1965, p. 151). More generally still, research on the personal and interpersonal aspects of laboratory training reflects all the signs of robust activity. The applied consequences of such effort are clear, for example, in the Tentative Guidelines (National Training Laboratories, 1965) developed for stranger laboratory experiences. It is not that network members have lost their zeal to be creatively free in designing laboratories. Rather, in a growing number of particulars, research and experience have tended to come to some relatively sharp points of agreement.

Third, relevant research about organizational applications, even where it does exist, has important design limitations. The point applies in widely different degrees in various areas of concern. Thus a good deal of the research on personal learning in laboratories has a strong focus on such outcomes as the before/after change in an individual's ability to empathize with others. Commonly, input or process variables receive less attention, and particularly when they concern the specific properties of specific training groups. Exceptions to this rule exist both early (Glidwell, 1958) and late (Harrison, 1965), but the generalization still holds rather more than less. The outcome bias also appears in many other guises. For example, as trainers have become more self-confident about the sanguine nature of the processes they monitor, sharply less attention has been paid to conceptualizing about such inputs as group dimensions, which "can be gotten in books." Sharply more attention has been paid to the "feeling" aspects of the experience, which outcomes are of course largely novel to a particular T-group. For many training purposes this tendency to focus on end results is largely gain, but the scientific costs are patent.

The outcome bias also characterizes research on laboratory approaches to organization change and development, with several interesting reservations. Thus the outcomes emphasized most in research about change programs in organizations tend to cover a narrow range and/or to be restricted to the feeling realm. Of course, many narrow measures of the success of laboratory approaches to organization change can be cited. Whether changes in (for example) patterns of interaction are complemented by payoff changes in effective work relations, however, is an elusive and problematic issue. Hence the operational measure of program success tends to be in the feelings of organization members about the program. If members "like" what is going on — however that is determined, and particularly if highly placed individuals do the liking — that may be validation enough even over the relatively long run. Liking is an important outcome, to be sure, and for some purposes even the most important. But other outcomes also are of scientific and practical interest.

Finally, the complex and chancy nature of crucial events in organizations often leaves change agents exhaustedly satisfied if "things seemed to work out pretty well, on balance." This outcome bias I can well understand, as a participant in several major efforts in which events far beyond the change program affected it substantially. Straightforward summary is possible, then. With very rare exceptions (Barnes & Greiner, 1964; and Friedlander, 1967), change programs in large organizations have not been validated in the broader sense of tracing their influence on such desirable states as high productivity or low employee turnover. Sloth does not explain the condition; rather, complexity and confounding variables make any such global validation very difficult. Similarly, very few change programs in large organizations (Argyris, 1962) have looked closely at input variables or at specific processes of the groups involved. There has been a bias toward the study of limited "outcomes."

Phenomenal "Wheels Within Wheels": A Summary

If briefly, this paper should make three points definitely. First, integrating small groups into large formal organizations is solidly a "wheels-within-wheels" business. Second, although significant routes for progress seem patent, uneven advances have been made toward that complex but orderly model that scientists usually seek in nature. Unlike Einstein, students of the group are not yet ready to ask of our alternative deductive theoretical formulations whether they would esthetically please God. We have trouble enough crudely reconciling even the major emphases of our own findings. But there seems some hope that we are not doomed to be behavioral Rube Goldbergs or modern counterparts of the medieval scientist-alchemist Theophrastus Bombastus ab Hohenheim. Third, various "applied" uses of group theory and methods add urgency to the need for "basic" research.

Bibliography

Abruzzi, A. *Work, workers, and work measurement.* New York: Columbia University Press, 1956.

Adams, S. Status congruency as a variable in small group performance. *Social Forces,* 1953, **32,** 16–22.

Alexander, C. N., Jr. Ordinal position and sociometric status. *Journal of Abnormal and Social Psychology,* 1966, **29,** 41–51.

Altman, I. The small group field. In R. V. Bowers (Ed.), *Studies on behavior in organizations.* Athens, Georgia: University of Georgia Press, 1966. Pp. 64–86.

Argyle, M., Gardner, G., & Cioffi, F. The measurement of supervisory methods. *Human Relations*, 1957, 10, 295–313.

————. Supervisory methods related to productivity, absenteeism and labour turnover. *Human Relations*, 1958, 11, 23–40.

Argyris, C. *Integrating the individual and the organization.* New York: John Wiley & Sons, 1964.

————. Interpersonal barriers to decision making. *Harvard Business Review*, 1966, 44, 84–97.

————. *Interpersonal competence and organizational effectiveness.* Homewood, Illinois: Irwin, 1962.

Barnes, L. B., & Greiner, L. E. Breakthrough in organization development. *Harvard Business Review*, 1964, 42, 139–165.

Bass, B. M. *Organizational psychology.* Boston: Allyn & Bacon, 1965.

Baum, B. H. *Decentralization of authority in a bureaucracy.* Englewood Cliffs, N. J.: Prentice-Hall, 1961.

Baumgartel, H., & Sobol, R. Background and organizational factors in absenteeism. *Personnel Psychology*, 1959, 12, 431–443.

Bennett, E. B. Discussion, decision, commitment and consensus in groups. *Human Relations*, 1955, 8, 251–274.

Blake, R. R., & Mouton, J. S. *The managerial grid.* Houston, Texas: Gulf Publishing, 1964.

————, & Sloma, R. L. The union-management intergroup laboratory. *Journal of Applied Behavioral Science*, 1965, 1, 25–57.

Blake, R. R., Shepard, H., & Mouton, J. S. *Managing intergroup conflct in industry.* Houston, Texas: Gulf Publishing, 1964.

Bowers, R. V. (Ed.). *Studies on behavior in organizations.* Athens, Georgia: University of Georgia Press, 1966.

Bradford, L. P., Gibb, J. R., & Benne, K. D. *T-Group theory and laboratory method.* New York: John Wiley & Sons, 1964.

Bright, J. R. *Automation and management.* Boston: Harvard University Graduate School of Business Administration, 1958.

Bugental, J. F. T., & Tannenbaum, R. Sensitivity training and being motivation. In Schein, E. G., & Bennis, W. G., *Personal and organizational change through group methods.* New York: John Wiley & Sons, 1965. Pp. 107–113.

Burack, E. H. *Technology and management organization.* Chicago: Illinois Institute of Technology, 1966.

Calvin, A. D., Hoffman, F. K., & Harden, E. L. The effect of intelligence and social atmosphere on group problem solving behavior. *Journal of Social Psychology*, 1957, 45, 61–74.

Capra, P. C., & Dittes, J. E. Birth order as a selective factor among volunteer subjects. *Journal of Abnormal and Social Psychology*, 1962, 64.

Chandler, A. D., Jr. *Strategy and structure.* Cambridge, Mass.: M.I.T. Press, 1962.

Cleven, W. A., & Fiedler, F. E. Interpersonal perceptions of open hearth foremen and steel production. *Journal of Applied Psychology*, 1956, 40, 312–314.

Dalton, M. *Men who manage.* New York: John Wiley & Sons, 1959.

Dember, W. N. Birth order and need affiliation. *Journal of Abnormal and Social Psychology,* 1964, 68, 555–557.

Dohrenwend, B. S., & Dohrenwend, B. P. Stress situations, birth order, and psychological symptoms. *Journal of Abnormal and Social Psychology,* 1966, 71, 215–223.

Dubin, R., Homans, G. C., Mann, F. C., & Miller, D. C. *Leadership and productivity.* San Francisco: Chandler, 1965.

Fleishmann, E. A., & Harris, E. F. Patterns of leadership behavior related to employee grievances and turnover. *Personnel Psychology,* 1962, 15, 45–53.

Fleishmann, E. A., & Peters, D. R. Interpersonal values, leadership, attitudes and managerial "success." *Personnel Psychology,* 1962, 15, 127–143.

Friedlander, F. The impact of organizational training laboratories upon the effectiveness and interaction of ongoing work groups. *Personnel Psychology,* 1967, 20, 289–307.

Frank, J. D. Training and therapy. In Bradford, Gibb, & Benne, *op. cit.,* 1964. Pp. 442–451.

Gibb, C. A. *The emergence of leadership in temporary groups of men.* Unpublished doctoral dissertation. Urbana, Ill.: University of Illinois, 1949.

Glass, D. C., Horwitz, M., Firestone, I., & Grinker, J. Birth order and reactions to frustration. *Journal of Abnormal and Social Psychology,* 1963, 66, 192–194.

Glidwell, J. C. In D. Stock & H. A. Thelen. *Emotional dynamics and group culture.* New York: New York University Press, 1958. Pp. 122–126.

Golembiewski, R. T. *The small group.* Chicago: University of Chicago Press, 1962.

―――. *Men, management, and morality.* New York: McGraw-Hill, 1965a.

―――. *Organizing men and power: patterns of behavior and line-staff models.* Chicago: Rand McNally, 1967.

―――. Small groups and large organizations. In March, J. G. (Ed.), *Handbook of organizations.* Chicago: Rand McNally, 1965b. Pp. 87–141.

――― & Blumberg, A. Confrontation as a training design in complex organizations: Attitudinal changes in a diversified population of managers. *Journal of Applied Behavioral Science,* in press.

Gomberg, W. Democratic management. *Trans-Action,* 1966, 3, 30–35.

Guest, R. H. *Organizational change.* Homewood, Illinois: Irwin-Dorsey, 1962.

Harrison, R. Group composition models for laboratory design. *Journal of Applied Behavioral Science,* 1965, 1, 409–432.

Heinicke, C., & Bales, R. F. Developmental trends in the structure of small groups. *Sociometry,* 1953, 16, 7–38.

Herbst, P. G. *Autonomous group functioning.* London: Tavistock, 1962.

Hopkins, T. K. *The exercise of influence in small groups.* Totowa, N. J.: Bedminster Press, 1964.

Lakin, M. Human relations training and interracial social action. *Journal of Applied Behavioral Science,* 1966, 2, 139–145.

Leavitt, H. J. Unhuman organizations. In H. J. Leavitt & L. Pondy (Eds.),

Readings in managerial psychology. Chicago: University of Chicago Press, 1964.

Lewin, K., Lippitt, R., & White, R. K. Patterns of aggressive behavior in experimentally created "social climates." *Journal of Social Psychology,* 1939, **10**, 271–299.

Likert, R. *New patterns of management.* New York: McGraw-Hill, 1961.

Luke, R., & Seashore, C. *Generalizations on research and speculations from experience related to laboratory training design.* Washington, D. C.: National Training Laboratories, January 1966.

McArthur, C. Personalities of first and second children. *Psychiatry,* 1956, **19**, 47–54.

McGrath, J., & Altman, I. *Small group research.* New York: Holt, Rinehart & Winston, 1966.

Mann, F. H. Toward an understanding of the leadership role in formal organization. In Dubin, *op. cit.,* 1965. Pp. 68–103.

———, Indik, B. P., & Vroom, V. *The productivity of work groups.* Ann Arbor, Michigan: Survey Research Center, 1963.

Melman, S. *Decision-making and productivity.* New York: John Wiley & Sons, 1958.

Miles, M. B. Changes during and following laboratory training. *Journal of Applied Behavioral Science,* 1965, **1**, 270–285.

———. The T-group and the classroom. In Bradford, Gibb, & Benne, *op. cit.,* 1964. Pp. 452–476.

Moment, D., & Zaleznik, A. *Role development and interpersonal competence.* Boston: Harvard University Graduate School of Business Administration, 1963.

Nagle, B. F. Productivity, employee attitude, and supervisor sensitivity. *Personnel Psychology,* 1954, **7**, 219–233.

National Training Laboratories. *Outcomes of basic human relations laboratories.* Washington, D. C.: National Training Laboratories, March, 1965.

Odiorne, G. The trouble with sensitivity training. *Journal of the American Society of Training Directors,* 1963, **17**, 9–20.

Parisi, D. G. The impact of a change in information technology. Unpublished doctoral dissertation, Northwestern University, 1966.

Penniman, C. Reorganization and the internal revenue service. *Public Administration Review,* 1961, **21**, 121–130.

Porter, L. W. Job attitudes in management, IV: Perceived deficiencies in need fulfillment as a function of size of company. *Journal of Applied Psychology,* 1963, **47**, 386–397.

——— & Lawler, E. E. The effects of "tall" versus "flat" organization structures on managerial job satisfaction. *Personnel Psychology,* 1964, **17**, 135–148.

Sayles, L. D. *Behavior of industrial work groups.* New York: John Wiley & Sons, 1958.

———. *Managerial behavior.* New York: McGraw-Hill, 1964.

Schachter, S. *The psychology of affiliation.* Stanford, Calif.: Stanford University Press, 1959.

Schein, E. H., & Bennis, W. G. *Personal and organizational change through group methods.* New York: John Wiley & Sons, 1965.

Schutz, W. M. *FIRO: A three-dimensional theory of interpersonal behavior.* New York: Rinehart, 1958.

Seashore, S. E. *Group cohesiveness in the industrial work group.* Ann Arbor, Mich.: Survey Research Center, 1954.

Shepard, H. A. Changing interpersonal and intergroup relationships in organizations. In J. G. March (Ed.), *Handbook of organizations.* Chicago: Rand McNally, 1965. Pp. 1115–1143.

Slater, P. E., & Bennis, W. G. Democracy is inevitable. *Harvard Business Review,* 1964, **42,** March-April, 51–59.

Smart, R. B. Alcoholism, birth order, and family size. *Journal of Abnormal and Social Psychology,* 1963, 66, 17–23.

Thibaut, J. W., & Kelley, H. H. *The social psychology of groups.* New York: John Wiley & Sons, 1959.

Triandis, H. C. Notes on the design of organizations. In Thompson (Ed.), *op. cit.,* 1966. Pp. 56–102.

Tuckman, B. W. Personality structure, group composition, and group functioning. *Sociometry,* 1964, **27,** 469–487.

Turner, A. N., & Lawrence, P. R. *Industrial jobs and the worker.* Boston: Harvard University Graduate School of Business Administration, 1965.

Turner, A. N., & Miclette, A. L. Sources of satisfaction in repetitive work. *Occupational Psychology,* 1962, 36, 25–31.

Vroom, V. H., & Mann, F. C. Leader authoritarianism and employee attitudes. *Personnel Psychology,* 1960, **13,** 2.

Walker, C. R., & Guest, R. H. *The man on the assembly line.* Cambridge, Mass.: Harvard University Press, 1952.

Woodward, J. *Management and technology.* London: Her Majesty's Stationery Office, 1958.

Worthy, J. C. *Big business and free men.* New York: Harper & Row, 1959.

———. Organization structure and employce morale. *American Sociological Review,* 1950, **15,** 169–179.

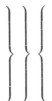

Personality and Organizational Behavior Studies[1]

L. K. WILLIAMS

New York State School of Industrial and Labor Relations
Cornell University

As has been noted elsewhere in this symposium, a classification scheme or taxonomy has several requisites including a principal requirement of having an underlying ordering principle. One of the niceties of the zoological system, for example, is that an evolutionary or developmental process provides much of the ordering. In our attempts to deal with personality and organization, it would be helpful if we had a developmental concept to assist us but it appears that at best we have various developmental constructs in the field of personality and a very limited developmental literature in the area of organizations. It is possible, however, that the concept development can provide one of the many keys to organizing the material that might be included under the caption, "Personality and Organization." This paper is a primitive attempt to view personality and organization by utilizing developmental or growth themes and concepts.

The field of personality and organization suffers both from neglect and disorganization. As is the case with other areas investigated in this symposium, much of the appropriate literature is problem-oriented, rather than theoretical, and was not designed to contribute to a field such as personality *and* organizational behavior. It includes such organizational behavior problems as selection, placement, turnover, leadership, group problem solving, and mental illness. In terms of levels it goes from problems of dyads to the supporting values for certain political science forms. The available literature is found in personnel psychology, clinical psychology, social psychology, personality theory, social organization, political science, and a host of other fields not normally related one to another.

Some of the most comprehensive literature on personality and organizational behavior is probably to be found in the cross-cultural anthropology and personality literature, which seldom is utilized or integrated with attempts to look at personality functioning in the organization. Yet it is probably this literature that most closely meets one of the requisites of such a field: the simultaneous consideration of personality and the structure and functioning of the system. The notion of adaptive personality in terms of classical studies still make exciting reading for the student entering the field of personality and organization: such studies as those concerned with plains and woods Indians, where openness, bravado, interpersonal cooperation, and similar personality concepts are prerequisite for survival in one culture and dysfunctional in the other.

This paper is but one of many attempts to evaluate the field of personality and organization, and no claim is made that the review has been exhaustive or that the suggestions for research and subsequent taxonomic consideration have been tested.

The paper is concerned, first, with the problems of the merger, that is, personality and organizational behavior; next, with an overview of some of the findings; and, finally, as suggested above, with some notions about the use of developmental concepts as a way of conducting research, instigating theory, and hopefully providing a better taxonomy or classification process.

Problems of the Merger

One of the basic problems of personality studies within organizational systems lies in the instruments currently available. While most of the instruments have their origin in the trait approach to personality, some of the most popular have been primarily designed for screening pathological from nonpathological cases. As a consequence, although the parameter being investigated may be important for organizational behavior, such instruments are usually sensitive only at the point of classifying all individuals capable of institutional or systems functioning in one category, and those individuals who are incapable of getting along in their particular society, culture, or institution in another category. Nearly all instruments with origins in the abnormal personality area fall down terribly in making distinctions among individuals who are functioning in the types of organizations which we typically investigate. Moreover, the terms and concepts are not often amenable to any operational definition in organizational terms, although they may be useful in dealing with the mental illness problem in the organization. A review of literature using such instruments as the MMPI or the Rorschach offers little insight into systems of organizational functioning *per se*.

Many of the personality instruments have no specific base in personality theory, but rather were designed for such practical problems as placement and selection in business firms. Most of the preference inventories such as the Kuder or Strong interest tests and others, while perhaps providing data that are rich for understanding personality and organization, do not in and of themselves present dimensions that are readily linked with any true personality theory; they are generally based on the notion of accommodation or convergence of the personality and some specific role rather than the function of that role in a system. Essentially, the question asked in this type research is: "What does a person who does a certain kind of job look like?" It is not the task of such research to ask whether one *should* look like that in order to maximize the efficiency or effectiveness of an institution or role. Conclusions drawn about organizations or group processes are based upon surviving, although not necessarily successful, holders of roles.

As noted above, most of the instruments have been empirically derived and are only occasionally related to personality concepts embedded in a "good" personality theory. They are usually rather static in nature in that they do not account for the growth process of personality. In fact, in most research that uses instrumentation of this type, changes in values, beliefs, and preferences are seen as problems of reliability of the instrument and not as a reflection of personality change. Few, if any, of the dimensions in this area have any direct theoretical convergence with organizational theory in either process or structural terms.

It should be noted that many of the personality variables available for study in organizations — and hence candidates for a taxonomy — lack the conceptual clarity required to make them a good parameter for studies across systems. The authoritarian personality is but one example. The operational definitions, usually in terms of ethnic prejudice or xenophobia, exhaust but a small portion of the variance potential under the theoretical concept of authoritarianism. Moreover, there is the problem of labeling one end of the dimension, but leaving the other end completely confused. While many students of personality and organization might like to use this variable, many hold back because "nonauthoritarian" is still a vague definition and permits labels such as "democratic," "permissive," "unprejudiced," "open-minded" for the other end. It should be noted, in passing, that a search for linear dimensions may also be a misguided effort. It is remotely possible that there are two or more alternative extremes to "high-authoritarianism."

Another problem in the field of personality and organization is the fact that those personality instruments intended for use within organizational systems are too often developed with college sophomores who typically provide the researcher with highly consistent personality scales that break down consideraby when tried in the "real world." This may be a problem of demand characteristics so that sophomores try to give the professors back the scales they are looking for. It may be a problem of identity crisis, where college students go out of their way to provide a consistency in their responses around preference or value items, or it may be that this is a select population that has more consistent abstract belief patterns than the man on the street. For any or all of these reasons, personality inventories based on college students are seldom reproducible in the field. In this vein, it should also be noted that personality research with individuals in work organizations has typically been done with white Anglo-Saxon Protestant males or other selected groups in selected organizations in the United States.

Much of the concern for personality has been in a rather indirect or disguised process in that the predominately used variables in this area are still sex and the rural-urban continuum. Studies of job satisfaction, turnover, or practically any other hard criterion of organizational performance almost always indicate a sex difference. Females nearly always either like or dislike something more or exhibit more or less of some behavior than males. In each case there is a relationship between sex and some aspect of organizational behavior but this only classifies and does not explain the distinction in values held by them.

Similarly there are constant findings of significant differences between rural- and urban-born individuals in the literature. The assumption about the values and beliefs of the rural-born in terms of the Protestant ethic or some similar constellation of values is usually an inference rather than something specifically measured in the context of the research.

In summary, a basic problem of the merger of personality and organization lies in the imperfect tools we have for measuring personality. Imperfect theories and a lack of corresponding parameters wherein personality and organizational variables can be simultaneously investigated add to the difficulties.

Overview of Findings

Studies based on organizational concepts with either process or structural terms are perhaps of more help than those which have a personality base for understanding and creating a literature of personality and organizational behavior. This literature is less likely to use the trait approach, that is, looking at specific needs, values, preferences, and has been addressed more to the concept of growth, competence or mental health in the organizations.

Perhaps the most fully developed area of research in this area involves leadership and personality. Twenty odd years of research attempting to measure or 'train in' leadership qualities have indicated essentially the futility of a single trait approach and yet current findings — such as those of Foa (1957); Vroom (1959); and Williams, Whyte, & Green (1966), to name but a few — have indicated the necessity of using certain personality dimensions as modifying variables in a theory of personality and leadership, particularly as research across groups and cultures is conducted. The initial impact of this research was a clearer picture of leadership, even though little was discovered about personality. Perhaps now that the concept of leadership is more fully developed than many of the other concepts within the organizational behavior, more work can be done on the convergence of personality and organizational theory using our knowledge of leadership to bootstrap our way into better theory and hence a better taxonomy.

In most of the writing on the specific topic of personality and organization, there is an implicit value concerning the self-actualized individual, nonneurotic individual, or fully adjusted individual, where the outcome from the point of view of organizational theory is the design of a system or systems to allow for a total adjustment as distinct from accommodation of the individuals in the organization. Were we to follow through in this way, all leaders would look alike or would act alike and presumably all organizations would have very similar systems structures and processes. Within this area there is often the underlying assumption that, if the structure and process of the system are redesigned to allow for a maximum growth, then the individual will grow. Or in other words, the values, beliefs, and core personality of the individual will blossom and come into line with the "perfect" organization. This is more a value than a theoretical position and as yet remains untested.

With the exception of some mental health research the typical personality and organization literature deals with a select number of "social value" traits of personality. The implicit definition of personality being "effect upon others." Given the practical concern of most organizations with morale and an underlying unwarranted assumption in our culture that conflict is bad, typical dimensions used are sociability, aggressiveness, dominance, and submission, and most recently the ubiquitous achievement motive or need for achievement. The latter dimension — that is, need for achievement — seemingly is getting the greatest play in the current research literature, although still bedeviled by the fact that it is a very difficult variable to measure for females and that achievement seems to be more of a process variable or style of approach variable than a specific need.

What else have we learned in a decade of research? Much of the research on personality and organization has come out of the training field wherein attempts are made to change values, beliefs, and preferences so that they are more in line with a perfect organization or system which "the trainers have in mind." If there is one thing we have learned about organizational structure and personality, it is that structural changes need to be consistent with the personality process and must reward those values or beliefs which one is trying to inculcate. The whole area of attitude change has indicated very clearly that values and beliefs will be reasonably consistent with those structural properties that enforce or punish a particular value or belief, whether we want to or not, we appear to have arrived at a state where we cannot talk about personality without talking about the organizational or systematic arrangements in which individuals are going to operate.

Very much unanswered in the research is the question of the permeability of values, beliefs, and preferences. How much can a personality be changed as a function of immersion in an organization? Breer and Locke (1964), for example, have indicated that such values and beliefs about cooperation and individualism can be specifically changed, at least in the laboratory, depending upon whether cooperation or individualism pays off in a work process. This is a rather fascinating area of research about the nature of work and suggests that various work arrangements can and do affect the values of the participants.

Field studies on organizational change definitely suggest that there are "personality changes" within organizations as individuals encounter crises and go through major change activities.

The literature available in this area suggests that personality change in the formal work organization is not unlike that in other areas of personality change. Change is most likely to occur, if at all, where there is a traumatic, visible change in roles, not unlike a "puberty rite." There can be considerable personality change, using the definition of personality as social value, if individuals interacting with a specific role tolerate, permit, or expect personality change. It is probably for this reason that individuals moving into organizations where they are totally unknown, individuals who have had a traumatic experience in their background known to others such as serious illness or death in the family, and those who have been away to courses or training processes which others agree are aimed at personality change will have the greatest potential for "personality change."

In summary, much research on personality in organizations has been oriented toward personal growth, mental fitness, or self-actualization as seen by those who are engaged in the training or change process. While there is little hard data, there is seemingly ample evidence that personality change does take place within the organizational context and that the changes are a product of both the individual and the system to the degree to which the system allows or enforces personality change.

Toward a Model

It is not a new idea that unhealthy people, unhealthy groups, unhealthy organizations, and even unhealthy societies share very similar values and beliefs as well as ways of behaving.

Therapists interested in bringing competence to their clients have an amazing similarity in terms of the concepts used and in their description of the dysfunctional case. For example, on the dysfunctions of the bureaucracy, authors such as Bennis (1966) or Argyris (1957) point to mistrust and submissiveness as both supporting values and evidence on the incompetence of the bureaucratic form. Writers on poverty and the community note the need for changes in the interpersonal levels of the poverty stricken in terms of raising the level of interpersonal relations, which are characterized as highly distrustful and fatalistic. Similar concepts of interpersonal relations are used to describe other cases such as the ultraconservative, the dogmatic liberal, the underdeveloped society, and the wallflower.

Seemingly, every therapist, change agent, manager, or parent has a desire to aid growth, competence, or health, the latter two being concepts with numerous similarities. The problem for each is that of defining competence and of finding that leverage on the client which will bring about growth.

While this is not necessarily a treatise on action programs, I would like to suggest that examination of such programs in organizational behavior provides considerable guidance in the nomination of appropriate personality variables for the study of personality and organization.

The developmental literature is not value free by any means, and one way of producing dimensional candidates for examination is to search the literature for the "good guys" and, implicitly, the "bad guys." The problem of values becomes much more severe in practically any model which attempts to describe a fully matured system, be it an individual or an economy. Either out of pity or smugness, researchers tend to agree on the characteristics of an arrested personality, group, factory, or economy, to take but a few examples, and most of the theoreticians implicitly if not explicitly attempt to describe the healthy, functioning systems. There is usually consensus as to what constitutes a primitive or initial phase of a developmental sequence. Therefore, one can start a "laundry list," such as the one included here, of dimensions or variables to describe developing systems by searching for the agreed "bad guys" as a way of establishing relevant dimensions for consideration, even though there may be total disagreement as to what the opposite end of the developmental sequence looks like or should look like.

FIGURE 1. Developmental Dimensions

I. Cognitive — Perceptual and Learning

Bimodal and/or Binary	Multiple
Absolute	Relative
Concrete	Abstract
Rigidity	Flexibility
Demand for certainty	No demand for certainty
Intolerance for ambiguity	Tolerance for ambiguity
Immediate reinforcement	Delayed reinforcement
Immediate gratification	Delayed gratification
Regular reinforcement	Aperiodic reinforcement
Closeminded, stereotyping	Open minded, nonstereotyping
Narrow category width	Broad category width
Limited time perspective	Extended time perspective

II. Values, Beliefs and Motives

Fatalistic	Nonfatalistic
Pessimistic	Optimistic
Nature/man	Man/nature fate control
Past or present orientation	Future orientation
Fear of failure	Achieving
Particularistic	Universalistic
Security-seeking	Risk-taking

III. Interpersonal and Institutional Relationship

Mistrust	Trust
Xenophobic	No fear of strangers
Autocratic-Authoritarian	Democratic-Nonauthoritarian
Ascriptive	Achieving
Subsistence and scarcity	Abundance and saving
Traditional	Modern
Prejudiced	Nonprejudiced

Figure 1 involves an eclectic collection of concepts or terms from various developmental ledgers. It is but a sampling of the dimensions or concepts available, and filling in with additional dimensions is a game which anyone can play. The only order implied involves the successive levels of concepts going from the individual and the learning-perceptual process to levels which involve organizations or societies — and the use of the left side of the figure to connote the initial state or position in a developmental or growth sequence.

The labels for our dimensions are separately open to question, but the assumption is made that the developmental positioning of each dimension is more right than wrong and that the parameters used here have tradition if not logic as a support for their inclusion.

As a heuristic model, the intent of the list is to suggest relationships within and between levels so as to incorporate those terms which are usually used only in a descriptive sense into a more dynamic model; as such it suggests directions or propensities for change. Moreover, each dimension included has a potential operationalization in both personality and organizational terms.

Level I: Cognitive, Perceptual, and Learning Dimensions

At this level, the available literature suggests that the first distinction made by an individual in development is essentially binary or bimodal in nature. In the labeling or cognitive process, the most primitive form is a distinction between those events, phenomena or individuals which belong or do not belong to a class or label. This would involve such labels as: "family," "not family;" "animal," "not animal;" "good to eat" and "bad to eat;" and the like. The development of the self-image follows similar lines, and a distinction is between the "me" and "not me," where the individual learns the extensions of his capacity and control. This is at once a cognitive and perceptual process which later becomes elaborated in terms of further distinctions within any class of events or in forming categories, and in this literature there is at least the implication that those who persist on bimodal responding, seeing the world as black and white or overstereotyping, present cases of arrested development where growth lies in the direction of flexibility, permeability, multiple categories for screening life, or a capacity for abstract as distinct from concrete concepts in the evolution of the perceptual, cognitive process of the individual.

There is some connection between the above, and social learning theories such as that of Rotter (1954). Such learning theories, specifically with regard to reinforcements, involve the concept that initially immediate reinforcement is required in order to affect behavior and even to develop concepts, but later on, greater distance may intervene between an act and its reinforcement. Stated another way, primitive systems are seen as needing immediate feedback, and more advanced, mature systems as functioning with delayed feedback.

It is on this last point that there is perhaps some connection between concept formation, perception, and learning, in that the "bad guys" have a high need for certainty or intolerance of ambiguity and a very rapid system of closure in making a definition of a decision about new stimuli.

In general, then, the primitive or incompetent at this level is characterized by: the need for quick reinforcement or information in order to continue activities, intolerance or anxiety when stimuli or cues are ambiguous; a tendency, when we are describing the social activity of such individuals, to stereotype; lack of flexibility in the capacity to admit new information, quickness in forming judgments, without the willingness or capability to suspend judgment, decision, or activities.

Level II: Values and Motives

The work on values, motives, and attitudes tends to be less developmental in nature than the research and theorizing in perception and cognition. In fact, socialization is usually leaned upon as a way of describing the transmission of these values, although it is a construct of limited utility in describing the origin of values. Nevertheless, linkages have been established between what has been described above as the primitive level of cognitive development and some of the value attitudinal dimensions in the literature. This is particularly so in the area of traditionalism versus modernism, or in such cross-cultural research as that of Kluckhohn, Murray, and Schneider (1953), where the primitive society or social group is seen as having such undesirable characteristics (for most modern people's values) as fatalism, nature over man as against man over nature, ascription rather than achievement as a means of assigning roles, immediate or past-time perspectives rather than future-time perspectives, and so forth. Borrowing from this literature, others have been able to recast future orientation as against present orientation in terms of immediate or delayed gratification or in terms of inner and external controls (see, for example, Mischel, 1966). Stereotyping, rigidity, desire for certainty, or intolerance for ambiguity are often linked with traditionalism when this concept is used to describe a group or society, or organization.[2]

Many motivational models of need achievement such as the level of aspiration or the more recent work by McClelland (1961) and Atkinson, et al., (1958) imply a mechanism of successive goals where the individual is capable of perceiving discrete steps and adapts his choices or behavior as a function of current success and failure, thus linking perception and motivation and behavior. It should be noted that those described as high in fear of failure are less prone to engage in such successive level setting in terms of their own behavior; they either avoid or do not see intermediate probabilities of success, or at least do not see them as related to their own behavior in the same way as do

---

[2] It should be noted that the discussion and research on modernity in the sociological literature usually involves nearly all of the value dimensions as used in this paper (see Kahl, J. (1967) and Inkeles, A. (1966) for recent examples).

those characterized as having high achievement orientation. We also noted that the child-rearing practice associated with achievement is one where success and failure are both experienced and where the environmental return is not a complete win-lose matrix or absolute process.

Looking at Figure 1, it is also possible to recall other types of research which in one way or another suggest a close link between immediate gratification and such values as fatalism. It can be argued that if one sees the world as being capricious or a matter of luck — one is more prone to take what one can when he can get it and not trust in the future of others. This, then, is reason enough not to delay gratification nor to be really concerned with the future. It is only rational to plan for the future if one feels that he will be able to respond to or master nature. Therefore, a system which uses immediate gratification only as a reinforcement process should not have future orientation emerge as the predominant value.

Stated another way, these are not really separate dimensions but rather there is some conceptual overlap existing between all of the dimensions of Levels I and II noted in the figure.

Level III: Interpersonal and Institutional Relationships

This is a somewhat artificial category, but involves interpersonal values as distinct from values toward life in general and certain values and behavior with regard to institutional settings. Some of the dimensions involved are authoritarianism, interpersonal mistrust or xenophobia, low cooperation, and, perhaps, inner-direction rather than other-direction. The relationships between this level and the previous levels can be found rather readily in the literature, where those high in authoritarianism or those low in interpersonal trust are seen as being supported by rigid close-minded perceptual systems or values. Looking cross-culturally, we note that primitive systems or underdeveloped cultures are often described as having authoritarian leadership forms supported by ascriptive values and processes with absolute concepts of justice and distribution. In fact, one might even note that under the most authoritarian leadership form, even the concept of leadership is such that there is only a leader and nonleaders, or, stated another way, the leadership may not be divided among the various individuals but is a singular role. This is consistent with definitions of charismatic leadership.

Low interpersonal trust has been linked with authoritarian political structures in such works as that of Almond and Verba (1963). Other relationships indicated in the literature on traditional authoritarian systems describe such systems as being supported by or consisting of certain forms of low cooperation, values associated with immediate gratification, fear of the unknown, or xenophobia, and low tolerance for ambiguity. It is also possible to consider relationships between distrust and fatalism such that it is necessary for individuals in a system to have mutual reliance and trust before reciprocal relationships will be engaged in which have any extended form of payoff. This would also include such concepts as division of labor where certain activities are not visible to other participants in the activity.

The above is intended to indicate (albeit sketchily) some relationships between the dimensions included. Next we shall examine some of the organizational correlates merely as examples of a systems growth model.

Ambiguity

Human systems appear to differ in their capacity to handle ambiguity as do humans. Budner (1962), Balk (1967), and others writing on this subject have noted that creative groups and systems must develop a tolerance for ambiguity. Related to this are systems that tend to have only binary decision processes and recruit similar individuals to them. In one study, by Balk and Williams (1962), it was found that law students tended to be much more prone to being bimodal perceivers than liberal arts students, and this also affected a number of behavioral choices including the grading process in courses.

Essentially systematic dimensions in this involve the mode and scope of stimulus classification and response processes.

Gratification–Reward Process

Mischel (1966) and others have indicated reliable differences between individuals in their preferences for immediate *versus* delayed rewards. The amount and timing of feedback is but one property of systems that appears to be related to this dimension. To give but one example, the effectiveness of compensation systems such as wages and bonuses is undoubtedly related to systems members' capacity to delay gratification. Underdeveloped systems, if this observation is correct, would reinforce their members more frequently and closer to the event being reinforced than would be the case in highly developed systems.

Time

Most social systems have to be concerned with time. Jaques (1956), for example, has indicated that individuals in a firm are paid in terms of time span managed. Elaborating on this, Goodman (1966) has indicated that industrial units can be calibrated in terms of time span of planning and has indicated that engineers with a short time perspective are well adapted to manufacturing assignments, but reject or are rejected by research and development units which tend to have a longer time span. Several individuals have noted that a major problem of industrialization in underdeveloped cultures involves the time commitment requirements. Thus it is quite possible to measure differences within and between systems in terms of time orientation and time evaluation.

Trust

Interpersonal trust studies have indicated, for example, a relationship with membership in extremest organization, type of conflict resolution process adapted, and type of political system supported (see for example, Goldsen, et al., 1960). In a cross-cultural leadership study, Williams, Whyte, and Green (1966) showed a significant relationship between interpersonal trust and preferred supervisory style. Only among high-trust Peruvians were democratic leaders preferred. In fact, low-trust individuals indicated that they were not members of a work group, despite what the organizational chart said, thus suggesting a parameter of leadership relations that starts autocratically and becomes "man-to-group" democratic, with at least one intermediate stage of "man-to-man" democratic.

System dimensions would include such phenomena as visibility of roles and the monitoring of behavior, conflict resolution procedures, and group cohesiveness.

Where and How to Look

Underlying this exposition is that institutions are maintained by values of the participants, and that changes either in the institution or in the values system will result in change in the complementary unit.

Not too long ago, I had the dubious pleasure of acting as consultant to an organization that, according to its own description, had become childlike in its interpersonal relations. A number of individuals in a northeastern plant were embarrassed to note that they were in a "dog-eat-dog" situation, that they distrusted each other considerably, and that they were only working from day to day rather than thinking ahead in their activities. They felt that this was abnormal and did not know how the factory had gotten into this spot. Their statement was, "We're not really like this, but we've become childlike or animal-like over the years."

I found this situation not unlike a description of the peasant society by Foster (1965). Foster notes that most peasant societies operate under an environmental and organizational condition of scarcity. The prevailing orientation is that of limited good or that in which the individuals are in combat with nature and playing a zero-sum game, where if someone wins, someone else must lose. The concept of an ever-expanding pie as a function of cooperation is missing, and the predominant values are ones of distrust, envy, short-time perspectives, and fatalism.

The factory situation mentioned above had the same predominate value system, and further investigation indicated that the factory was operating on a scarcity basis. Prior to my arrival, accounting principles had been installed in such a way that people had to compete for what everyone considered to be an insufficient budget. At the time of my entry into the system, members thought the process was impossible to reverse, and everyone was admittingly living on a day-to-day schedule, viewing his organization life in a most fatalistic manner.

The important point, as far as this article is concerned, is that the system had regressed to a more primitive set of values and beliefs. Moreover, the organization later changed its budgetary procedures, and the system was removed from the burden of extreme scarcity. Qualitative measures taken at a later time, through interviews, suggested a rather drastic reversion of values within the system closer to the desired previous state of cooperation, long-time perspective, and interpersonal cooperation.

This is not meant to indicate that personality in those aspects that we can measure, such as values and beliefs, is perfectly changeable, but does suggest there is an ordering in which movement is possible up and down certain parameters depending upon the nature of the system. The boundaries of such change, of course, are extra-organizational, and are determined in part by cultural constraints on such values and belief systems.

By and large, this exposition has examined the relationship between a number of the specific organization variables and some personality parameters and has excluded the environment in which the organization exists. Obviously, environment is an extremely important factor in examining the structure and functioning of an organizational system and is perhaps even broader than the concept of culture, in that, within any given culture, hostile environments exist for certain organizations and not for others. Highly competitive organizations such as some professional sports groups or magazines sales teams, for example, even within the context of the reasonably developed culture of the United States are two obvious examples of systems whose reward processes, time orientation, and other processes are closer to the underdeveloped than to the developed end of the dimensions in question. While it is not the purpose of this article to examine external constraints on individual or organizational values and behavior, the following is an indication of how the environmental dimensions can be considered in the context of exploring the isomorphic conditions between individual and organizational parameters.

FIGURE 2. Conditions of Personality, Organization, and Environment

State	Personality System	Organizational System	Environment
1	Developed	Developed	Developed
2	Underdeveloped	Underdeveloped	Underdeveloped
3	Underdeveloped	Developed	Developed
4	Underdeveloped	Developed	Underdeveloped
5	Underdeveloped	Underdeveloped	Developed
6	Developed	Underdeveloped	Underdeveloped
7	Developed	Developed	Underdeveloped
8	Developed	Underdeveloped	Developed

Figure 2 is a schematic presentation of personality, organizational, and environmental systems and indicates some of the possible relationships. In addition to denoting a personality and organizational system, it also brings into account the environment in which a system is found. Environment includes, but is not limited to: the culture system; religious, economic, political, legal, and other institutional systems; and relevant organizations (that is, competitors and complementers). While only the labels "developed" and the "underdeveloped" are used, we should remember that these labels refer to continua and, therefore, that the diagram represents theoretical or "pure" cases for purposes of exposition.

States 1 and 2 are balanced conditions. As noted above, they actually refer to a whole continua of balanced conditions wherein these are merely the extremes. State 1 represents some form of an ideal for many change agents, and state 2, while it might have certain values in processes which one would find very "undemocratic," represents an organization quite in tune with the environment. It is quite possible that people with more "developed" values in the personality system would feel very uncomfortable and would leave the organization in question.

States 3 through 7 are unbalanced conditions where one would anticipate or hypothesize change. State 4, for example, might represent the situation we often find in attempting to export management principles into certain underdeveloped countries. In this case, the American way of doing things assumes responsibility on the part of individuals, delayed gratification, and longtime-span orientation. In such an instance there is nearly always modification of the organizational system in order to make it match the values and beliefs of the members who must participate, such change usually being fully in line with other organizational models available in the culture.

State 7 might be thought of as an organization with a reasonably participative model of behavior, with individual members who trust one another, where there is an extended time orientation and similar matching of personality and organizational goals. If this system is confronted by an extremely hostile environment — for example, conditions of scarcity with high competition and a general mistrust of people outside with regard to members and purposes of a system in question — a natural prediction is that the organization may not be very effective or efficient and that the processes of the organization and subsequently the values of many of its members will change to be more in line with the environment.

Finally, we might consider State 8, which represents to some degree current discussions of bureaucracy within the culture of the United States, where individuals desire a high degree of participation and responsibility but where the organization is highly specific with regard to the activities of individuals and is seen as blocking individual initiative and growth. The outcome in this case is either alienation from work or high turnover of individuals who find the organizational framework antithetical to their own beliefs or values. This outcome, of course, assumes that the individual members are unsuccessful in any attempt to modify the organizational system.

Rather than discuss all possible permutations and combinations, the above illustrations should suffice to indicate the requirement for bringing the environment into a discussion of personality and organization and to suggest that the interaction of these latter two systems can result in modifications of either the organizational system or the personality system in rather predictable directions.

Turning again to general considerations, it is reasonable to conclude from all of the developmental literature that the institutional or system return to the individual can modify values, but when the discrepancies are too great, there is an attempt to modify institutions.

This is reasonably obvious in looking at the limited institutional transfer literature, for example, on the importation of the British or American trade unions structure to underdeveloped countries, where depending upon the values of that culture the structure becomes modified to fit the culture. In fact it is just this transfer process that can and should provide illuminating material in the value prerequisites of certain social forms or institutions.

Finally, it should be noted that within the developmental literature very few of the dimensions have intermediate stages. Seldom is anything described between what has been defined as the initial and the matured phase of any dimension. If the institution or system can be changed, a natural evolutionary process should emerge where one can identify both intermediate institutional or system forms and intermediate levels of change with regard to those personality dimensions suggested in this paper.

The Theory X'er, the Autocrat, the Bureaucrat, the underdeveloped country, the factory, and the community appear to have a lot in common. If nothing else, — everyone wants to make them "better." If we determine what "better" is and how to get there in discrete steps, we may have many of the dimensions we are looking for.

Summary

This has been a brief presentation of the problems of simultaneously investigating personality and organization. It has been noted that one of the problems of the merger has been that the dimensions used for the investigation of personality and organization are not necessarily grounded in either good organizational or good personality theory.

For the purpose of developing a taxonomy some underlying scheme is necessary in order to bring order to the data already available. What has been proposed is the notion of development or evolutional growth, and through an examination of the developmental literature it is suggested that there is a reasonable degree of agreement amongst change agents and theorists with regard to the underdeveloped end when one is considering either personality or organization. Moreover, an evolutionary form is either implicit or explicit in most of these writings, wherein the individuals and organizations are supposed to develop toward a set of values and processes very similar to those usually detailed under such concepts as "modernization" or "the Protestant Ethic." It is suggested that the use of a growth or developmental model may be of some utility in developing a taxonomy of personality and organizational variables, particularly in pointing toward intermediate stages of system or organizational development in keeping with the intermediate stages that can be found for personality development.

Included in this paper have been a number of dimensions which can be used for the simultaneous investigation of personality and organization.

Bibliography

Almond, G., & Verba, S. *The civic culture*. Princeton, N. J.: Princeton University Press, 1963.

Argyris, C. *Personality and organization*. New York: Harper & Row, 1957.

Atkinson, J. W. (Ed.). *Motives in fantasy, action and society*. Princeton, N. J.: Van Nostrand, 1958.

Balk, W. *Certain social psychological aspects of supervisory performance quantification in large work organizations*. Ph.D. dissertation, New York State School of Industrial and Labor Relations, Cornell University, 1967.

———— & Williams, L. K. Perception of ambiguous stimuli using the APT test. (Unpublished manuscript, 1962.)

Bennis, W. G. *Changing organizations*. New York: McGraw-Hill, 1966.

Breer, P., & Locke, E. *Task experience as a source of attitudes*. Homewood, Illinois: Dorsey Press, 1965.

Budner, S. Intolerance of ambiguity as a personality variable. *Journal of Personality*, 30, 1, March 1962, 29–45.

Foa, U. G. Relation of workers expectations to satisfaction with supervisor. *Personnel Psychology*, 10, Summer 1957, 161–168.

Foster, G. M. Peasant society and the image of limited good. *American Anthropologist*, 67, 2, April 1965.

Goldsen, R., et al. *What college students think*. Princeton, N. J.: Van Nostrand, 1960.

Goodman, P. *A study of time perspective: Measurement and correlates*. Ph.D. dissertation, New York State School of Industrial and Labor Relations, Cornell University, 1966.

Inkeles, A. The modernization of modern man. In *Modernization: The dynamics of growth*. New York: Basic Books, 1966.

Jaques, E. *Measurement of responsibility*. London: Tavistock Publications, 1956.

Kahl, J. *The measurement of modernism: A study of values in Brazil and Mexico*. Austin, Texas: University of Texas Press (in press).

Kluckhohn, C., & Murray, H. with the collaboration of Schneider, D. *Personality in nature, society, and culture*. New York: Knopf, 1953.

McClelland, D. C. *The achieving society*. Princeton, N. J.: Van Nostrand, 1961.

Mischel, W., & Masters, J. Effects of probability of reward attainment on responses to frustration. *Journal of Personality and Social Psychology*, 1966, 3, 4, 390–396.

Rotter, J. B. *Social learning and clinical psychology*. New York: Prentice-Hall, 1954.

Vroom, V. H. Some personality determinants on the effects of participation. *Journal of Abnormal and Social Psychology*, 54, 1959, 322–327.

Williams, L. K., Whyte, W. F., & Green, C. S. Do cultural differences affect workers' attitudes? *Industrial Relations*, 5, 3, May 1966, 105–117.

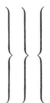

The Elements of Organizational Performance[1]

STANLEY E. SEASHORE
and EPHRAIM YUCHTMAN

Survey Research Center
Institute for Social Research
The University of Michigan

In 1964 there was proposed a conceptual framework for the assessment of organizational performance (Seashore, 1965). This proposal was developed in response to the repeated failure of managers to form reliable and valid estimates of their own organizations' performance and the repeated failure of researchers to locate stable and generally applicable relationships between predictor variables, on the one hand, and single organizational performance variables, on the other. This conceptual scheme also was a response to the fact, often noted by others, that organizations seem to have many goals, not one, and that these goals are often incompatible with one another, changing in priorities and in realization over time. The objective in this formulation was to seek some way to find order, perhaps simplicity of order, among the numerous and miscellaneous variables that are used by managers, researchers, and the general public when they attempt to define and evaluate the performance of an organization.

The proposed conceptual framework assumed that variables descriptive of organizational performance could be ordered into a hierarchical network based upon the distinction between longer-term

---

[1] This investigation has been supported by the National Science Foundation (Grant GS-70), and by the anonymous firm that provided, at considerable expense to itself, the data used in the investigation. A somewhat different version of this paper appears in Seashore and Yuchtman (1967).

output variables, on the one hand, and on the other shorter-term variables descriptive of output behavior and of various organizational states and processes. We conceived of a hierarchical model as follows.

1. At the top of the hierarchy is the "ultimate criterion" — some conception of the net output performance of the organization over a long span of time in achieving its formal objectives, whatever they may be, with optimum use of environmental resources and opportunities. Such an ultimate criterion may never be measured, except possibly by historians, yet some concept of this kind is the basis for evaluation of lesser criteria.

2. Below the ultimate criterion there may be a roster of penultimate criteria, relatively few in number, having the following characteristics: they are "output" or "results" criteria, referring to things sought for their own value; they have trade-off value in relation to one another; they are in turn wholly caused by partially independent sets of lesser performance variables; their sum in some weighted mixture over time wholly determines the ultimate criterion. We suggested that these criteria would be factorially independent of one another, although probably correlated in observed performances, and that some of the component variables would be universal, others unique to certain classes of organizations.

3. Below this roster of key criterion variables, there would be a large number of subsidiary variables, with the following characteristics: some would refer to subgoals or means for achieving goals, while others would refer to organizational states and processes; they would have interrelationships of many kinds (independence, positive or negative correlation, causation, covariance, interaction, modification, and so forth); they would comprise distinguishable but overlapping subsets with each subset containing a full determination (causation) of its own penultimate criterion of organizational performance. The variables in the lower levels of the hierarchy would represent relatively short-term performances and transitory states and processes of organizational life, responsive to environmental changes and to phases of organizational development. They would, accordingly, present complex time-related changes often of a phasic or cyclic type.

The merits of such a conceptual scheme, whatever its defects, are considerable. The scheme emphasizes that no *one* criterion (except the unmeasurable ultimate criterion) can reasonably be used alone to represent organizational performance; at the very least, account must be taken of the full roster of penultimate criterion variables. The scheme emphasizes that organizational performance is complex, involving probably hundreds of variables. The scheme allows for both elements of universality and elements of uniqueness. The scheme acknowledges the elementary but notably ignored fact that organizational performances fluctuate with time and that few single variables, if any, can be expected to reveal much constancy over time, even though the network may have stable features.

Ideally, we should like to measure directly performance in relation to the ultimate criterion. Traditional treatments of the criterion problem have led to the choice of some one measurable criterion to represent this ultimate criterion. The present scheme, however, suggests that we must start with a large number of variables describing the performances of organizations and then examine the pattern of relationships among them in order to infer from this pattern the underlying dimensions of performance. These underlying dimensions could then be interpreted to be the penultimate "goals" of the organizations. These goals would be inferred from the actual behavior of the organizations, not from ideal states, norms, or cultural entities. Given the assumption that the ultimate goal is not a part of actual processes of current organizational life and is thus an unmeasurable construct, it follows that effectiveness can be assessed only in terms of the position of an organization on all of the penultimate dimensions. In line with this thinking, we undertook an empirical investigation. Given a set of data descriptive of many aspects of performance for a set of organizations over a span of time, we could then by statistical tests investigate:

1. Whether there is a set of penultimate performance variables, factorially pure, that account for much of the total variance in performances.
2. Whether the factors are strongly correlated with, and therefore potentially caused by, sets of subsidary variables representing organizational states and processes but not goals.
3. Whether the set of factors is constant across a number of similar organizations (not tested in our analysis).
4. Whether this set of factors is constant over some span of time.
5. Whether the performance of a single organization is variable over time within the set of constant factors.
6. Whether the conceptual content of the factors suggests that some of them may be "universals," others "uniques."

Such an analysis leads to an assessment of whether it now seems reasonable to hope that there might be identified a roster of conceptual variables, limited in number, discrete in meaning, comprehensive in coverage, partially universal in applicability, that can be the taxonomic framework for comparative organizational studies. Such an analysis has been largely completed, and some of the results will be presented next.

The data refer to 75 independently owned and managed life insurance sales agencies located in different communities throughout the United States. They range in size from about 10 to 60 salesman members plus supporting staff, and are thus technically small business organizations, although they are considerably larger than the average business enterprise in dollar volume. All have been in business for a number of years, and none have had a recent disruption such as change of territory or of ownership. The data are all from firm records and, although more elaborate than is usual, are of kinds normally kept by business firms. An eleven-year span of time is encompassed, the earliest data being for 1952, the latest for 1962. The analyzed performance variables, 76 in number, were selected from an initial roster of over 200 variables; variables were eliminated on the grounds of duplication (statistical identity), unreliability of measurement, insufficient variance, dubious accuracy, and similar statistical quality reasons. We think this is an extraordinary set of uniform comparative organizational data, for most smaller firms are hard pressed to find in their records even a dozen performance indicators of statistical quality suitable for analysis. The data, however, are highly restricted: they refer to organizations of rather uniform size, all sharing similar formal business goals, all employing similar methods and resources, and all data refer to "hard" indexes of performance computed in standard ways.

Organizational Performance Factors

The empirical design that is implied by the conceptual framework, and the rather complex set of data associated with it, both call for factor analysis as an appropriate statistical model for our purpose. Accordingly, the selected 76 performance variables were factor analyzed, using the principal component solution, and later rotated according to the varimax method. This yielded about 15 factors that account for over 90 per cent of the total variance. Out of these, we have succeeded in labeling, or giving meaningful identification to, the 10 factors listed in Table 1. They account altogether for about 70 per cent of the total variance. The kinds of variables contributing to each of these factors are suggested also by Table 1.[2]

---

[2] The technical information is not complete here, but was published in considerable detail early in 1967. The following points, however, may be useful in the present context. The "final" matrices for analysis include, with a few unavoidable exceptions, only items having equal-unit scalar properties and either normal or rectangular dis-

TABLE 1. Performance Factors: Insurance Agency Organizations

Factor	Assigned Name	Indicator Variables*
I	Business volume (Including both accumulated volume and current increment in volume)	Number of policies in force, year end (4) New insurance sold, dollar volume (5) Renewal premiums collected, dollars (10) Number of lives insured, year end (17) Agency manpower, number of agents (26)
II	Production cost	Production cost per new policy (61) Production cost per $1,000 of insurance (62) Production cost per $100 of premium (63)
III	New member productivity	Average productivity per new agent (35) Ratio of new agent vs. old agent productivity ("New agent": less than 5 years service) (36)
IV	Youthfulness of members	Ratio of younger (under 35) to total membership (45) Ratio of productivity of younger members to agency total (46)
V	Business mix (Many low-value transactions vs. fewer high-value transactions)	Average premium per $1,000 (13) Per cent of new policies with quarterly payments (14) Per cent of business in employee trust (76)
VI	Manpower growth	Net change in manpower during year (27) Ratio of net change to initial manpower (28)
VII	Management emphasis	Manager's personal commissions (52)
VIII	Maintenance cost (Refers to maintenance of accounts, not of physical facilities)	Maintenance cost per collection (64) Maintenance cost per $100 premium collected (65)
IX	Member productivity	Average new business volume per agent (47)
X	Market penetration	Insurance in force per capita (16) Number of lives covered per 1,000 insurables (19)

* Variable identification (serial) numbers in parentheses are included to aid cross-reference between tables.

Table 2 shows (for 1952) the factor loadings upon each of the 10 factors for those variables we chose to use as factor indicator variables. With a few marginal exceptions, easily visible to the eye, each of the selected indicator variables loads strongly on one and only one factor,

---

tributions. Preliminary factor analyses limited to data of various statistical properties (that is, omitting ratio scales, omitting items so that no more than one came from each source of basic data, and so forth) produced factor structures of such similarity that we feel assured that no serious distortions arise from such causes. Orthogonal rotation was required because the matrix included a large number of high inter-item correlations and the factor structure is complex; the unrotated factors were, in our judgment, uninterpretable.

with nonsignificant loadings on all other factors; the only instances of significantly shared loadings occur for variables having a loading on Factor I, volume, in addition to their factor of main loading. This is, of course, a simplified table. Among the 53 variables not represented are some with no significant loadings, some with significant loadings on two or more of the factors. The indicator variables were used to calculate factor scores for each of the organizations.

TABLE 2. Factor Loadings for Selected Indicator Variables*

Indicator Variables	I	II	III	IV	V	VI	VII	VIII	IX	X
Policies in force (4)	86	—	—	—	—	—	—	—	—	—
New sales (5)	88	—	—	—	—	—	—	—	—	—
Renewal premiums (10)	92	—	—,	—	—	—	—	—	—	—
Lives insured (17)	83	—	—	—	—	—	—	—	—	—
Manpower (26)	87	—	—	—	—	—	—	—	—	—
Cost per sale (61)	—	72	—	—	—	—	—	—	—	—
Cost per $1,000 (62)	—	91	—	—	—	—	—	—	—	—
Cost per $100 premium (63)	—	82	—	—	—	—	—	—	—	—
Productivity per new agent (35)	—	—	73	—	—	—	—	—	—	—
Ratio new/old productivity (36)	—	—	89	—	—	—	—	—	—	—
Ratio young/old agents (45)	—	—	—	86	—	—	—	—	—	—
Ratio young/old productivity (46)	—	—	—	89	—	—	—	—	—	—
Premium per $1,000 (13)	41	—	—	—	79	—	—	—	—	—
% quarterly payments (14)	—	—	—	—	69	—	—	—	—	—
% employee trust (76)	47	—	—	—	80	—	—	—	—	—
Manpower increase (27)	—	—	—	—	—	84	—	—	—	—
Ratio increase to total (28)	—	—	—	—	—	82	—	—	—	—
Manager's commissions (52)	—	—	—	—	—	—	89	—	—	—
Cost per collection (64)	—	—	—	—	—	—	—	86	—	—
Cost per $100 premium (65)	52	—	—	—	—	—	—	74	—	—
New business per agent (47)	—	—	—	—	—	—	—	—	93	—
Insurance per capita (16)	40	—	—	—	—	—	—	—	—	83
Lives per 1,000 insurable (19)	—	—	—	—	—	—	—	—	—	82

* Decimals omitted; loadings under .40 omitted. Data are for the year 1952. N = 75 organizations.

The point to note from Tables 1 and 2 is that there is a set of factors that satisfy ordinary hopes and requirements with respect to (1) having identifiable factors that plausibly can be described in ordinary business language, (2) having for each factor one or more variables that have highly discriminating factor loadings and which thus can be used as indicator variables, (3) having a set of factors comprehensive enough to leave a relatively small residual variance.

TABLE 3. Factor Loadings for Indicator Variables in 1952, 1957 and 1961*

Variable Numbers	I '52	I '57	I '61	II '52	II '57	II '61	III '52	III '57	III '61	IV '52	IV '57	IV '61	V '52	V '57	V '61	VI '52	VI '57	VI '61	VII '52	VII '57	VII '61	VIII '52	VIII '57	VIII '61	IX '52	IX '57	IX '61	X '52	X '57	X '61
4	86	86	86	—	—	—	—	—	—	—	—	—	—	—	—	—	—	—	—	—	—	—	—	—	—	—	—	—	—	—
5	88	91	86	—	—	—	—	—	—	—	—	—	—	—	—	—	—	—	—	—	—	—	—	—	—	—	—	—	—	—
10	92	95	94	—	—	—	—	—	—	—	—	—	—	—	—	—	—	—	—	—	—	—	—	—	—	—	—	—	—	—
17	83	89	82	—	—	—	—	—	—	—	—	—	—	—	—	—	—	—	—	—	—	—	—	—	—	—	—	—	—	—
26	87	85	80	—	—	—	—	—	—	—	—	—	—	—	—	—	—	—	—	—	—	—	—	—	—	—	—	—	—	—
61	—	—	—	72	82	82	—	—	—	—	—	—	—	—	—	—	—	—	—	—	—	—	—	—	—	—	—	—	—	—
62	—	—	—	91	94	90	—	—	—	—	—	—	—	—	—	—	—	—	—	—	—	—	—	—	—	—	—	—	—	—
63	—	—	—	82	90	89	—	—	—	—	—	—	—	—	—	—	—	—	—	—	—	—	—	—	—	—	—	—	—	—
35	—	—	—	—	—	—	73	79	74	—	—	—	—	—	—	—	—	—	—	—	—	—	—	—	—	—	—	—	—	—
36	—	—	—	—	—	—	89	94	88	—	—	—	—	—	—	—	—	—	—	—	—	—	—	—	—	—	—	—	—	—
45	—	—	—	—	—	—	—	—	—	86	91	78	—	—	—	—	—	—	—	—	—	—	—	—	—	—	—	—	—	—
46	—	—	—	—	—	—	—	—	—	89	92	89	—	—	—	—	—	—	—	—	—	—	—	—	—	—	—	—	—	—
13	41	42	42	—	—	—	—	—	—	—	—	—	79	76	70	—	—	—	—	—	—	—	—	—	—	—	—	—	—	—
14	—	56	42	—	—	—	—	—	—	—	—	—	69	42	69	—	—	—	—	—	—	—	—	—	—	—	—	—	—	—
76	47	50	43	—	—	—	—	—	—	—	—	—	80	52	73	—	—	—	—	—	—	—	—	—	—	—	—	—	—	—
27	—	—	—	—	—	—	—	—	—	—	—	—	—	—	—	84	92	91	—	—	—	—	—	—	—	—	—	—	—	—
28	—	—	—	—	—	—	—	—	—	—	—	—	—	—	—	82	90	89	—	—	—	—	—	—	—	—	—	—	—	—
52	—	—	—	—	—	—	—	—	—	—	—	—	—	—	—	—	—	—	89	88	87	—	—	—	—	—	—	—	—	—
64	—	—	—	—	—	—	—	—	—	—	—	—	—	—	—	—	—	—	—	—	—	86	81	74	—	—	—	—	—	—
65	52	55	—	—	—	—	—	—	—	—	—	—	—	—	—	—	—	—	—	—	—	74	68	86	—	—	—	—	—	—
47	—	—	—	—	—	—	—	—	—	—	—	—	—	—	—	—	—	—	—	—	—	—	—	—	93	86	81	—	—	—
16	40	—	—	—	—	—	—	—	—	—	—	—	—	—	—	—	—	—	—	—	—	—	—	—	—	—	—	83	86	82
19	—	—	—	—	—	—	—	—	—	—	—	—	—	—	—	—	—	—	—	—	—	—	—	—	—	—	—	82	85	83

* Decimals omitted; loadings under .40 omitted. N = 75 organizations.

Stability of Factor Structure

Factor analytic studies frequently have been attacked on different grounds. Some of the criticisms have to do with the fact that most of these studies are based on data collected from some population at one point in time. This raises the problem of the stability of the factor structure over time. It makes, obviously, little sense to work with factors, even as merely statistical artifacts, if they fail to reappear upon successive analyses of the same kind of data over the same population. A successful replication of a given factor structure, however, tells us at least that regardless of some possible changes in the specific relationships within the pattern of the correlation matrix, the major dimensions underlying that pattern remain, more or less, the same. This should give more confidence in working with such factors similar to that of personality theorists working with individual traits.

The data available in the present study made it possible to perform factor-analyses for three different points of time: 1952, 1957, and 1961. The high degree of similarity among the three factor structures over the ten-year period is suggested by Table 3. This table shows the factor loadings for the indicator variables for each of the three different years. It will be noted that the results are so similar that figures for any one year may be substituted for any other year. This re-emergence of the factor structure is taken by us to support the fruitfulness of working with these factors as hypothetical constructs.[3]

Stability of Organization Performance

The stability of the factor structure over a span of ten years does not arise from stable performances on the part of the individual agencies. Table 4 represents this conclusion in the form of correlations between each factor score and itself for each of three time periods, 1952–1957, 1957–1961, and the ten-year interval, 1952–1961. These correlations, when considered as reflecting the reliability of relative performance among these organization, are not uniform in magnitude.

Factor I (volume) represents an aspect of organizational performance that is highly stable over time. Over a period of ten years during

---

[3] It seems worthwhile to note that our data were also subjected to a different multivariate method of analysis that has been developed by Guttman and his associates in Israel and Ann Arbor. (L. Guttman, in press, 1967.) This nonmetric method is known as "the smallest space analysis." The application of this technique to our data produced a striking confirmation of our factor structure. Each of the relatively distinct clusters of points comprising the Euclidean space is readily identifiable as one of our factors. This adds assurance that our factors are not wholly artifacts of some specific analytic technique.

TABLE 4. Stability of Agency Factor Scores over a Ten-Year Period*

Period	I	II	III	IV	V	VI	VII	VIII	IX	X
Five years, 1952–1957	96	41	−13	21	67	15	36	60	71	91
Five years, 1957–1961	95	67	15	30	82	22	67	33	71	89
Ten years, 1952–1961	91	33	02	16	63	05	28	24	53	82

* Factor scores for each organization were computed using the indicator variables shown in Table 2 with equal weights. Figures above are similar to "retest reliability" coefficients. Decimals omitted. N = 75 organizations.

which the average volume of business rose very substantially (more than two standard deviation units from the starting distribution in 1952) the several organizations maintained virtually the same relative positions. Factor X (market penetration) is another factor of performance displaying high inter-organizational stability over a time of great change in absolute level of market penetration. Factor V (business mix) can also be regarded as a relatively stable aspect of organizational performance. These three factors are stable in part because they are accumulative performances. Volume, for example, begets further volume for the reason that a life policy once sold continues to produce income for some years, and for the reason that new customers once sold tend to buy more insurance themselves and to recruit friends as new customers; market extension begets further market extension for the same reasons; a choice of market strategy tends to perpetuate itself as continuation and new business is generated by the old in like kind. In short, these are in part *self-caused* performances and therefore perpetuate themselves, with the result that major changes in relative performance among the organizations come about only over some rather long time period. The stability of these factors no doubt arises as well from the persistence of those subsidiary (causal?) performances which originally gave rise to relatively high-volume or low-volume increment rates.

Factor III (productivity of new members) is a rather different class of organizational performance with respect to stability over time. The "reliability" of this performance over a five- or ten-year period is virtually zero. The negative correlation for one five-year time interval is nonsignificant in this instance, but represents a possible cyclic or phasic phenomenon: organizations that take on and train many new members in one time period may take on few in the succeeding period. If all these organizations have the same periodicity (a fact not yet determined) and if they are randomly phased, then we may expect very large negative factor score correlations for time intervals matched to the periodicity. If substantiated this would again be an instance of an organizational performance "causing" itself, but in a negative manner.

Factor IV (youthfulness) may similarly be a phasic or else cyclic organizational performance, as is Factor VI (rate of manpower growth). These two factors share with Factor III a reference to membership maintenance, development, and growth. The instability shown for five-year intervals is probably phasic, and may have a periodicity that is not uniform for all organizations nor for all three factors of performance or all initial sizes of organizations.

The remaining factors, II (production costs), VII management emphasis) and VIII (maintenance costs) are intermediate in their stability over time. It may be that these aspects of performance, along with the performances presumed to be phasic or cyclic, have the burden of adaptation in organizational life — that is, to sustain growth in volume and in market penetration, or to modify the character of the organization's business strategy, in response to environmental demands and opportunities. One may propose that these internal performances in the case of selling organizations become modified over short-time intervals in service of the longer-term improvement of the market position.

It should be noted that Factor VII (management emphasis) is, first, a dubious factor, being defined by a single variable and, second, it may be a factor that is unique to owner-managed small sales organizations.

"Predictability" of the Factor Scores

Before relating the meanings of these factors to our conceptual scheme, we now turn to a supplementary set of data: in 1961 a questionnaire survey of all members of 33 of these organizations provided a number of indexes representing various internal states and processes of their organizational lives. These permit us to explore the predictability of our several factors of performance from variables of kinds not ordinarily treated themselves as performance variables. Table 5 represents a selected few of these variables and their correlations with the ten performance factors for the year 1961 (the year of the questionnaire survey) and for the subsequent year, 1962. We shall remark upon only a few of the features of this material.

One point to note is not very evident to the eye, but is statistically verified: the survey data correlate more strongly with performances in the following year than they do with performance concurrently with the survey. Out of 14 pairs of correlations in this table, of which at least one of the pair is statistically significant (a correlation of .32 is significant at the .05 level), there are 10 where the correlation for 1962 is higher than the correlation for 1961, 3 are the same, and 1 is lower. While most of the differences within the pairs are statistically non-

TABLE 5. Correlations between Representative Structure/Process Variables and Factor Scores in 1961 and 1962

| Factors | Manager's Supportiveness | | Upward Communication | | Manager's Power | | | | Total Control | |
| | | | | | Expert | | Reward | | | |
	1961	1962	1961	1962	1961	1962	1961	1962	1961	1962
I Volume	35	37	20	25	34	41	25	31	27	31
II Production cost	—	—	—	—21	—	—	—41	—49	—	—30
III New manpower productivity	27	20	30	56	—	—	—	20	—	30
IV Youthfulness	34	50	—	—	36	36	—	25	26	33
V Business mix	—	—	—	—	—	—	—30	—	—28	—22
VI Manpower growth	—	45	—	—	30	25	—	22	—	30
VII Management emphasis	—	—	—	22	23	24	—	—	—	—
VIII Maintenance Costs	—	23	—	—	—	—	—46	—31	—	—
IX Average production	—	—49	—	—	—	—	—	—	—	—
X Market penetration	33	33	32	32	—	—	44	48	58	61

Correlations less than r = .20 omitted; decimals omitted. Data are for 33 insurance sales agencies. Factor scores are computed from indicator variables shown in Table 2, with equal weights. Organizational structural/process variables are based on member questionnaire responses obtained in 1961. Correlations of .32 are significant at the p = .05 level.

significant, the between-year difference for the total set is highly significant. Such a trend suggests the presence of a causal rather than merely a covariant relationship between the "predictions" and the criteria. With time-series performance data, we can determine some of the features of managerial and member behavior that plausibly can be said to be causal in relationship to organizational performances. This trend highlights, in addition, the limitations inherent in data collected at one point of time, on which many studies are based. If we had at our disposal the correlation matrix for 1961 only, we would have to conclude that most of the social-psychological variables treated here have very little to do with dimensions of organizational peformance. The results obtained for 1962, however, indicate that a significant portion of the variance in performance is accounted for by such social-psychological variables. One may ask if the relationships are still more strong by the third year, or if each predictor has its own characteristic period of effect.

Second, it may be noted that each of the ten performance factors is significantly related to some of our selected predictors, not significantly related to others. This selectivity in correlation suggests that our hypothesized network of lower-order performance variables (examples here treated as predictors) may in fact assort itself into subsets, each subset having potentially a causal relationship to one of the higher-order performances. For example, "supportiveness" (on the part of the owner-manager as seen by the members) is significantly related to business volume, productivity of youthful agents, manpower growth, and market penetration, but is *not* related to production cost performance, business mix, or owners' devotion to management.

Third, we note that some organizational processes and states have strongly favorable relationships (presumed to be causal) with certain of the performance factors and strongly unfavorable relationships with others. One example again is "supportiveness" on the part of the owner-manager: high support appears to be associated in the succeeding year with such desirable outcomes as high business volume, high acquisition and retention of manpower, high market penetration, having a relatively youthful force; at the same time supportiveness by the manager is associated strongly with low average productivity per agent. The covariance among these factorially independent variables is evident. A managerial practice (supportiveness) may affect some aspects of organizational performance favorably, others unfavorably. The set of performance factors therefore *must* be treated as an intact set if one is to make reasonable interpretations. Had we been adhering to the usual past practice of examining single pairs of predictors and performance criteria — for example, support and average agent productivity — for a single time we would have come to the false conclusion that managerial support strongly diminishes individual agent peformance. With data for even two years, we are enabled to see better the trade-off relationships among the ten factors of performance.

We suggest that much of the confusion and contradiction in past studies of managerial and organizational practices associated with performance arises from reliance upon single indicators of performance rather than upon a coherent and comprehensive set of criterion variables. There is no future for us in pursuing odd pairs of variables; we must treat comprehensive sets and networks of variables in order to understand these events, for they comprise an intact system of variables.

The Conceptual Framework Reconsidered

The foregoing fragmentary and perhaps tedious exploration of empirical results has now been carried far enough for our purpose. We have indicated several points of strong support for a conceptual framework of the kind initially outlined, and have pointed to compelling kinds of evidence that forbids further work with conceptions of lesser scope. On one vital point, however, our empirical results flatly contradict our opening propositions and force us to a reconsideration of them.

The moment of insight occurred while we were considering whether our ten performance factors could plausibly be described within the specifications of our conceptual framework. One of these specifications — a crucial one, we thought — was that the penultimate performances would have the character of autonomous *goals*, things sought for their own value, things valued in themselves, goals of kinds that allow one to say that their achievement justifies the creation, existence, and continuation of the organization.

Some of the resulting performance factors do indeed seem to have this character. High volume of business, low production costs, high market penetration, and some others can readily be accepted as expressing the central values and purposes of the key people in a sales organization. Others of our factors, however, cannot be so interpreted. Is it a *goal* of a sales organization to have a relatively large part of its productivity coming from youthful members? Is it a *goal* of these organizations to have a relatively high proportion of new members? Even more oddly, how can we say that some choice as to preferred type of business is a goal of these organizations, when the people themselves do not agree on whether one end of the scale is "better" or "worse" than the other?[4]

---

[4] The business mix factor refers, roughly, to the choice of emphasis upon selling many

Even the dimensions that can plausibly be described as "goals" present a problem in theory, for we have difficulty showing that they are in fact goals of the organizations. Neither we nor others concerned with similar problems have provided a sound rationale for demonstrating that such goals are in fact properties of the organization. If the proposed goals do not, in some sense, belong to the organizations, then it is rather arbitrary to assess organizational effectiveness in reference to such goals. We must show that such goals belong to the organizations and that they are not merely transient goals adopted by various interested persons or groups, or by the investigators themselves. Parsons (1956), for example, attempted to escape from this problem by proposing a functional analysis that also fails to adhere to the organizational frame of reference; for Parsons, organizational effectiveness in the final analysis lies in the functional contribution of the organization to meeting the needs of the larger society. This solution is not tenable, for it merely shifts the same problem to a higher level of social organization. Others, Etzioni (1960), for example, have tried to retain the effectiveness concept while remaining within the organizational frame of reference, but have then found it impossible to provide an operational means for identifying criteria that correspond to their theoretical definitions of effectiveness.

The solution we offer to this problem is advanced with some trepidation, for if our reasoning is correct, then we shall disturb the thinking and language habits of many people in all kinds of organizations. The solution arose from the task of discovering what it is, if anything, that our ten factorial dimensions have in common. What they have in common is that, without exception, they represent the getting of resources for organizational functioning from the organizations' environments.[5]

---

policies of relatively low unit value as against selling fewer policies of high unit value. While a high-value unit of sale is obviously advantageous in itself, the net goodness of one emphasis or the other, or some intermediate balance, depends upon which strategy best utilizes the existing staff and accessible market toward the end of optimal resource-getting.

[5] "Environments" is in the plural form to indicate that the proposed conception of organizational effectiveness will require the differentiation of environment into types or classes with respect to the nature of resources involved and the means for organizations to realize these resources. An example is the case of members of an organization whom we view as an integral part of the organization with respect to their role defining and role carrying activities, but as part of the organization's environment with respect to abilities, motives, other memberships, and other characteristics that are potentially useful but are not utilized by the organization in role performance. An effective organization will incorporate more of the individual member's personality into the organizational system, thus acquiring additional resources from this part of its environment.

The volume factor, for example, indicates the extent to which the agencies have acquired money, clients, and manpower, all of which are scarce and valued resources needed by the organization. The cost factors reflect the efficiency of the agencies in conservation of available resources, that is, prevention of unnecessary waste. Average member productivity can be viewed as a measure of the agencies' success in extracting resources (selling effort, selling ability) from the members.

This perspective on organizational performance is consistent with the system concept of organizations. According to that concept, organizations as systems are continuously engaged in processes of exchange with their environments. Much of the stuff that is exchanged in these transactions falls into the category of scarce and valued resources of kinds potentially useful to other social systems as well. There is thus competition for these resources, and under competitive conditions the ability to secure and use resources reflects the relative effectiveness of the organization *vis-à-vis* other social structures. The significant outcomes of organizational behavior, whether anticipated or not, whether voluntary or constrained, are always influenced by and lead to changes in the ability of the organization to mobilize resources from the environments. Effectiveness in organizations can thus be viewed as the relative bargaining position of organizations in relation to resources over which there is competition. We define the effectiveness of an organization as its *ability to exploit its environments in the acquisition of scarce and valued resources to sustain its own functioning.*

This general definition must be qualified in two ways. Some organizations exist in relatively rich environments, others in poor environments; we must therefore assess effectiveness in relation to environmental potential. The second qualification is that the *ability* to exploit the organization's environment cannot be equated with *maximum use* of this ability in the short run, for an organization might then destroy its environment and reduce its longer-run potential for favorable transactions. We must invoke an *optimization* concept.

An interpretation of our ten performance factors for sales organizations can illustrate these ideas: these sales organizations are maximizing their ability to get resources when they optimize, as an interdependent set, the ten performance factors we have isolated. This optimizing process involves balancing off some exploitative strategies against others, for example, increased market penetration against temporarily higher production costs, short-run gains against deferred gains, exploiting the manager for current sales as against exploiting him for staff growth and development. The optimum pattern of performance for each of the organizations may be unique to the extent that their histories and environments differ, and they may fall into a limited number of types of alternative general strategies that are equally effective so long as each type maintains its own internal balancing principle. Nonoptimization of performance would occur to the extent that some performance factors were under- or over-realized in relation to the others. A gross imbalance could result in the extinction of the organization, that is, total loss of its ability to derive resources from its environment.[6]

This conception of organizational effectiveness has escaped attention because of our traditional preoccupation with the concept of "goal." We have thought too simplistically that organizations have goals that can be identified and that become the yardstick for assessing organizational effectiveness. This imputation of purposiveness to organizations has misled us. While profitability, for example, or growth, or productivity, seem attractive and superficially plausible as goals of an organization, it is apparent from empirical studies, our own included, that in persisting organizations profit is never safely maximized, growth is never safely maximized, and productivity is never safely maximized; as "goals" they become destructive when approached, and they therefore are goals only (a) with reference to certain classes of interested persons (owners, customers, employees, and so forth) or (b) with reference to society at large (which must exploit the organization as best it can if it needs the output without destroying the organization), or (c) with reference to some particular limited time span or phase of the organization's life (that is, a temporary concentration of effort toward restoring balance among the total roster of necessary performances — a transient goal to be moved toward, but not actually reached).

Returning now to the main theme of this conference — that of exploring the possibilities of developing a meaningful and useful system of concepts for describing and comparing organizations — we can conclude by saying that in describing organizational performance or effectiveness, we must first of all reject conceptual schemes that link organizational effectiveness solely to the values of some one or another element in the environment of organizations; instead the standards of effectiveness are to be sought with reference to the organization itself. Second, we require that our ultimate conceptual scheme avoid the trap of imputing goals, or other expressions of the teleological principle, to organizations, for they are not "trying" to do anything — they merely exist and function.

We note that botanists can classify and describe flowers very well in terms of accommodations to environmental resources and internal

---

[6] We are aware that this is a very sketchy outline of the conceptual position we are advancing. A more detailed and better documented statement is in preparation.

processes, without imputing goals to flowers. Zoologists can deal taxo-nomically with living systems within their domain. Similarly, psy-chologists are coming to conceive of human effectiveness in terms of "adjustment" and "self-realization," not goal attainment. The sugges-tions we have offered here appear to follow a well-trodden path laid out by the more advanced disciplines relating to the behavior of open systems.

We do not propose that our ten factorial dimensions for these sales organizations constitute a universal roster of such dimensions applicable to all kinds of organizations. It does seem possible, however, that several of them have this universal meaning while others may be unique to these and similar organizations. It is the next task to apply similar procedures to other populations of organizations in an effort to find those dimensions that may confidently be used to compare organizations.

Bibliography

Etzioni, A.   Two approaches to organizational analysis: A critique and a suggestion. *Administrative Science Quarterly*, 1960, 5 (2), 257–278.

Guttman, L.   A general nonmetric technique for finding the smallest Euclid-ean space for a configuration of points. *Psychometrika*, in press, 1967.

Parsons, T.   Suggestions for a sociological approach to a theory of organiza-tions — I. *Administrative Science Quarterly*, 1956, 1 (1), 63–85.

Seashore, S. E.   Criteria of organizational effectiveness. *Michigan Business Review*, 1965, 17 (4), 26–30.

———— & Yuchtman, E.   Factorial analysis of organizational performance. *Administrative Science Quarterly*, 1967, 12 (3), 377–395.

PEOPLE, } GROUPS, AND } ORGANIZATIONS { **III**

METHODOLOGICAL SUGGESTIONS AND
THEORETICAL ALTERNATIVES

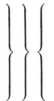

A Multifacet Approach to Classification of Individual, Group, and Organization Concepts

JOSEPH E. McGRATH

Psychology Department
University of Illinois

Molière once said: "For more than forty years I have been speaking prose without knowing it." It is much the same with facet analysis. For a long time, many of us have been using the logic of facet analysis, more or less systematically, without knowing it, until Guttman (1957) gave it a name and a formal theoretical base, and he and his associates (see Foa, 1961) showed its wide applicability. This paper is a plea for even wider application of facet analysis — or rather, of portions of it and their extensions — as a broadly useful tool for classification of social psychological concepts.

Toward this aim, the paper is organized into three sections. The first section sketches the key features of an approach to classification which will be termed "multifacet classification." This approach builds on, and extends, certain features of the *input logic* of formal facet analysis (facet design), although it does not necessarily require the data analysis logic of the facet approach.

The second section elaborates by illustration. It outlines a series of "case studies" in which the multifacet classification approach has been applied. The content of these applications include: a method for integration of research information in the small group field (McGrath & Altman, 1966); a system for interaction process analysis; a framework for a criterion system for investigation of mental hospital patient recovery; and a technique for analysis of role relationships in groups and organizations.

The third and final section tries to draw out some implications of the proposed approach, and to point out its weaknesses as well.

The reader should be aware that this is unquestionably a "working paper." All but one of the applications treated in the case studies are incomplete. All failed in some respects, though succeeding in others. What is crucial here is not these specific applications, nor the facets and categories used in them, but an underlying theme: social psychologists should use their *a priori* concepts more often — and more systematically — as the basis for organizing their material.

Some Principles for Multifacet Classification

No general treatment of the logic of classification is presented here. Other papers in this volume (such as Altman's) treat the broad methodological problem "How classify?" far more extensively and elegantly than we can. Instead, our concern will center on certain assumptions about what makes classification systems useful and generalizeable, and show how these "classification principles" are met by the multifacet approach.

1. *Objects should be classified in terms of all relevant properties or facets.*

Our first premise about classification is that most aggregates of objects — be they concepts, events, or pieces of data — have more than one property upon which they can fruitfully be classified. Furthermore, those relevant properties are seldom highly, much less perfectly, correlated with one another. Thus, there is a need for classification in terms of multiple properties.

In the ideal case, where all relevant properties are quantifiable in terms of ratio or interval scales, this notion leads us to the search for the clusters of properties which "go together" and which denote the main factors, axes, or dimensions of a multidimensional space. This kind of reasoning underlies traditional factor analysis methodology, and that approach has had extensive use, and some success, as an *a posteriori* classification device, although its value as a tool for identifying the underlying (genotypical) structure of a space remains much in dispute.

Note that factor analysis requires "strong" measurement of all properties on ratio or interval scales (and incidentally applies a "strong" model for combination which considers only linear covariation). However, many of the variables we wish to deal with in social psychological research are analyzable (at least as yet) only in terms of nominal or ordinal categories. More importantly, the *most* factor analysis can tell us is about the pattern in which the things we "put in" go together. It is mute about the more critical question for classification, namely: what things should be "put in" in the first place. For classification, we need a multiproperty input logic as well as a systematic procedure for assessing results.

2. *Each property or facet should be analyzed into a set of collectively exhaustive categories or values.*

Our second premise about classification is that *every relevant property* or dimension or facet of the aggregate to be classified should be applied to *every object in the set;* furthermore, that each object in the set should be characterized in terms of some one value or category on each property or dimension. This premise is fundamental to the business of classification and runs counter to the logic of much classification in the social sciences, especially those classification efforts which yield typologies.

This premise means, for example, that if we have a set of objects to be classified and a set of classification properties or facets, we may *not* proceed to denote one subset of the objects as "having Property A" and another subset as "having Property B." Rather, we must categorize the entire set with respect to Property A: for a certain subset it is "present," or present at a given level of magnitude; and for the remaining subset it is "absent," or present at less than a certain level of magnitude. Similarly, we must classify *all* objects in the set with respect to Property B.

This may have implications for both the names and meanings we assign to our concepts. For example, if our objects are divided into "children" and "adults" we do not have two properties (that is, "childrenness" and "adultness"), but rather two values (that is, "high" and "low") of one property ("age"). A less obvious and trivial example might be drawn from the area of interaction process analysis (which is the subject of one of the case studies in the next section). The most general and popular existing system for interaction process analysis, the Bales (1950) system, may violate the classification premise we are here discussing in at least one respect. Bales's system classifies (each of a set of) acts as having *either task or socioemotional* consequences for the group. The premise here expounded would maintain that every act be classified with respect to its task function *and* with respect to its socioemotional function. This, of course, may require the addition of a "zero" value as a category for some properties. For example, we might categorize each act as socioemotionally positive, or negative, or "affect neutral." It may be that most acts which have task-relevant content do fall into the socioemotional "neutral" category. But this in an *empirical* question, which need not be predetermined by using a classification system which precludes the "occurrence" of an act which serves both task and positive or negative socioemotional functions.

Application of the principle would have saved a lot of anguish in our discipline's past history. Many theoretical efforts based on "Type A" *vs.* "Type B" typologies have failed to gain general usefulness because cases with the attributes of *neither* A nor B *or* of *both* A and B readily arise. They might have fared better if the presumably bipolar types had instead been conceptualized as a two-facet space — high A *versus* low A on the one hand, and high B *versus* low B on the other. The classification could still have been used for the original purpose of comparing "pure" or "opposed" types (now, the diagonals of the 2 x 2 space). At the same time, the theorists would have been able to account, readily, for the cases which did not fit the bipolar types, and they would have been forced to specify the defining properties of their types more analytically.

Examples of cases of this problem might include such well-known types as rural *versus* urban settings, *gemeinshaft versus gesellshaft* conditions, formal *versus* informal groups, competition *versus* cooperation conditions, coacting *versus* interacting groups, task-oriented *versus* interpersonal-oriented leadership, democratic *versus* authoritarian leadership, affiliation *versus* achievement motivation. In each of these cases, it would seem, the presence of the conditions defining *one* of the types *does not logically preclude* the presence of some or all of the conditions defining the "opposite" type; nor does absence of the conditions for one type guarantee presence of the conditions for the other. Hence, the *logic* of our classification system should *permit* the occurrence of either, neither, or both of the "opposed" types, whatever the empirical frequency of the "neither" and "both" conditions may turn out to be.

3. *Each property or facet should have a mutually exclusive set of values or categories.*

Our third premise is that each object should be characterized in terms of *one and only one* value or category of each property or facet. Most classificatory efforts in social psychology have adhered staunchly to this principle, perhaps because multiple coding (in the sense of multiple classification of a single object into two or more categories of a given facet) leads to numerous problems in analysis due to the non-independence of cases which it involves. Besides the methodological "bite" that comes from violating this principle, attention to it can also be useful in helping to elaborate a classification system. If a given object seems to belong in both the high and the low categories on a given property, for example, it is clear that *more than one* underlying element is involved, and specification of those underlying elements as separate properties or facets for classification can improve the system.

4. The logical relationship among categories of a facet should be specified.

For continuous variables measured with ratio or interval scales, this principle is automatically fulfilled. The categories of many social psychological properties, though, represent ordered sets or even nominal categories with no apparent unidimensional relationship. At a given point in development of a problem area it may not be possible to adhere to this principle for the categories of all useful properties, but, as in the case for the preceeding principle, serious attention to discerning the interrelations among categories of a facet can lead the investigator to a fuller understanding and elaboration of the logic of his classification system.

There are many forms of logical relations among categories besides the traditional one of "greater" (quantity or magnitude) usually reflected in scaling concepts. For example, we may define an ordered set of categories of a facet where the ordering principle is successive inclusion: A includes B, B includes C, C includes D, and so forth. Use of the categories *individual, group, organization, society* for a "level of reference" facet (McGrath and Altman, 1966) is a case in point. This arrangement is sometimes called a "nested facet." Such an order relation implies transitivity: A includes B, B includes C, therefore A includes C.

Sometimes, too, nominal categories with no apparent order relation among them are ordered on an underlying continuum which has not yet been discovered. An example would be the ordering of the primary colors *prior to* light wave theories. Concern for the order relation among categories may lead to the discernment of such an underlying continuum, which in turn leads to improvement and even "extension" (through the ultraviolet, and infra-red) of the system. Examples of this kind of success in finding the underlying continuum on which nominal categories are related, however, do not abound in the social sciences. Perhaps this is because of our willingness to accept unrelated nominal categories as "sufficient" tools for our relatively crude analyses.

5. The logical relations among the multiple facets should be specified.

Ideally, the facets should be logically independent or orthogonal (although, of course, it is often the case that the investigator is predicting empirical dependencies between facets). Facet analysis, in fact, is defined in terms of a series of logically independent facets which are the axes of a Cartesian space.

Being "independent" means that categorization in terms of any one facet does not constrain categorization on any other facet — that is, every possible combination of facet values taking one value from each facet, can occur. It is often the case, however, that certain logical contingencies do exist between categories of one facet and those of another. It may be that being in Category 1 of Facet A implies being in Category 3 of Facet B, or precludes being in Category 4 of Facet C. If there is total contingency between the entire set of categories of one facet and those of another — that is, if being in Category 1 of Facet A implies being in Category 1 of Facet B, A2 implies B2, A3 implies B3, and so forth — then Facets A and B are logically equivalent and should be combined.

Short of total equivalence, though, it is often useful to have logically separate facets with partial contingency between categories. This reduces the elegance of the system and generates some null cells in the Cartesian space, but it may not have substantial consequences for the usefulness of the classification system. Indeed, the attention given to the logical relations between categories across facets probably adds to the "goodness" of the system even if it leads to specification of some contingencies and null cells.

6. The facets, collectively, should be logically exhaustive of the domain of interest.

This principle, of course, is never to be fully realized in an empirical science with fallible measurement. It amounts to demanding that the set of facets, collectively, accounts for 100 per cent of the variance in the phenomena to be classified. While unattainable, it is a valuable *aim* to guide the development of any classification system.

This principle of classification points up what is perhaps one of the main advantages of a multifacet approach. If the facets are orthogonal, and the categories of each facet are mutually exclusive and collectively exhaustive, then the system is (for the time being) logically closed; while at the same time it can readily be expanded, by adding new facets, without substantially upsetting the prior system. Moreover, if certain facets turn out to be relatively useless, the system can be reduced by eliminating the classification on that facet, leaving the basic system undisturbed. The same is true of adding, eliminating, or combining categories within a facet.

All of this implies, of course, that there is some criterion by means of which we can assess the "usefulness" of categories, sets of categories, facets, and sets of facets. This most crucial problem, "validation" of the classification system, is discussed next.

7. *The principle of concordance or contiguity.*

One crucial determinant of the value of any *a priori* classification system is the extent to which its user can assess its "usefulness." We here presume that the value of a classification system is directly proportional to its efficiency in systematically ordering the set of objects to which it is to be applied. Just what "systematic ordering" will imply depends, in part, on the nature of the set of objects being classified, and the purpose of the classification system. In one of the illustrations to be presented, for example, we were attempting to classify tests of research relationships in order to systematically order the existing knowledge in the small-group field. In another of the illustrative case studies, we were attempting to classify communicative acts in a group interaction context in order to describe the interaction process. In the first case, systematic ordering meant accounting for variation in outcomes of empirical tests of relationships between variables studied in the small-group field. In the latter case, systematic ordering meant accounting for variance in interaction patterns (between groups, among group members, and among group-task conditions), which might be predictive of group effectiveness and member adjustment.

Regardless of the purpose of the system or the nature of the objects to be classified, though, it seems clear that the major aim of any *a priori* classification ought to be to order the objects in terms of their logical properties in such a way as to be predictive of their ordering on (meaningful) empirical properties. In essence, the classification system should put together things which are alike, both in the *a priori* properties of the classification system and in meaningful empirical properties which are measured independently of the classification procedures.

One basic principle for assessing the usefulness of the facet approach has been termed "the contiguity principle" by Foa (1958) and "the principle of concordance" by McGrath and Altman (1966).[1] In essence, it asserts that things classified as alike are alike (from the point of view of the classification system), that the degree of classification similarity for any two objects is an index of the degree of their similarity, and that the degree of similarity of any two objects is predictive of the degree to which they will exhibit common empirical properties (for example, relate to the same things, be affected by the same things, and so forth).

The concordance principle is both an assumption useful in developing a classification system and an hypothesis for testing the efficacy

[1] The contiguity or concordance principle is only one of a set of potential principles for assessing the usefulness of a facet classification. For one example of an alternative principle, see Foa (1966), and Foa, Triandis, and Katz (1966).

of the system. In the latter capacity, the concordance hypothesis predicts that the *a priori* ordering of phenomena in terms of the properties of the classification system will show high concomitance with empirical orderings of these same phenomena on properties not included in the system. It takes the degree of such concomitance as indicative of the degree of validity of the system. If the concomitance is high, then the classification system contains facets and categories which are meaningful distinctions relevant to empirical properties of the objects being classified. In other words, the system has classified as (logically) alike things which are (empirically) alike, and has classified as different things which are (empirically) different. If such concomitance does not occur, then the classification system fails in its major purpose of systematic ordering (although it still may be useful for purely descriptive purposes).

By extending this notion of concordance, it is possible to evaluate the usefulness of any given facet by assessing how much it contributes to the systematic ordering of the objects on the empirical properties of concern. Likewise, it is possible to assess the additional (empirical) "discriminability" obtained from any given subset of categories of a facet. These kinds of assessments can best be explained by examples, as provided in the next section, especially in the case study of integration of small group research literature.

Case Studies of Multifacet Classification

This section describes four applications of the multifacet approach to classification. They deal with a range of types of social psychological phenomena and represent a variety of classification purposes. They also exhibit different degrees of completion, from the (completed) application to integration of small-group research information (Case Study No. 1) to the role-system application (Case Study No. 4) now only in its early pilot stages.

We are not particularly "selling" these specific classification systems, nor the facets and categories which they utilize. Our interest here is in illustrating the principles discussed above and in indicating the wide applicability of this general approach. Also, we will use the case studies to point up certain weaknesses of the approach, and to illustrate the kinds of data analysis systems which can be coupled to the input logic of the multifacet approach.

Case Study No. 1: Integration of Small-Group Research (McGrath and Altman, 1966)

Quite a few years ago, Altman and I set out to "clean up the mess" into which the body of small-group research literature seemed to us to have fallen. At this time, we were indeed speaking the "prose" of facet analysis without knowing it. We began building a comprehensive system for classification of *research information* about small groups, based on the following rationale.

The unit of research information was taken to be the statistically tested relationship between two or more variables. For purposes of clarity, we construed one variable (the agent) as relating to the other (the resultant), without intending any necessary causal inference. We also recognized that a given variable (say, cohesiveness) might be agent variable in one relationship (for example, "cohesiveness increases morale") and resultant variable in another (for example, "competition increases cohesiveness").

Secondly, we assumed that variables differ from one another in terms of certain properties of the *operations* by which measures of those variables are obtained. The choice of operational, rather than substantive, terms for classification was the keystone of our approach. It permitted us to develop a system which, in general, fulfilled the principles discussed above. We did, however, keep record of the substantive nature of each variable, and it subsequently turned out to be highly valuable as we shall see.

We focused on six parameters, properties, or "facets" of the data collection procedures which operationally define variables. A datum was defined as a judgment by some source about some attribute of some object or set of objects. The key facets of the judgment are:

1. *Object,* or level of reference: Member, group, and surround (including individuals, groups, and inanimate objects in the environment). Note that since our focus was on groups, we dealt with one system level above and one below the group level. This would seem to be a minimum. If the focus had been on organizations, then it could have been critical to deal analytically with the "surround" of the organization, (community or society) as well as with its parts: individual and groups.
2. *Mode:* This distinction has to do with whether the datum refers to a *state* or an *action* of the reference object.
3. *Source:* This refers to whether the datum is generated by an individual who is a *member* of the subject group (distinguished as to whether it is the same member as the object, or a different member), by the *group* as an entity, or by the *investigator* (or his surrogate, or his surrogate-instrument).
4. *Viewpoint:* This refers to the frame of reference from which the source judges the attribute of the object: own (*subjective*);

other (*projective*); or *objective* (that is, from a point of view external to the subject group).

5. *Task:* This refers to the form of judgment involved in the datum: *description* (that is, how *much* of the attribute does the object have) *versus evaluation* (that is, how near the *preferred* amount of the attribute the object has).

6. *Relative — Irrelative judgment:* This refers to whether the object is being judged as a single stimulus on the attribute, or in terms of a comparison with other objects on the attribute. (This parameter was later dropped because the data showed no variability on it — hence it did not add to the discriminability of the system.)

We also defined two modes of combination by which specific data are sometimes combined into indexes of variables (we termed them "indexing operations"): *summation* (including averaging) and *comparison* (including subtraction, ratios, and so forth). These added enormously to the complexity of the system and, as it turned out empirically, they contributed relatively little discriminability to the system. Hence, we dropped them for our purposes, although they ought to be included for conceptual completeness.

We considered the relational term — that is, the statement of presence, degree, and direction of the relationship between agent and resultant variables — primarily in terms of an arbitrarily selected probability value (.05), although we also classified and retained other information about the relational term.

The six data facets, each with varying numbers of categories, generate a six-axis Cartesian space with an enormous number of "cells." A single "cell" defines a specific class of variables in terms of a specific category of each of the six facets. All variables falling in a single variable class, or cell, are assumed to be alike, regardless of their substantive heterogeneity.

There are some null cells in the Cartesian space, because of contingencies between categories of different facets. For example, only when the object was a group member was it meaningful to distinguish a member source into "self" *versus* "other." As another example, we imposed the constraint that investigator, as source, could only use an objective viewpoint. However, even with these contingencies, there are still a very large number of real cells, or potential classes of variables.

Since the unit relationship deals with an agent variable of one class in relation to a resultant variable of the same or a different class, and since variables of each class can serve as either agent or resultant, then if there are K classes of variables, there is a K by K matrix, of which each cell is a class of relationships. The diagonal of that matrix represents relationships between two variables of the same class.

From the point of view of the classification system, two variables which have the same (six-facet) classification are instances of the same class of variables. A test of a relationship between two variables of the same class is an index of reliability. Hence, we would expect relationships within a variable class (along the diagonal of the relationship matrix) to be highly related. Similarly, two variables which are classified as alike in all respects but one are *more alike* than two variables which differ on two, three, or more parameters. Hence, we would expect the former pair to be more highly related than the latter.

A generalization of this notion is the principle of concordance or contiguity, namely, that the matrix of relationships can be properly ordered in terms of the similarity of the variables being related within each relationship class, and that this ordering will be predictive of the extent of relationship between the variables of the various relationship classes.

We then applied this classification system to about 12,000 relationships from 250 studies (which had been drawn as a random sample from a bibliography of over 2300 titles of small-group studies). Having classified each variable involved in all these relationships into one of the classes defined by the six data facets (and the indexing operations), we then classified each relationship class in terms of the degree of concordance or contiguity of the variables in it. If both variables were classified differently on *all* parameters, the relationship class had zero concordance; if they were classified the same on only one parameter, then concordance was one. There was maximum concordance of a relationship class when the two variables were classified alike on all parameters. We then plotted the relationship between this index of concordance and *the proportion of times empirical tests of that relationship had been found to be significant at $p < .05$.* We termed this the "batting average" of that relationship class.

The relationship between concordance and batting average was strong. Improving the index of concordance (for instance, by taking into account indexing operations, and by weighting certain facets and the distance between categories of certain facets in various ways) failed to increase the relationship. Analysis using one facet at a time showed that the facets contributed differentially to the concordance/batting average relationship. The *object* facet was dominant, followed by *mode,* then by *source. Viewpoint* was virtually coextensive with *source.* The *task* and the *relative/irrelative* parameters failed to differentiate.

The degree of "predictability" can be represented by the following statement: Using *object, mode,* and *source* parameters only, combined in their most powerful sequence, the relationship class with maximum concordance had statistical significance ($p < .05$) 57 per cent of the time, while the relationship class with minimum concordance had significance ($p < .05$) only 26 per cent of the time, regardless of the substantive content of the variables involved in these relationships.

From certain points of view our effort was a smashing success. The system "worked," in that it provided a systematic *a priori* ordering (*concordance* in terms of our facet classification), which corresponded to a substantial degree with a systematic empirical ordering (proportion of significant relationships) of the same set of objects (that is, research relationships). Furthermore, the particular facets and categories which worked best are those of most substantive interest, and they worked in ways which can be sensibly interpreted (see McGrath, 1963; McGrath & Altman, 1966).

But lo! the system had many problems, weaknesses, and inadequacies as well. First of all, it was both over-complete (including facets which didn't matter) and incomplete. We realized afterwards that there were certain additional facets which we had not included. In particular, we failed to deal adequately with temporal factors, with varying definitions of levels of manipulated variables (for example, how "high" is "high cohesiveness," in one study as compared to another), and with certain types of complex data analysis (for example factor analysis loadings). Finally, it was far too cumbersome in form and too exotic in terminology, to be effectively communicated to our small group research colleagues. In the end, we translated our variable classes from operational terms *back into substantive terms* in order to present a summary of the field useful to others.

There are many other lessons to be learned about classification from both successful and unsuccessful aspects of our endeavors toward classifying small group research information. Some of these can be illustrated more effectively by considering several other multifacet classification efforts which raise some of the same problems and some new ones.

Case Study No. 2: A Multifacet System for Group Interaction

One of the most troublesome areas of the small-group research field is the matter of group interaction process. While to my way of thinking it is conceptually crucial (that is, it is "the black box," but we *can* look into it directly), at the same time, it is a relatively untended area of study and one very difficult to research.

There are numerous systems for interaction analysis, many of them special purpose systems. By far the best general system, as well as the most widely used one, is Bales's interaction process analysis — even though that system is now approaching 20 years of age. It is in part so successful, I feel, because it is the kind of system that might well have been guided by facet thinking. (Perhaps Bales, too, "spoke facet analysis" without knowing it!) Its main flaw seems to be that it is single facet, defining *one set* of mutually exclusive, collectively exhaustive categories into which all communicative acts are to be classified. Not only are there other potentially relevant attributes of interaction "external" to Bales's IPA, but more important, it seems to me that his twelve categories represent several distinct facets, folded into one. Bales himself treats them as six pairs, two sets of six, and four sets of three categories, from various points of view, which suggests that the twelve categories are indeed several facets folded together.

We have attempted to develop a multifacet system for interaction analysis. Its rational is as follows: There are three main interpersonal processes that take place in group interaction: Communication (that is, transmission of information), influence, and affect(that is, the "flow" of positive or negative feeling). There is a fourth, intra-individual process, for which we shall use Bales's term "tension management."

Every act that occurs in an interpersonal situation has some bearing on each of these processes, rather than on one and only one of them as the Bales system (and most others) maintains. Note that all these processes are represented in the Bales system, though with varying emphasis. The central point here, however, is that Bales treats them as alternative processes, while we are treating them as simultaneous processes.

Each of these processes may have multiple aspects. For example, influence may be reflected in terms of interruption (floor control), in terms of statements which structure subsequent process or content, and so forth.

The early and crude version of this system was developed for special case use in the study of negotiation groups (Julian & McGrath, 1963; McGrath & Julian, 1963), and emphasized influence and affect. Its partial success led us to develop the approach more fully, leading to an interaction analysis system with thirteen facets (which can be grouped into six sets).

A. *Personnel Facets*
  1. *Actor.* Categories are each group participant.
  2. *Target.* Categories are each group participant, plus group as a whole.

B. *Temporal Facets*
  3. *Serial position.* Categories are the serial number of each act in a session.

4. *Duration.* Categories are units of duration (for example, seconds) of a single act.

C. *Influence Facets*

   5. *Floor control.* Categories refer to various ways an individual can "get the floor" such as: interrupting another, seizing an unoccupied floor, keeping the floor for a further act, and so forth. The categories are ordered in terms of the degree of assertiveness which they imply.

   6. *Process control.* Categories refer to whether the act designates or influences who the next speakers will be, and how the group will proceed.

   7. *Content control.* Categories refer to whether the act has implications for bounding the universe of discourse, encouraging or discouraging various topics, and so forth.

   8. *Relation of act to prior act.* Categories refer to whether the act continues, modifies or abruptly shifts the topic of the prior act.

D. *Information Facets*

   9. *Level of information.* Categories here are Bales's information, opinion, evaluation.

   10. *Mode.* Categories here include Bales's "asks for" (interrogative) and "gives" (declarative), and also include "agrees" and "disagrees."

   11. *Topic.* Categories include *task, group members, group process, environment.* Further subdivisions of categories, especially task, can be tailored to specific problems.

E. *Affect Facets*

   12. *Affect.* Categories include strong positive, mild positive, affect neutral, mild negative, strong negative.

F. *Intrapersonal Facets*

   13. *Tension management.* Categories include strong display of tension, mild tension, nontension, mild tension release, strong tension release.

This system is applied by categorizing each act that takes place in an interaction setting in terms of one and only one category on each of the thirteen facets. A unit act is defined as a verbal output by an individual; a new act occurs when classification of the behavior requires a shift in category for any one (or more) of the facets. A new speaker, or new target, or new topic, or a shift from agreement to "asking for," or a shift from "group" to "task" topics — any of these signal the beginning of a new act. (Naturally, the temporal facets of serial position and duration are not used to define a unit act, but are merely recorded for acts defined in terms of shifts in the other eleven facets.)

We attempted to apply this system to each of two sets of recorded group interaction data: (1) a subsequent study of negotiation groups, and (2) a series of staff conferences in a mental hospital setting. It was partially successful in both cases. In the former case, results replicated prior findings using the preliminary system (McGrath and Julian, 1963; McGrath, 1966). In the latter case, using only a limited portion of the data, results showed significant differences, in amount and distribution of activity by topic, by actor, by hospital unit, and by each of the two-way interactions. Furthermore, the differences in interaction pattern between hospital units were concomitant with differences in patient discharge rates for the units over a two year period (McGrath, 1967).

But, again, the inadequacies and disadvantages of the multifacet classification system must be noted. First of all, its use requires an enormous investment of time and personnel resources. The system worked best when the coder had both tape recordings and typed verbatim transcripts available. Reliability of coding is difficult to estimate with accuracy, but seems to be about the level of reliability attained by most process analysis systems, namely, moderate to weak. It *can* be applied to groups ranging from three to twelve participants, but difficulty in its use increases greatly as group size increases. The data processing and analysis task is formidable, if not frightening. Indeed, the completeness and "elegance" of its thirteen-facet structure is both its main attraction (from a conceptual point of view) and its main limitation (from a practical point of view). It is true, of course, that a user can choose to omit one or more facets, either in initial coding or in subsequent data analysis (as we did for the staff conference data), thus reducing the task to more manageable proportions. It is this flexibility, perhaps, that renders the system worthy of further development.

We also attempted to develop a less elaborate classification schema which could be applied more economically but which still retained the notion of simultaneous operation of three basic interpersonal processes, and still retained the fundamental facet-structure.[2] This simplified interaction system considered three main parameters of an act: activity, assertiveness (potency), and valence (evaluation). The coding process used a two-dimensional grid (actually, an equilateral triangle resting on its "point," since we decided on *a priori* grounds that the range of evaluation was not independent of the level of potency). The vertical axis represented degrees of potency, *intensity* of the act, from 0 to a

[2] This work was done in collaboration with Mr. Ronald Kent, whose efforts are gratefully acknowledged.

maximum intensity of 5. The horizontal axis represented degrees of positive or negative affect, from strong negative (—3), through affect neutral (0, centerline), to strong positive (+3). Activity, of course, was represented by the total *number* of acts. More precisely, each participant was recorded somewhere on the grid for every 5-second time interval (hence a unit act is defined as 5-seconds of time). "Activity" is the number of non-zero entries for a person (or for a group) in a fixed time period. (For example, with 5-second intervals, a given person can have from 0 to 12 "acts" per minute; a three-person group, collectively, can have from 0 to 36 "acts" per minute. In any case, *some* tally is made, at zero or higher magnitude and at some degree of +, 0, or—valence, for each person in each 5-second time interval. Hence, there are 12 recordings per minute per person, 36 per minute for a three-person group.

This time-based, four-facet (actor, activity, potency, evaluation) interaction system was applied to recordings from some of the three-man negotiation group data and from a set of three-man laboratory task-groups (Morris, 1965; Hackman, 1966). Tentative results suggest that the simplified system can be applied with relative ease, yields solid reliability, and may be capable of distinguishing between sets of groups working on different types of tasks (that is, problem-solving, discussion, production, and negotiation). It is a gross system, though, and loses all information about content and mode of communications, about structuring and process activity, and so forth. It reflects simply the tempo (activity), heatedness (potency), and emotional flavor (evaluation) of the interaction — "the music, but not the lyrics, of the song." Still, its feasibility renders it attractive, and suggests that with further refinement it may be a valuable tool.

Case Study No. 3: A Criterion System for Mental Hospital Patient Recovery

One of the most difficult features of research on mental hospital patients is the lack of a clear, and broadly accepted, criterion of "recovery" or "improvement" or "health." Studies assessing overall hospital (or system) effectiveness sometimes use such criteria as turnover, cost per patient, or discharge-readmission rates. Research to evaluate effectiveness of in-hospital therapy programs (when such evaluation is done at all) is likely to lean heavily on criteria measured by staff ratings, and/or by the patient's own report of symptoms. Controlled experiments on perception, learning, and so forth, done within the mental hospital setting, are likely to use as criteria relatively specific measures (for example, speed, errors) of performance on tasks or tests closely related to the experimental treatment.

These criteria are different — and different in more respects than one — so that it is not suprising that results of their use do not always seem to add up to a cumulative body of knowledge about mental health. Because of these differences, an attempt was made to impose a multi-facet classification on these phenomena, as a step toward generating a system, or related set, of criterion measures (McGrath, 1965).

Three main facets of the criterion space were posited:

1. *Source of data.* There are at least four sources of potential criterion data on patient recovery, as follows: self-report by the patient (interviews, questionnaires, and so forth); ratings by ward personnel who have observed patient behavior over time; observation of patient behavior within specific "standard" (test-ing or experimental) situations; observation of patient behavior in "free" situations.

2. *Modes of behavior.* This facet refers to the nature or content of of the behavior to be examined. For convenience, four "behav-ior modes" were tentatively postulated: the motor, the cogni-tive, the emotional, and the social.

3. *Levels of immediacy* (of measurement). This facet refers to the temporal and situational reference of the criterion measures on an "ultimate-proximate" continuum. Three levels were ten-tatively postulated.

     Level 1 — measurement of direct and immediate conse-quences of a specific experimental or therapeutic activity.
     Level 2 — measurement of consequences of overall hospital stay.
     Level 3 — measurement of adjustment to long-run, out-of-hospital conditions.

This facet structure was initially put forth as a conceptual guide to encourage development of multiple and conceptually related criterion measures for research in mental hospital settings. It has since influenced the design of one large-scale experimental study of over 400 patients involved in a move to a new building. In that study, parallel measures of patient social, motor, and other behavior were developed for three of the sources of data: patient self-report, ward personnel ratings, and direct observation in a "free" (ward-lounge) situation. Furthermore, these measures were gathered at each of four points in time: initial (three weeks prior to the move); after an experimental manipulation (interaction experience and responsibility training) but one week before the move; three weeks after the move; and six weeks after the move.

This particular set of data opens the possibility of using multitrait-multimethod analysis (Campbell & Fiske, 1959) as a systematic method for data analysis. The three sources of data are, of course, different methods. The various kinds of behavior (some 23 specific behavior items) are traits, and each is measured by each of the three methods. Therefore, a multitrait-multimethod (MTMM) analysis for data from any one measurement occasion should let us assess (1) to what extent there are systematic clusters of traits which hold over methods (and these method-stable clusters can then be used to define the "modes" of the facet-space); and (2) to what exent such "patient-behavior" data is an artifact of method, or source of data.

Note, though, that these data contain a third axis, occasions. We can apply the MTMM approach using occasions as methods and behaviors as traits. Here, methods variance is an indicator of stability over time, which we would expect to be high for our control group. Alternatively, we can use *occasions* as traits and *sources* as methods. Here, convergent and discriminant trait validity means systematic differences over time, regardless of method, which we would expect for our experimental groups. These analyses are now in progress. Availability of a three-way analysis paradigm, for simultaneous assessment of behaviors, sources, and occasions, would add appreciably to the information obtained, as we will see in the fourth case study.

Case Study No. 4: A Multifacet Analysis of Role Relationships

Role theory is an area which has offered great promise for advancement of our knowledge of social-psychological phenomena for several decades, but in which there has been relatively little systematic work. Jackson's (1965) work is a notable exception. The recent comprehensive treatment of role concepts by Biddle and Thomas (1966), which unfortunately was not available at the time we began our role-analysis efforts, may well be instrumental to a real growth of systematic work on roles. Incidentally, Biddle and Thomas also "speak" facet analysis, and their classification of role concepts is a monumental application of the multifacet approach.

We are currently attempting to impose a multifacet structure in the role area, not in terms of classification of general role theory concepts (as Biddle and Thomas have done in the role area, and as McGrath and Altman have done in the small group research area), but rather in terms of classification of patterns of role relationships. That is, we are not using multifacet classification as the basis of a *metatheory* (as per Biddle & Thomas, McGrath & Altman, and the "patient recovery" criterion system by McGrath). Rather, we are here using multifacet classification to generate (and define) a substantive theory, as facet analysis is used by Foa (1961), and as it was used in the inter-action process case study.

We began by considering three main facets involved in a given person's set of role relations.

1. The *role partner(s)* involved in the relationship. This facet is itself analyzable into various subfacets, having to do with sex (relative to the focal person), age (relative to the focal person), kinship (relative to the focal person), and so forth.

2. The *behavior attributes* relevant to the role relationship. These include levels of each of several formal properties of roles (for example, subordination-superordination, positive-neutral-negative affect, high and low communication, diffuse *versus* specific relations, universalistic *versus* particularistic relations, and so forth).

3. Several different kinds of *cognition* are involved in the role concept. Here, we are working with four: the focal person's (FP) expectations about his own behavior about the role partner (RP); his perception of his actual behavior re RP; his expectation for RP's behavior about him; and his perceptions of RP's actual behavior re him. These four "modes," of course, can be treated as two facets, each with two categories (expectation *versus* perceived behavior, and FP's *versus* RP's), rather than as one facet with four categories.

Of course, there is another facet implicit in this system: various types of respondents — more accurately, the combination of the respondent (type) and the role partner (type) represents a type of role-pair.

Our plan is to ask a series of respondents (sampled with respect to age, sex, and perhaps other variables) to indicate the extent to which they consider each of a series of behavior attributes (sampled with respect to power, affect, and other "formal" properties of role relations), appropriate in their behavior toward each of a series of role partners (sampled with respect to age, sex, kinship, work relation, and so forth).[3] Respondents will be asked to respond in terms of self-expectations, own actual behavior, behavior expected of the other, and other's actual behavior.

Then, we plan to apply Tucker's three-mode factor analysis (Tucker, 1963) to these data. The three modes, to begin with, will be: respondents, role partner, and behavior attributes, analyzing each of the four modes separately. Subsequently, we hope to apply the same

---

[3] This work is being done in conjunction with Mrs. Margaret Blackburn, whose efforts are gratefully acknowledged.

procedure to a different set of three modes: respondent-partner, behav-ior attribute, and mode of response.

Three-mode factor analysis differs from ordinary two-mode factor analysis, even when it is applied to only two modes, in that it generates a three-mode core of types. The types on each mode are defined in terms of combinations of categories of the other two modes. Thus, we should be able to define types of role partners in terms of clusters of respondent-attribute combinations. Similarly, we should be able to define types of attributes in terms of clusters of respondent — role partner combinations (that is, role pairs). At a more complex level, we should be able to determine for what clusters of attributes mutuality, complementarity or other forms of reciprocal expectations hold, and to find for what role pairs mutuality *versus* complementarity is expected, for various sets of attributes.

These kinds of specifications, it seems to me, will represent a marked advance in systematic description of complex role structures. They are possible by linking the input logic of a multfacet classification to the newly available analysis logic of Tucker's three-mode factor analysis. While this effort is still in its preliminary stages, it is already apparent that it requires an extremely cumbersome set of judgments by each respondent. As with case studies one and two, its complexity is both its chief conceptual strength and its chief pragmatic weakness. Hopefully, the burdensomeness of the respondent's task can be reduced as we are able to define, and sample from, sets of equivalent role partners and equivalent attributes.

Some Concluding Comments

Data Analysis for Multifacet Classification

One central point of this paper is that the input logic of facet analysis can be coupled with a range of data analysis methodologies. The right data analysis method for use with multifacet input depends on the nature of the particular set of data and the purposes for which it is being classified.

Formal facet analysis typically utilizes the principle of contiguity and correlational procedures to order cells of the facet structure (or to assess the *a priori* order imposed on them). Early applications of facet analysis were limited to facet-category sets whose structure could be described in relatively few dimensions, in such structural patterns as simplexes, circumplexes, and radexes. Recent work by Lingoes (1964) toward programs for analysis of small spaces, may well reduce this limitation considerably.

The facet-analysis techniques permit the investigator to find the empirical ordering (or validate his *a priori* ordering) of categories within and across facets. It also permits an empirical "weighting" of relative contributions of facets, and of relative "distances" between categories of a facet. Hence, it permits a detailed and intricate exploration of the total space defined by the facets and categories which are included. Moreover, the investigator can make at least a rough estimate of the degree to which the total set of facets accounts for the variability in the data to which it is applied. Hence, the investigator has some notion of the extent to which he has succeeded in specifying a collectively exhaustive set of facets which account for "all" the variability of his phenomena.

The input logic of facet analysis is also akin to that of Campbell and Fiske's (1959) multitrait-multimethod (MTMM) analysis, although far more general. The applicability of MTMM is probably most apparent when one of the major facets is methodological (for example, the source facet in Case Study No. 3 and several facets in Case Study No. 1). But the logic is applicable in any case, since what is "method" and what is "trait" in the MTMM analysis depends on how the investigator chooses to construe his data.

MTMM is a useful logical tool for identifying which categories of a facet are, and which are not, empirically distinct from one another. At present, though, the MTMM appears to be limited to work with two facets — one construed as traits, the other as methods — although it is possible to fold the categories of two or more facets together into either the trait or the method facet. There is no apparent way, within MTMM, to relate facets to one another, except perhaps by "folding" categories of several facets together into a single "trait" facet and comparing them by means of their relation to the "methods" facet.

Tucker's (1963) three-mode factor analysis is designed, specifically, for dealing with three major facets simultaneously.[4] Three-mode factor analysis differs from traditional factor analysis (even when applied on only two modes) in that it generates an "inner core" on each mode (facet). This inner core specifies the distinctive "types" (clusters of categories) on that mode, in terms of interaction of the categories of the other two modes. Thus, three-mode factor analysis is an empirical assessment procedure which permits the ordering of categories within facets and, simultaneously, relates facets to one another.

---

[4] In principle, it is possible to generalize the rationale to develop an N-mode factor analysis for N larger than 3, although computational procedures for doing so have not yet been developed (Tucker, personal communication).

It should not be overlooked that the familiar procedures of analysis of variance, particularly factorial type designs, are instances of facet structures. Hence, all of the data analysis methodology associated with analysis of variance is potentially applicable to analysis of data classified by multifacet approaches. Indeed, while analysis of variance has a number of limitations, it has several distinct advantages as a method for analysis of data classified in a multifacet system. First, it is a truly multidimensional method on the input side, which can be applied for four, five, or even more facets. Secondly, it permits the investigator to assess the discriminability of categories within a facet (by supplementary statistical tests) and the (empirical) relationships between facets. Moreover, it permits the assessment of effects of facets taken two, three, four, and more at a time (that is, interaction terms) within the context of their effects as single facets. Finally, it provides the investigator with a direct estimate (per cent variance accounted for) of how close he is to the criterion of accounting for all systematic variance in the data.

Some Limitations

It goes without saying that a multifacet approach is *not* a magical solution to all our problems of classification. Up to this point, emphasis has been on the advantages of this approach. Here, we want to note some of its weaknesses.

First of all, in each of its applications, the extreme elaborateness of the classification structure, strength in terms of conceptual elegance, is accompanied by an extreme cumbersomeness which raises serious problems of feasibility within limited resouces.

While this cumbersomeness has seriously hurt our efforts at a practical level in each of the illustrative case studies, I am inclined to discount it as a major weakness of the approach — a mere practical problem. I see the major contribution of the multifacet approach as theoretical — it is a way of conceptualizing and analyzing a problem area — which is not entirely lost even when substantial compromises must be made to work within limited resources. Nevertheless, its elaborateness is a clear negative in a "cost/effectiveness" assessment of its value.

A second weakness has to do with the kinds of properties which cannot be handled without violating one or more of the "principles" enunciated in the first section of this paper. Particularly difficult is the fifth principle, calling for orthogonality of facets so that classification on one doesn't constrain classification on another. Often there are important distinctions on a given facet which only apply within one of the categories of another facet (see, for example, Case Study No. 1). While one can live with this constraint, it not only reduces the elegance of the system, but also makes it more difficult to relate outcomes across facets.

Still another problem is posed by inability to order categories of a facet. When this is the case — and it often is, for all but two-category facets in our still nebulous problem areas — it seriously limits the applicability of a concordance principle at the single-facet level; although concordance over all facets can still be assessed (for example, the McGrath-Altman small-group integration).

But by far the most serious limitation of the multifacet approach — and of any input-logic — is that it provides no precise technique for determining what parameters or dimensions or properties or facets should be built into the system. The initial selection of facets remains an act of "magic," of artistic creativity if you will, which sets ultimate limits on the fruitfulness of the system. What a multifacet approach does, however, is to force the theorist to develop his system by applying a series of systematic logical principles, and these tend to help him eliminate, revise, and add relevant facets and categories. They will not guarantee that he won't overlook a truly crucial facet, nor will they insure against his treating as crucial a facet which is truly trivial. These safeguards must depend on the investigator's knowledge of the domain of concern — and on his horse-sense. The multifacet approach is only a method for systematizing the elaboration and articulation of the creative ideas of the scientist-classifier — and then evaluating how "good" the resulting system is! It is a very valuable method, I feel, for performing these very difficult functions of elaboration and assessment. But we should never lose sight of what it is not. It is a supplement to, but not a substitute for, the creative act by which the scientist-artist discerns what are the important similarities and differences in his field of study.

Concluding Comments

The method here presented is not in itself new. Rather, we have tried to specify, explicitly, a logic for conceptual development of classification systems by means of methods most of which have long been available. The basic theme of the paper is an exhortation for more use of systematic, *a priori* methods as input logic. Presentation of the case studies, which were successful in varying degrees, was done to indicate the broad range of classification problems to which the proposed approach can be applied, as well as to point up some of the main problems to which it leads.

Supplementing this basic theme is the suggestion that there are a range of available tools which can be used to assess the empirical structure of the data classified into any given multifacet conceptual structure.

Among these are formal facet analysis and the principle of contiguity or concordance, multitrait-multimethod analysis, three-mode factor analysis, and analysis of variance.

It is probably true that social psychologists could profit by relying more heavily than we have on our *a priori* concepts as a basis for the input logic by which we structure our concepts and our data-gathering operations. This is only true, though, under two very important conditions. First, we must be able to make our *a priori* concepts systematic and operational. Second, we must build into our methodology one or more methods for systematically assessing, hence modifying, our input logic on the basis of empirical evidence. Without such methods for "validating" classification schema, our classification systems can become as sterile as the four humours and the twelve Zodiacal signs, no matter how complex and elegant they may be. But with effective methods for evaluating and modifying classification systems via empirical evidence, then perhaps someday soon our field can reach the level of Mendeleev's chemistry or Linneaus' phylogenetic structure.

Bibliography

Bales, R. F. *Interaction process analysis: A method for the study of small groups.* Cambridge, Mass.: Addison-Wesley, 1950.

Biddle, B. J., & Thomas, E. J. *Role Theory.* New York: John Wiley & Sons, 1966.

Campbell, D. T., & Fiske, D. W. Convergent and discriminant validation by the multitrait-multimethod matrix. *Psychological Bulletin,* 1959, 56, 81–105.

Foa, U. G. The contiguity principle in the structure of interpersonal relations. *Human Relations,* 1958, 11, 229–238.

———. Convergences in the analysis of the structure of interpersonal behavior. *Psychological Review,* 1961, 68, (5), 341–353.

———. Perception in behavior in reciprocal roles: The ringex model. *Psychological Monographs,* 1966, 80, (15, Whole No. 623).

———, Triandis, H. C., & Katz, E. W. Cross-cultural invariance in the differentiation and organization of family roles. *Journal of Personality and Social Psychology,* 1966, 4, (3), 316–327.

Guttman, L. Introduction to facet design and analysis. In *Proceedings of the fifteenth international congress of psychology, Brussels,* 1957. Amsterdam: North Holland, 1958.

Hackman, J. R. Effects of task characteristics on group products. Technical Report No. 5, June, 1966, University of Illinois, Contract AF 49(638)–1291.

Jackson, J. "Structural characteristics of norms." In Steiner, I. D., & Fishbein, M. (Eds.), *Current studies in social psychology,* New York: Holt, Rinehart & Winston, 1965.

Julian, J. W., & McGrath, J. E. The influence of leader and member behavior on the adjustment and task effectiveness of negotiation groups. Technical Report No. 17, October, 1963, University of Illinois, Group Effectiveness Research Laboratory.

Lingoes, J. C. Smallest space analysis — G-L(SSA-I). *Comp. Rept.,* 1964b, 3, 1–20, The University of Michigan Computer Center, Ann Arbor, Michigan.

McGrath, J. E. Systems of information in small group research studies. *Human Relations,* 1963, 16, 263–277.

———. A methodology for design of a criterion system for social psychological research in a mental hospital setting. Research Report No. 66–2, December, 1965, Danville V. A. Hospital.

———. A psychological approach to the study of negotiation. In Bowers, Raymond V. (Ed.), *Studies on behavior in organizations: A research symposium.* Athens: University of Georgia Press, 1966.

———. Patterns of communication in diagnostic staff conferences within neuropsychiatric units of a V. A. hospital. Research Report Danville V. A. Hospital (in preparation).

———, & Altman, I. *Small group research: A synthesis and critique of the field.* New York: Holt, Rinehart & Winston, Inc., 1966.

McGrath, J. E., & Julian, J. W. Interaction process and task outcome in experimentally-created negotiation groups. *J. Psychol. Studies,* Vol. 14, No. 3, September, 1963, 117–137.

Morris, C. G., II. Effects of task characteristics of group process. Technical Report No. 2, July, 1965, University of Illinois, Contract AF 49(638)–1291.

Tucker, L. R. Implications of factor analysis of three-way matrices for measurement of change. In Harris, C. W., (Ed.), *Problems in measuring change.* Madison, Wis.: University of Wisconsin Press, 1963. Pp. 122–137.

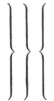

Experimentation in Translevel Interaction[1]

KARL E. WEICK

*Laboratory for Research
in Social Relations
University of Minnesota*

Suppose that several investigators were to observe an experimental laboratory filled with college sophomores. Suppose further that the exercise which is underway is a straightforward discussion task in which five participants have to agree on a plan of action. All discussion groups are treated identically with one exception. In one set of groups a simple majority is sufficient to adopt a plan of action while in the other groups the final plan must be accepted unanimously.

Now, what relevance does this simple situation have when one is concerned about processes associated with groups versus individuals, or between sets of individuals within groups? One answer is that different criteria for agreement may be sufficient to create aggregates which represent two distinct levels. This possibility exists because of subtle differences in interdependence. The aggregate that has to reach unanimous agreement must assess the preferences of all members and accommodate the differences. Considerable interdependence is required for success. The majority rule imposes fewer demands for interdependence and generates a more individualistic orientation. Individuals can be ignored as long as a majority exists. In short, the simple device of a change in decision rules may establish sets of persons who act more or less like a small group. The crucial point in this illustration is that the decision rule can serve as a technique to induce levels in settings which are otherwise equivalent. Furthermore, once the setting has been sensitized to levels, various hypotheses can be tested.

Throughout this paper, the terms "levels phenomena" and "levels issues" will be used. The term "levels" refers to the fact that as one

[1] Preparation of this paper was facilitated by Grant GS-1042, administered by the National Science Foundation.

moves from cells to political states or nations, systems show progressive increments in complexity and capacity (Miller, 1965). Furthermore, emergent features appear at a given complexity level that do not exist at simpler levels. Empirically, emergents can be distinguished by means of the criterion proposed by Milburn, namely, "Does this operationally defined concept, not available at simpler levels of complexity, contribute significantly to the predictability of dependent variables?" (Milburn, 1967, p. 24).

The phrase "levels issues" refers to issues on which investigators might differ in the level of complexity at which they conceptualize the outcomes. In general, levels issues involve the question of denotation (Allport, 1962). More specifically a levels issue is one in which investigators feel more or less constrained to explain the results in terms of the specific level at which they were obtained. If, for example, an investigator asks several persons in a group, "How attracted are you to the other members?", he may average the scores and talk about group cohesion, a concept that is one step removed from the level involved in data collection, or he may talk about liking among individuals. The problem here is that we do not always know what the empirical referent is for the term "group," that is, the precise agent that is cohesive.

The general theme in this paper is that the value of a levels perspective is often unclear because the empirical referents for concepts are unclear. We are in agreement with Allport who has labeled the individual and the group as the "master problem of social psychology":

Some way must be found to describe in general terms that layout of conditions surrounding and involving individuals which we have called the group, and to formulate, in the precise yet *universal* manner of science, what actually goes on in the situation we call "collective action" (Allport, 1962, p. 7).

Most experimental settings contain implicit theories about levels. Inherent in any experimental setting are properties which are found in groups, organizations, and societies. Thus, many experimental settings actually incorporate multilevel properties even though most investigators have ignored this fact. It is instructive to take an existing taxonomy of stimulus situations such as those proposed by Sells (1963) or Indik and examine the extent to which a multiperson experimental setting contains properties which are included in the taxonomy. Typically one finds that several dimensions contained in these taxonomies assume some value *other than zero* in the experiments.

If, for example, one were to compile all of the studies which show that persons who are similar like each other more than those who are dissimilar (see Lott & Lott, 1965, for such a review), and then assessed the extent to which the experiments contained individual, group, organizational, and societal properties, several facts would be discovered. First, the hypothesis is supported when dimensions associated with nonindividual levels are salient. Second, different nonindividual dimensions appear in different studies. Third, and perhaps most important, if it is true that experiments contain properties which represent more than one level, and if these sets of properties overlap only partially, then it can be argued that the hypothesis of similarity and attraction has survived not only several experimental tests, but more important, it holds true when nonindividual dimensions can influence the process.

With this brief overview in mind, we are now in a better position to state the central theme of this paper. It attempts to initiate a consideration of ways in which experimental methodology can be applied more directly to problems highlighted in the preceding papers.

To discuss the relevance of experimentation, it is necessary to examine several assumptions pervading the thinking about the levels issue. Many of these assumptions, if retained, can block an effective experimental methodology. Our concern is with issues that have drawn attention away from central questions, and also with potentially central questions that have not been asked so far. After detailing some of these reservations, we will examine a few experimental research strategies which converge on the levels issue.

Diversionary Issues

Upon close inspection it turns out that levels issues, prosaic as they sometimes appear, actually constitute a volatile arena in which divergent scientific values converge. Because people have failed to recognize this property of the levels problem, many subtle methodological arguments are waged under the guise of "neutral" discourse. For example, systematic thinking about levels issues sometimes is replaced by efforts to justify certain objects of study. Thus one finds frequent arguments that groups are real, that groups' products exist, that individual predispositions are not the sole determinants of action, and so forth. No one seriously doubts such conclusions even though their importance may be questioned. But granting the conclusion, it is unlikely that arguments given marginal support through intricate statistical manipulations would be persuasive. A listing of dimensions which presumably are unique to multiperson units is not sufficient to justify extensive research *if* such lists cannot be coupled with empirical findings demonstrating that these dimensions do make a difference.

Aside from the preoccupation with justification, other diversionary issues are debated whenever questions of level arise. Many discussions of levels argue that a holistic approach is preferable to an atomistic approach, that functional analysis is preferable to structural analysis (Wheeler & Perkins, 1932), and that the law of parsimony is misleading. How may these methodological preferences be diversionary? While these preferences have considerable merit, they sometimes become entrenched and divert attention from alternative research strategies. Furthermore, each of the preferences is actually open to considerable dispute.

Two examples may clarify this latter point. The whole-part issue is especially salient in discussions of levels phenomena. Investigators are understandably reluctant to fragment a whole such as a group since the part, even when it is understood, may function differently when it is placed alongside other parts. There is also legitimate concern about the common assumption that parts combine in a summative rather than an interactive manner. But the flaw in this line of thinking is that investigators may err in the opposite direction. They find themselves in the position of maintaining an extreme form of the holistic doctrine, namely, ". . . a whole is itself part of a larger whole, and so on; since only wholes and not parts must be studied, in order to study any complex it is necessary to study the whole universe" (Luchins & Luchins, 1965, p. 331). This latter form of the holistic viewpoint is as much in violation of the Gestalt emphasis as is the total disregard of wholes. The extreme form of the holistic argument misses the point that a Gestalt tends to be self-enclosed, finitely extended, and characterized by determinable laws. As Kohler cautioned (1938, p. 30), ". . . the *size* of an area beyond which interaction between a process and its surroundings may be ignored is a matter for specific determination."

The principle of parsimony also enters discussions of levels. While the assertion "it is vain to do with more what can be done with fewer" (Mason, 1962, p. 118) appears to have face validity, there are several reasons why such a prescription is ambiguous, unworkable, and incompatible with many objects of study (Luchins & Luchins, 1965, pp. 352–364). But in their eagerness to criticize Occam's razor, persons who concern themselves with complex phenomena sometimes forget about the importance of simplicity in scientific inquiry. The criterion of simplicity is closely related to the falsifiability of a theory. The simpler a theory, the easier it is to test its falsehood; the more complex, the more difficult its refutation. This problem is especially common among theories involving levels which often consist of complex sets of disjunctive statements—several statements connected by the word "or". This creates problems because of conditions that must be met to disprove a series of disjunctive statements. "A disjunction is true as long as one of its components is true and is false only if all of its components are false" (Luchins & Luchins, 1965, p. 363). A common form in which theories about levels are stated is that a given outcome is a function of the individual *or* the situation *or* both. As long as evidence exists for one portion of the statement, the entire statement is logically plausible.

It would be well to restate the points being made. It is not being argued that methodological and conceptual preferences associated with levels issues are necessarily wrong. What is being asserted is that these preferences are not as defensible as they sometimes appear. Persons who implement these preferences forego more gains than they may realize, and entrenchment may hinder the solution of levels problems. When attempts have been made to conduct experiments involving levels, these attempts have been imposed on assumptions and values that defeat experimental aims. Thus it is not surprising that, so far, experimental methodology has not been very successful.

Nondiversionary Questions

Perhaps more important than diversionary questions, are questions which directly involve the problem of levels, but which remain unanswered.

Spurious Use of Size

One may question, for example, whether the concept of levels is the most useful way to categorize stimulus situations. Size is a crucial variable running through most proposals for ordering stimulus conditions. However, persons who have studied size in the small-group field (Kelley & Thibaut, 1954) contend that it is not a useful means to organize small group-work because so many variables change when size is altered. While one remedy is to pay closer attention to these correlates of size and to state them with more precision, it is possible that other bases for categorization might be more productive. It is not immediately clear what an alternative categorization might involve. It is possible that rather than size, physical and/or psychological distance might serve as a basis to organize stimulus situations. Stimuli would be categorized in terms of their proximity in time and space to an actor. From this point of view, it is conceivable that an organization might be a more immediate environment than a small group. Given the recent interest in territoriality (Hall, 1966) and the effects on persons of physical distance, it is possible that events which are sorted out along dimensions of distance might be both orderly and predictive. But, even if one is committed to size, it is not necessary to adhere to large-scale increments. Instead of discussing ill-defined increments such as those associated with groups, organizations, and societies, it is conceivable that much smaller gradations in size could assume greater importance. For example, existing studies of size suggest that the increments in complexity between groups of two and three, and three and four, and four and five persons are substantially greater than are increments from five to six, and so forth. While such a conclusion is based on interpretation of size studies in ways not intended by their designers, there does seem to be some plausibility to this conclusion and it seems to be sufficiently useful that further studies of supposedly small groups might be analyzed for their relevance to levels issues.

Ambiguous Criteria of Society

It is frequently difficult to conduct experiments involving levels because it is difficult to tell which level has been established. An example may illustrate this problem. Suppose that we watch five people interact over an extended period of time. Initially, the persons act like five individuals; interdependence is minimal. As time passes, two of the five persons form a pair, then a second pair forms, then the isolated person joins one of the dyads so that now we observe a group of two persons interacting with a triad. Finally, both groups unite into a single interdependent unit of five persons. Now the question is, what levels are represented at the different stages in the history of these five persons? The initial answer would probably be that we see a steady progression from individuals, through groups, to sets of groups (organizations) with the five persons finally emerging as an incipient society. This assumes that society is the most unified setting and exerts the most uniform influence over the persons. But it is not self-evident that unification is the most crucial feature of society. Just the opposite may be true, namely, societal levels afford the most explicit differentiation among persons, in which case the final stage in the five-man group is as remote from a society as is the first stage.

It seems clear that at all levels processes of integration and differentiation occur. Society may be the most integrated level in the sense that it exerts the most uniform influence, but the fact that this influence is nonspecific, plus the fact that distinctive societal tasks must be executed, also places a premium on differentiation. The argument here is that persons who discuss levels often act as if increasing integration is associated with higher levels. However, differentiation may also increase as one ascends levels. Given this possibility, it becomes more difficult to state to which of several levels a particular experiment is relevant. It may be more useful to talk about stimulus situations in terms of those which generate integration and/or differentiation rather than situations which are distinctive because of their size.

It is clear that within an experimental setting it is possible to establish conditions under which individuals develop different patterns of interdependence over time. In this sense laboratory experiments, if they continue for a sufficient length of time, are potentially capable of paralleling natural instances of levels. The problem is that even if the laboratory is sensitive in this way, and even if various patterns of interdependence, dependence, and independence can be created, it is difficult to know at what level the group is functioning or in what way the experiment engages the issue of levels.

Spurious Social Facilitation Effects

Even though there is evidence that group products exist and that different levels possess unique properties, a set of studies has recently emerged which may be troublesome for persons concerned with levels. These studies concern social facilitation as represented in the work of Zajonc (1965). They show that when persons perform a solitary task in the actual or implied presense of the other persons, their performance differs from that when the same task is performed in isolation. Zajonc argues that these differences in performance are mediated by differences in arousal. When an audience is present, dominant responses are more likely and subordinate responses are less likely to occur. In other words, the spacing between the various responses in a person's response hierarchy is magnified when an audience enhances the arousal level.

The issue of social facilitation bears directly on the issue of whether it is even necessary to talk about levels. It is commonly argued that when persons act in groups they behave differently than they do when they are alone and that this demonstrates the existence of group effects. Notice, however, that the concept of social facilitation suggests that differential responding in groups is not necessarily evidence of unique group properties. Instead, what we observe is that *individual* patterns of responding change when arousal levels change. An unequivocal demonstration of group effects would require the investigator to employ *both* a nonsocial and a social source of arousal. If a group setting is important solely for its arousal value, then there should be no differences in performance when arousal stems from social and nonsocial sources. If, however, groups make unique contributions, then social and nonsocial sources of arousal should lead to *different* outcomes.

Absence of Significant Questions

Even though we may have implied that persons concerned with levels know what questions they are trying to answer, close examination suggests that this implication may be unwarranted. It is revealing to construct a list of questions which seem relevant to the issue of levels and then assess which of these questions have been studied.

The first question is, do levels correspond to entities with definite boundaries? If investigators cannot demonstrate that levels correspond to entities, then they may be studying elusive phenomena which will never stabilize sufficiently to allow the detection of lawful relationships. As Campbell has observed, "if discreteness and multiple-diagnosability of entities at the social level turns out upon examination to be lacking, then the possibility of a social science representing a separate level of analysis from the biological or psychological will be eliminated" (Campbell, 1958, p. 24). The important point is that the existence of entities is both a formal definitional and an empirical question.

If it is established that entities exist, then it is possible to examine the entities more closely. So far, examination has consisted mainly of explicating the distinctive structures and processes which characterize each level, and then establishing the extent to which these properties behave like a system. Most of the work with levels seems to center on this phase, but notice that some of this work may be inconclusive if the prior step, that of establishing the existence of an entity, has been bypassed.

Once the distinctive content of a given level has been established then it is possible to ask in what ways properties at different levels interact. It is this question where current thinking about levels seems to be more deficient. Those who argue in favor of a levels approach often criticize persons who study part processes assuming that parts combine additively to determine behavior. This criticism is warranted, but the irony is that persons who work with levels often make the same mistake. They elaborate the distinctive content of a given level, then assume that all levels influence action (an additive assumption). In other words, action is regarded as a function of the individual *plus* the group *plus* the organization *plus* the society. Right at the point where a levels analysis could improve prediction, it falters through the usage of an oversimplified combination rule.

Questions concerning (a) priorities among levels as determinants of action, (b) the interaction among levels in the determination of action, and (c) overlapping processes often are ignored. Failure to push beyond a simple summative view of levels seems partially due to an overly static concept of levels. Levels seem to be treated as if they were closed systems which assume *equal* status in the determination of action. It would seem important to replace this view with one which is more dynamic. Such a portrayal would involve the notion that as conditions change, different levels assume more or less importance as determinants of actions. For example, stimulus clarity may affect the extent to which different levels control action. It has been shown that when stimulus conditions became ambiguous, persons search more intently for some stable anchors to guide their actions. Since organizations and societies are often less well defined than are face-to-face relationships, it is probable that under conditions of high ambiguity, properties associated with small groups will assume more control over action than will properties of organizations or societies. Thus, it is not necessarily true that all levels of a stimulus situation are equally important under all conditions.

Admittedly the issue of interactive relationships among levels cannot be studied until the distinctive content of a given level is elaborated. In this sense, the issue of relations among levels may be a task for the future. However, our point is that closer ties between experimentation and the levels issue may permit investigators, within the same setting, both to explicate dimensions and to derive some clues as to the ways in which these dimensions fit together. Dual attention to issues of analysis and synthesis seems to be lacking from much of the existing work with levels. As a result, the final product often has elegance in being a thorough description of potentially important dimensions, but this thoroughness is obtained at the price of fewer leads regarding synthesis and interaction. If *both* questions remain salient during inquiry, then the usefulness of a levels analysis should increase substantially.

Swamping Conditions

One unfortunate by-product of a concern with levels issues is that much behavioral research has been relegated to the category of fragments. These fragments presumably are of limited value because they have been studied apart from their natural context. While processes may be altered as a function of their context, it seems that investigators who use the levels framework sometimes miss important leads which would increase the predictive power of a levels approach.

For example, earlier we mentioned the recurrent finding that as stimulus situations become more ambiguous, persons tend to behave in terms of that level which provides the clearest prescription for action. For want of a better term, we will label conditions of this kind "swamping conditions." These are conditions which serve to overpower or submerge other determinants of action and to render them less effective in the control of behavior. Several such conditions have been studied, but we will mention only a few. The importance of these conditions for research on levels is that when they occur, only partial sets of dimensions at various levels become influential. Certain dimensions survive as determinants of behavior; most do not. Thus an important set of questions which should heighten the power of a levels analysis concerns the conditions that restrict or expand the range of dimensions that control behavior. Furthermore, dimensions probably vary greatly in their utility for participants. Thus, it is possible that the more useful the dimension, the more resistant to change or exclusion it will be when stimulus conditions narrow the attention of participants.

The point we are making may be clarified if we cite other examples of swamping conditions. Evidence shows that as ambiguity increases, actions are increasingly controlled by personal dispositions (Sherif & Harvey, 1952). When situations are unclear, individual differences may override group determinants. Rosenberg (1965) has recently suggested that many persons have multiple group ties and that these ties tend to be complex, imposing incompatible demands. As a result, persons may be in a state of considerable ambiguity. It is hypothesized that as ties proliferate, the actions of persons are apt to be *more* rather than less under the control of individual differences. This is rather different from the more common assumption that as group ties increase, it becomes much more important to take account of group processes. Precisely because these ties are so extensive, the person can deduce few consistent guidelines from them. As a consequence, individual dispositions rather than group processes assume greater control.

Another swamping condition is that of arousal. A useful view of the effects of arousal on performance has been proposed by Easterbrook (1959). He is concerned with the effects of arousal on the utilization of cues during task performance. His argument, greatly simplified, is that under conditions of low arousal, persons can attend both to relevant and irrelevant cues with the result that performance is moderately efficient. As arousal increases, the range of cues which are used narrows, and irrelevant cues are ignored first. This means that performance should improve. However, if arousal continues to increase and reaches a point where all irrelevant cues have been excluded, then relevant cues, too, start to drop away, and thus performance deteriorates.

If we assume that cues for task performance are embedded in levels, then it is conceivable that when arousal increases, both task cues and dimensions within the related level may be excluded. Suppose that a person attends to inputs from the organization while he performs a task in which the most relevant cues are embedded in a small group. Both levels influence his actions, but perhaps only when arousal is low. Since the organizational inputs are peripheral for actual performance of the task, an increase in arousal should lead to the exclusion of these organizational inputs, and actions should be influenced by small-group dimensions. Notice that under some conditions these peripheral organizational cues do affect performance, so it is reasonable to argue that a thorough analysis of action requires that a person remain attentive to different levels. But all levels may influence performance only when arousal is slight. As arousal increases, all levels do *not* exert equal influence over performance, and only those dimensions directly involved in task performance will be retained. Thus, it is possible that the levels issue may be most relevant to routine activities performed under conditions of low arousal. When arousal increases, levels become fractionated and do not exert a consistent influence over performance.

We have tried to argue that one set of variables which may increase the precision of a levels analysis is swamping conditions. These conditions narrow the attention of researchers and also collapse the range of influence which controls the activities of their subjects. If one is interested in discovering similar variables on two or more levels, swamping conditions may obscure those that may actually exist under nonswamping circumstances. If levels are characterized in terms of their sensitivity to these conditions, then more precise statements can be made concerning which dimensions at which levels will control behavior under which conditions. And this, after all, seems to be what a concern with levels is all about.

Some Needed Shifts in Focus

The present discussion suggests several ways in which thinking about levels might be redirected. After listing a few of these suggestions we will examine possible experimental strategies which may implement this redirection.

So far, levels have been treated largely as independent variables. However, the preceding remarks imply that equal attention should be directed toward levels as dependent variables. While it is generally acknowledged that individuals affect society and that society affects individuals, most research has centered on the latter view (Inkeles, 1959, pp. 251–256). Interest in levels as dependent variables would involve learning more about ways in which individual dispositions compel persons to establish groups, organizations, or societies which are consistent with these dispositions. An example of this point of view is found in March and Simon (1958) who argue that a prominent characteristic of persons is limited rationality. Assuming that persons possess this property, then organizations consist of processes and structures which either enlarge rationality or permit persons to take action based on the limited views which they maintain.

A second change which might improve the precision of a levels approach would be to remove several concepts from their status as axioms. Many distinctions within the levels area are treated as axiomatic, and it seems that the translation of these axioms into empirical questions might promote some much needed clarification.

Even though the dimensions within a given level have been given considerable attention, less attention has been directed to the description of boundary conditions. It is often difficult to know when there is a transition from one level to another. Thus a third useful shift would be to direct greater attention to measures which indicate when a boundary between levels is crossed. Campbell (1958) has suggested that measures involving diffusion and reflection could be useful. Diffusion can be examined by means of information transmission. Relevant questions include: Where does a message go, how fast, with what deflections in rate? If the rate of information transmission is plotted across a set of persons, there should be a significant change in rate whenever a boundary is crossed. Message content might also change when a boundary is encountered. Reflection techniques assume that intact units have differential sensitivity to inputs. Thus when information is fed into coherent entities, it may be deflected or absorbed more quickly than when it is fed into loose aggregations. When differences in the opaqueness of a unit are detected, it is probable that a distinct level exists.

Boundaries can be detected in other ways. The extent to which persons view their contributions as interchangeable has been shown by Deutsch (1949) to differentiate groups with an individualistic or cooperative orientation. The sensitivity of reaction time to group structural changes (Burnstein & Zajonc, 1965), the ease with which newcomers are incorporated and socialized (Ziller, 1964) and proximity (Webb, et. al., 1966) should give information about boundaries. It is clear that each of these measures is subtle and involves discrete responses, but this is certainly no reason to avoid them.

A fourth suggestion is that convergent methods to study subprocesses (or lower-level processes) should be developed. Subprocesses have often been unduly maligned, and closer examination of them should provide additional clues about ways in which total processes function. These clues might be more apparent if several methods were used to study the same subprocess. The advantage of this strategy is that it shows the stability of the subprocess, and a subprocess that survives multiple tests probably is one that should be taken seriously by levels theorists.

Finally, levels should be viewed in less static terms. We have already suggested that it is difficult to apply a levels analysis when (a) levels data are combined in an additive manner, (b) the data are presumed to be self-contained, and (c) the data are assumed equally salient under all conditions. Given these assumptions, it is difficult to study the differential ways in which levels might affect behavior. A partial remedy would be to examine dimensions which are less tangible. Several existing taxonomies of levels consist of dimensions which are easily detected. Visibility, however, is not a guarantee of significance or importance. A person who analyzes stimulus situations in terms of tangible properties often observes dimensions which are relatively insensitive to changes in the environment.

Some Specific Methodological Strategies

We conclude with three brief examples of experimental strategies which might clarify some problems in the levels approach. Although these strategies are speculative, they suggest ways in which experimental methodology can be adapted to the levels approach; they address ambiguities in existing levels work; they permit greater control than is possible in more naturalistic settings, and they serve the dual functions of analysis and synthesis.

Extended Composition

A central assumption in the levels approach is that the individual *and* the environment must be taken into account when predictions are made. This assumption is implemented most clearly in experiments where personality dimensions and group dimensions are manipulated (Berkowitz, 1956). It is proposed that this type of experiment should be extended to other levels and that the bases of composition be expanded. Instead of placing individual and small-group dimensions in the same experiment, it should be possible to examine the interaction between a small-group dimension (recruitment process) and an organizational dimension (number of hierarchical levels), or between an organizational and societal dimension. As a variation, small groups of different types of persons (high and low dominance) could be composed with the crucial addition that organizations would also be formed utilizing different sets of groups. Within these settings it would be possible to test hypotheses relevant to levels such as the hypothesis suggested by McGrath and Altman (1966) that

. . . intersystem relationships vary in their strength as a function of the distance between systems. For example, it may be predicted that a higher number of relationships will occur between intrapersonal system variables and intrapersonal dynamics than between intrapersonal dynamics and intragroup structure. Effects in the latter case may be mediated by or interact with intervening system variables (McGrath & Altman, 1966, p. 38).

If investigators are more deliberate in the ways in which they compose groups and sets of groups, and are guided in such composition by dimensions which are associated with different levels, then interrelationships among levels should become clarified.

Bypass Design

An intricate but informative attack on levels issues could involve bypassing. For instance, a group of persons are constituted into an organization. Dimensions associated solely with the organizational level are created (Bass, 1963; Wager & Palola, 1964). The content of prior levels, the individual and the group, are purposely left unspecified. The question is, given a level which is specified and several levels which are not, which dimensions at the unspecified levels are activated, in what order, and with what modifications of the specified dimensions at the organizational level? Essentially we are trying to discover the specific dimensions that become salient during interaction. If we then assume that salient dimensions at the unspecified levels are functional, then it is possible to reverse the process to see if our hunches are correct. In the second stage of this design, we would construct a small group with just those dimensions which emerged during the original bypass experiment, instruct the participants to form themselves into an organization, and then examine whether the organization which emerges resembles the organization which was established during the first stage. Probably it will differ, but the important question is: Where do these departures occur? Departures may signify superfluous dimensions in the original organization. However, the most important information provided by this approach concerns mediating mechanisms, for example, dimensions at various levels which influence one another. Data generated by the bypass design also provide information about the compatibility of dimensions at various levels. If it is assumed that relationships which emerge in the bypass design are functional, then relationships other than these might be viewed as incompatible and when they are present, to impose sizeable strain on the actor. In other words, relationships which emerge in the bypass design would be treated as prescriptive. Departures from these relationships could be an indication of potential strain within the system. When incompatible dimensions are present, levels should exert a less consistent influence on behavior.

Behavioral Vacuum

This strategy is a variation of the bypass design which is intended to focus on a more limited set of issues. Suppose that two dimensions embedded in two different levels are specified for the actors. Preferably these dimensions are separated by several intervening levels. For example, an individual dimension and an organizational dimension are activated. The subject then is assigned a task, the performance of which requires that he treat the two dimensions as given and adduce additional information which binds these two points together in a meaningful, consistent manner. In short, he has to interpolate between two points embedded in different levels in order to complete an assignment. This design attempts to reconstruct the phenomenology of translevel phenomena and to identify intermediate dimensions which bind levels together for a given actor. As before, the actor starts his task with cryptic information about the environment, two disparate properties of the environment are specified, and it is his task to construct whatever additional distinctions he needs to perform the task. Some order can be imposed on his constructions if specific information about other dimensions is made available so that the subject can choose which information he wants. These choices should show how subjects obtain a sufficient view of the world to act. By controlling informational inputs and content of choices, it is possible to determine what information is desired, in what order, and how much the individual is willing to forego in order to obtain the information.

Rather than interpolate, the actor might be given only one cognition with the assignment to secure whatever additional information he needed to initiate and sustain task performance. This approach would serve to answer the question: Through how many levels does extrapolation penetrate and which dimensions are most crucial?

All three of these designs involve individual rather than group decisions. Furthermore, there is the implication that awareness affects the impact of levels. There is a distinct thread of rationality running through these suggestions. These two biases are not necessarily detrimental. These designs have been anchored in individual perceptions because this is a convenient *starting* point, group effects should be evident if the design unfolds as expected, and for reasons mentioned earlier, it is not essential to adopt elaborate assumptions about group variables until they are necessary. These designs, it should be added, are *not* designed to demonstrate the existence of group effects. That issue is irrelevant. Instead these designs attempt to show which items of information associated with different levels are needed by a person in order to act. It is assumed that as conditions change, actors are differentially sensitive to group and organizational inputs, and that forcing them to be explicit about their world will clarify this sensitivity. Furthermore, it will enable us to learn more about priorities among levels, points of overlap, and potential points of mutual influence among levels.

Conclusion

The purpose of this syposium has been to integrate findings associated with various levels of analysis. The preceding analysis suggests that integration will require some shifting of methodological and conceptual preferences, as well as greater attention to some neglected questions. Levels issues involve problems which are too important to be explored with a limited range of techniques and an antiquated set of assumptions. Development along some of the lines suggested in this paper might move us closer to the integration of concepts which we desire but clearly have not yet attained.

Bibliography

Allport, F. H. A structuronomic conception of behavior: Individual and collective. *Journal of Abnormal and Social Psychology*, 1962, 64, 3–30.

Bass, B. M. Experimenting with simulated manufacturing organizations. In S. B. Sells (Ed.), *Stimulus determinants of behavior*. New York: Ronald Press, 1963. Pp. 117–196.

Berkowitz, L. Personality and group position. *Sociometry*, 1956, 19, 210–222.

Burnstein, E., & Zajonc, R. B. Individual task performance in a changing social structure. *Sociometry*, 1965, 28, 16–29.

Campbell, D. T. Common fate, similarity, and other indices of the status of aggregates of persons as social entities. *Behavioral Science*, 1958, 3, 14–25.

Deutsch, M. A theory of cooperation and competition. *Human Relations*, 1949, 2, 129–152.

Easterbrook, J. A. The effect of emotion on cue utilization and the organization of behavior. *Psychological Review*, 1959, 66, 183–201.

Hall, E. T. *The Hidden Dimension*. New York: Doubleday, 1966.

Inkeles, A. Personality and social structure. In R. K. Merton, L. Broom, & L. S. Cottrell, Jr. (Eds.), *Sociology today*. New York: Basic Books, 1959. Pp. 249–276.

Kelley, H. H., & Thibaut, J. W. Experimental studies of group problem solving and process. In G. Lindzey (Ed.), *Handbook of social psychology*, vol. 2. Reading, Mass.: Addison-Wesley, 1954. Pp. 735–785.

Kohler, W. Physical Gestalten. In E. D. Ellis (Ed.), *A source book of Gestalt psychology*. New York: Harcourt Brace, & World, 1938.

Lott, A., & Lott, Bernice. Group cohesiveness and interpersonal attraction: A review of relationships with antecedent and consequent variables. *Psychological Bulletin*, 1965, 64, 259–309.

Luchins, A. S., & Luchins, Edith H. *Logical foundations of mathematics for behavioral scientists*. New York: Holt, Rinehart & Winston, 1965.

March, J. G., & Simon, H. A. *Organizations*. New York: John Wiley & Sons, 1958.

Mason, S. E. *A history of the sciences.* New York: Collier, 1962.

McGrath, J. E., & Altman, I. *Small group research.* New York: Holt, Rinehart & Winston, 1966.

Milburn, T. W. Problems in extrapolating from psychological experiments. Northwestern University, unpublished manuscript, 1967.

Miller, J. C. Living systems: Basic concepts. *Behavioral Science,* 1965, 10, 193–237.

Rosenberg, M. J. Image in relation to the policy process. In H. C. Kelman (Ed.), *International behavior.* New York: Holt, Rinehart & Winston, 1965. Pp. 278–334.

Sells, S. B. Dimensions of stimulus situations which account for behavior variance. In E. B. Sells (Ed.), *Stimulus determinants of behavior.* New York: Ronald Press, 1963. Pp. 3–15.

Sherif, M., & Harvey, O. J. A study in ego functioning: Elimination of stable anchorages in individual and group situations. *Sociometry,* 1952, 15, 272–305.

Wager, L. W., & Palola, E. G. The miniature replica model and its use in laboratory experiments on complex organizations. *Social Forces,* 1964, 42, 418–429.

Webb, E. J., Campbell, D. T., Schwartz, R. D., & Sechrest, L. *Unobtrusive measures: Nonreactive research in the social sciences.* Chicago: Rand McNally, 1966.

Wheeler, R. H., & Perkins, F. T. *Principles of mental development.* New York: Crowell, 1932.

Zajonc, R. B. Social facilitation. *Science,* 1965, 149, 269–274.

Ziller, R. C. Individuation and socialization: a theory of assimilation in large organizations. *Human Relations,* 1964, 17, 341–360.

Persons, Settings, and Larger Contexts

PAUL V. GUMP
Midwest Psychological Field Station
University of Kansas

A key problem in the set of problems with which we are concerned is the conceptualization of man's immediate environments. Until adequate methods are developed for the identification and description of the proximate environment, understanding of the behavior of individuals and of multisituational complexes will be retarded. Targeting upon the immediate context is not a mere research preference, but a necessity deriving from the contemporary scientific challenge. Increasingly, social science is being asked to describe such relationships as those between urban renewal and anomie, between kinds of company organization and employee loyalty, or between political systems and individual well-being. Investigators hope to establish and understand relationships between variables associated with extended, encompassing contexts and variables associated with the behavior and experience of individuals.

For purposes of exposition, let us present just two locations in our problem: the person and the gross context within which he may be found. This larger context may be his school, his company, or his community. The words "larger contexts" point to a complex of situations encompassing the individual — yet extending much beyond his proximate situation. Use of the word context also indicates that the phenomena of reference are relatively first-order, without the distillations and abstractions that are necessary to arrive at such concepts as organizations or systems. This larger context, upon analysis, will yield many organizations or systems; without analysis, it names and encloses a span of people and their behavior, together with the places and things which enable behavior. In one portion or another of this arena the individual will be perceiving and acting. Typical questions are: How do variations in the arena impinge upon the individual? How do his actions change with changes in the larger context?

A frequent approach to individual and context research measures some aspect of the arena and correlates it with some measured aspect of the person. The authoritarianism of a company might be related to employee satisfaction. Authoritarianism is operationally defined as the extent to which lower echelons of employees are included in decision-making meetings. A relation of high authoritarianism and low employee satisfaction might be discovered. The temptation would be to infer that employees react to exclusion from decision-making by becoming dissatisfied. For the purposes of our examples, let us postulate that employees did not care at all about how policy was decided, but cared about how it was communicated. Employee dissatisfaction resulted from sudden and unexplained changes in procedures. These changes could be anticipated in companies where employees were included in decision-making but *not* in authoritarian companies.

Sophisticated investigators would not commit the simple error described, but the example seems helpful to communicate the idea of premature correlation. It is quite possible to select a certain portion of a complex reality, measure it, find correlations with other measurements — even when properties other than those identified were responsible for the effects of interest. The difficulty in our fictitious example arose because of failure to understand how policy-decision events, events around the communication of policy change, and individual perceptions and reactions are connected and circuited. Often the connections between the variables in the gross context and the personal variables are filled through the assumption of intervening variables. And a popular site for intervening variables among psychologists is in the intrapersonal sector. For the example just given, intrapersonal sequencing might proceed this way: Because the lower echelon employees were left out of the decision-making meetings, they felt rejected. Because they felt rejected, they expressed dissatisfaction with the highly authoritarian company — a wrong inference. Given the example offered, it becomes obvious that no amount of "discovery" of intervening variables in the intrapersonal sector will help. The workers are reacting to sudden shifts of procedure. Until these impinging events are known, intrapersonal psychologizing not only is futile, but delays solution of the problem because it puts effort in the wrong place.

Another way of visualizing the difficulties of premature correlation is to consider problems in which one is asked to go from larger contexts to persons as presenting missing situational links. These situational units will provide the real locale of environment-and-transactions — which neither the total context nor the intervening variables can provide. The effects of contexts of different size upon individual behavior provide an illustrative issue.

If a gross context such as a school is involved, we can envision the large complex to which "size" refers: Large size means many students and teachers inhabiting a relatively extensive physical plant. Under conditions which are not yet completely understood, there is a positive relationship between size of school and dropout rates. Although we understand in a general way the features that a large school presents to students, we do not, therefore, understand just how the organizational qualities of size get through to them. We do know that students do not, at any one time, live in total schools, that, rather, they live in libraries, Spanish classes, and pep rallies, and that in these smaller, more proximate situations must occur the events which tell a marginal student whether to hang on or to drop out. Certainly we cannot believe that the school attributes of 2,000 students and a plant that covers two city blocks cause dropout behavior. Between the large school with its many rooms and inhabitants and the behaviors and attitudes of individuals are a number of specific time-place-behavior entities; the student lives in a succession of these entities; in a real sense, he does not live in a big school, nor does an assembly line worker live in the Ford River Rouge plant, nor a citizen live in New York City. Understanding of how the larger context relates to individual behavior requires knowledge of the parts, the inhabited subunits, of the context.

The necessity for dividing the large and complicated larger context into manageable portions is so obvious that it may seem banal to mention it. However, there are different ways to divide; we are pointing here to division into the concrete, nonabstracted, immediate contexts in which individuals live. Often the division is done another way: communications systems, role relationships, power networks, and other abstractions are used to mark off the larger complex. Concepts and methods for the study of these aspects of contexts are relatively well developed; it is often tempting to accept them as representatives of the actual pieces of the world in which individuals behave. However, these favorites of social science are not environments but analytic concepts referring to selected attributes of environments. For purposes of research, people can be considered as occupying roles in a hierarchy of roles, but these considerations are abstractions from realities which are both more concrete and more complicated than role descriptions. Students in the high school do have sociometric ties, but they live in hallways, academic classes, and football games; they don't live in the sociometric network. For this reason, the title of our presentation reads "People, *Settings*, and Larger Contexts" rather than "People, *Groups*, and Organizations." The position taken here is that the actual immediate contexts of persons are settings, not groups.

The belief that settings are the appropriate intervening links between individual behaviors and larger contexts rests upon two lines of thought. First, such a unit is observational rather than analytic. In dealing with the more complex real-world phenomena, it is presumed desirable that the parts have the character of entities in time and space and have their own boundaries and internal coherence. Categories or dimensions which are more abstract and which cut across numbers of these parts should be developed *after* one has grasped the more primary data available in these natural parts.

Secondly, research findings indicate that the behavior of persons is transformed via forces which reside in settings. If, for example, one follows the behavior of children as they change settings in a camp, or in a therapy installation, or in a small town, it is clear that setting shifts are accompanied by behavioral shifts (Gump & Kounin, 1959; Gump, Schoggen, & Redl, 1963; Raush, Dittmann, & Taylor, 1959, 1960; Ashton, 1964). Demonstration that the behavioral shifts are more extensive than those which common sense would suggest (such as walking on the sidewalks and sitting in the classroom) increases the evidence that the settings significantly coerce behavior.

The Conception of Behavior Setting

The proposed unit for the proximate context, for the "intervening situation," is the behavior setting as this unit is defined by Barker and Wright (1955). The presentation to follow first, illustrates and defines the behavior setting and the place of the individual within it; secondly, discusses samples of research employing the behavior setting concept; finally, summarizes the conceptual and methodological saliencies of this kind of ecological research.

The understanding of setting as employed here involves time, place, and thing elements coordinated to behavior phenomena; this coordination is expressed in the label used: *behavior setting*. Examples of behavior settings from a typical high school include: "after-school basketball game in the home gym," "Mr. Smith's Algebra I classes in Room 298," or "pre-Thanksgiving assembly in the auditorium." Urban high schools of the 2,000-student size will contain about 500 such behavior settings per year. The labels used to identify these settings were intended to convey both the milieu and the behavioral attributes of the setting: the word "assembly" points to the behavioral aspect but the setting also has a time — just before Thanksgiving, and a place — auditorium. Ordinarily, setting labels are shortened; frequently only the site is given. In a small town important behavior settings include: Pearl Cafe, Bank of Midwest, and Garnett's Grocery. The shortening of the label to a site designation does not change the fact that behavioral elements are a part of the setting; behavior is the *sine qua non* for a behavior setting. Thus Garnett's Grocery is a site open on weekdays from 8:00 to 6:00, containing merchandise *and* the behaviors of buying and selling. When the behavioral aspects cease — when the customers and Mr. Garnett have gone home — the behavior setting, Garnett's Grocery, has ceased to exist; only its hull remains.

A formal exposition of the behavior setting concept involves both structural and dynamic qualities:

. . . on the structural side, a behavior setting consists of one or more standing patterns of behavior-and-milieu with the milieu circumjacent and synomorphic to the behavior (Barker & Schoggen, 1966, p. 37).

The standing pattern of behavior is the behavior of persons *en masse*. Persons watch, cheer, and play at basketball; think about and discuss algebra in classrooms; listen to talks and sing songs in assembly; serve and consume food in the cafe. The behaviors have positions in time and space, and they are extraindividual realities; particular persons come and go, but characteristics of the standing patterns of behavior persist.

The milieu is a combination of site, or place, objects, and time. The milieu exists independently of anyone's perceptions of it, independently of the behavior to which it is coordinated. Furthermore, the milieu is circumjacent — or encompassing of — the setting's standing pattern of behaviors. Temporal and spatial boundaries enclose the behaviors. Finally, behavior and milieu have a structural similarity, a synomorphy. Boundaries of milieu and boundaries of setting behavior are congruent; the classroom door and the beginning of the period are place and time boundaries which mark where algebra (as opposed to gossiping and traveling in the hallway) begins. The fit of behavior to facts of milieu applies also to the interior structure of behavior settings. In algebra, blackboards (milieu elements) are synomorphic to teacher display of algebraic processes (behavior parts). Behavior and milieu synormorphies are so ubiquitous and so inevitable that we take them for granted. However, this essential fittingness between milieu and behavioral attributes makes it inappropriate to conceptualize behavior settings as entirely social or entirely physical.

The dynamic aspects of behavior settings refer to the relations between behavior-milieu synomorphs within one setting and between one setting and another. The array of identifiable synomorphs in a town, a school, or a factory is extensive: What is the criterion by which synomorphs are grouped to form settings? What separates one setting from another? This raises the dynamic issue which Barker describes as follows:

. . . Behavior-milieu parts of a behavior setting have a specified degree of interdependence among themselves that is greater than their interdependence with similar parts of other behavior settings (Barker & Schoggen, 1966, p. 37).

This conception will be elaborated further. But first it should be noted that an observer, without definitions and concepts, can usually discriminate where one setting begins and another ends. Although abstract considerations are applicable to the problem of setting boundaries, the entity quality of most settings requires only human perceptions. The beginnings and ends — both temporal and spatial — of drugstores and algebra classes are clearly marked; the question of just where the algebra setting stops and the cafeteria begins does not arise often. However, there are situations which make it clear that some standard must be established for determining what shall be included in a setting. Within the drugstore are found a fountain section, a pharmacy enclave, and a shopping area. Do these pieces of the store constitute three behavior settings or are they parts of one? The interdependence criterion cited above is used to answer such questions. If there were marked changes in the pharmacy area, would extensive related changes occur in the fountain and shopping areas? To the extent that changes would occur in adjacent areas, the areas are not independent and are not separate settings. To the extent that synomorphs within these areas are independent of variation in outside areas, they are separate settings. In the case of a small-town drugstore, application of interdependency measures reveals that the fountain, the pharmacy, and the shopping areas are parts of one setting. In a larger store, where specialized personnel and customers inhabit the pharmacy, where the "insulation" of the pharmacy from fountain is accomplished in a number of ways, interdependency measures would probably reveal pharmacy and fountain to be discrete behavior settings.

Exposition of the methods for measurement of interdependency of behavior-milieu synomorphs is beyond the scope of this presentation. Such methods have been described by Barker and Wright (1955). However, the notion of high synomorph interdependence within settings is essential to the behavior settings conception.

The immediate contexts of persons are behavior settings; these are ecological entities which exist in their own right. They have time and space coordinates; they are perceived as ecological units by persons acquainted with the environment in which they occur yet they exist independently of particular persons' perceptions. Behavior settings are "out there" phenomena.

The Place of the Person in the Behavior Setting

Since behavior settings exist only via the behavior of their inhabitants, one function of the person within the setting is that of component. Persons engage in those standing patterns of behavior which create and maintain the setting: the seller sells, and the buyer buys; the cheerleader leaps, and the pep club cheers. Persons lend themselves — and their behaviors — to the setting operations. Although all of the individual's behavior can be considered to occur in one setting or another, not all of this behavior is required by the setting. Usually some behavior will be participation in standing patterns of behavior, as in examples just mentioned, but other behavior may be irrelevant to the standing pattern of behavior — that is, it is not clearly a part of it nor antagonistic to it. The commuter may hum, whistle, or keep silent as he threads his way through traffic.

A second aspect of the person's place in the setting is that of an individual with his own life space, his own agenda for action. Within broad limits, the motivations of various persons in a setting can be quite heterogeneous. In the setting City Park, a teenager waits to meet his girl, a child arrives to ride his tricycle on the broad walks, and an elderly man surveys the passing scene. Quite a variety of motivations are tolerated within the same behavior setting; in fact, the variety contributes to the setting's stability.

The fact that the individual creates and maintains the environment he inhabits yields some problems in the tracing of cause-and-effect relationships. A simple and clean test of the effects of an environment upon an individual in the traditional independent-dependent variable format can create some difficulties in making inferences. What the setting does to a person depends upon what he does to it. We are accustomed to the model of an individual attempting an action, getting feedback, then reshaping the action. But there are also feedback loops running from settings to inhabitants and back again. Barker has referred to this as the E-O-E arc (Barker, 1965). Inhabitants of expressway settings who take a wrong turn will quickly confront a red warning sign

WRONG WAY

which correctly turning inhabitants may never see; they are processed differently by the E-O-E arc. The individual's place in the behavior setting is such that he is both context and inhabitant; to an extent, he creates his own environment. This dynamic inseparability of man and environment is, of course, not new. Taylor, writing of similar problems in human engineering, says that the man-machine combinations employed in this field necessitate a systems approach in which the man and the machine form a new unit which is hierarchically superior to both man and machine (Taylor, 1963).

To make the problem even more challenging, some persons in a setting are more influential in creating the context than others. In a classroom the teacher creates and arranges the sequences of much of the behavior setting that she inhabits; the influence of individual students upon setting events is relatively less. However, one fact can be demonstrated about the teacher's fate in her setting; although she may choose certain setting creations, once these are under way, the fact that she chose them does not lessen their impact upon her behavior. It may not be possible to separate what in the setting results from an individual's behavior and what results from factors foreign to himself, but it is possible to note that certain setting arrangements, whatever their origin, have certain results for individual behavior. As we hope to illustrate later, the teacher may indeed create her setting, but once certain events are set in motion, she is coerced just as are her students.

The place of the individual within the setting can, then, be described in terms of his penetration or position. Settings have audiences and actors, clients and doctors, learners and teachers. Persons who have power and responsibility in the setting can be termed performers. Common experience and research data (Barker & Gump, 1964) indicate that whether or not one is a setting performer has much to do with his behavior and experience within the setting and with his attitudes toward it.

Illustrative Research Anchored in the Behavior Setting Unit

Behavior settings, their number, kind, or interrelationships, can be employed as dependent variables in the investigation of larger arenas. For example, as communities, companies or schools change, this change is often reflected in the settings they contain. As schools consolidate, certain settings disappear and others are born; some may begin to function with new vigor, others can become anemic. Behavior settings may also serve as the site of independent variables, and the behavior of individuals can yield the dependent variables. For instance, one might study the qualities of campers' social interaction as the boys inhabit swimming versus craft settings (Gump & Sutton-Smith, 1955). Finally, there is the more extensive task of tracing effects from a larger arena (school, factory, community) to individual behavior; in this effort settings have a place as intervening situations. Such an investigation was undertaken by Willems (1965).

The basic lines in the Willems' investigation began at global environmental arenas (schools of contrasting size) and ended with behaviors and cognitions of individual high school juniors as these reacted to extracurricular settings. Attempts were made to test the influence of settings' qualities and of personal variables in this environment-to-behavior relationship.

A basic fact, clear from Willems' work and from other work that preceded it, is that as schools get larger, their settings also change. The shape of the institution changes along with its size. In particular, the larger schools have more people per setting while the small school has relatively undermanned settings. These settings' differences in the two institutions have far reaching implications; we will return to this issue later.

Willems was also interested in the experience of different kinds of persons in these contrasting school ecologies. One of the dimensions investigated was *marginality*. Marginal students were those whose intellectual attributes and home background histories indicated that they were relatively unsuited for high school life; that they were potential dropouts. Another dimension of the personal type was *audience sensitivity*. It was reasoned that social anxieties might cause students to avoid setting positions that gave them public visibility and responsibility.

A prime behavioral measure was the extent to which students occupied the more responsible, powerful positions in the settings, that is, the degree to which they became performers. Finally, Willems sought to increase understanding about how settings impinge upon individuals by examining the forces in the large and small schools operating to invite or press students into participation.[1]

Willems' data indicated that small school students were performers in almost twice as many settings as large school students; furthermore, marginal students in the small schools engaged in as many performances as regular students in the large school — and in three times as many as large school marginals. On the issue of performance, it was clear that "being marginal" was a severe handicap in the large school but not in the smaller ones.

Data from the audience sensitivity measure were random. No evidence could be found to support a relationship between audience sensitivity and occupation of focal positions. The quite reasonable prediction that persons who admitted to social fears would not be found

---

[1] Such forces were measured by a structured interview during which students were asked, regarding five representative settings in their school, "What, if any, were for you reasons for or pulls toward going to X *setting?*"

in responsible, before-the-public positions, failed. Several lines of explanation for this negative finding can be set out; one consistent with the general orientation of settings' theory is that personality attributes become different phenomena in different contexts and, with regard to certain dimensions, they can become irrelevant.

What accounts for the large and small school differences in number of setting performances? Why are marginal students in the large school so "out of it" as compared to marginals in the smaller schools? Willems' results were predicted on the basis of a size theory developed by Barker (Barker & Gump, 1964). In brief, this theory states that as settings employ decreased manpower, increased forces will press upon the members to undertake the essential tasks of the setting. And a necessary supplement to this basic idea is that persons available will tend to be used — whether or not they are favorably equipped for the setting tasks. In the undermanned settings, there will be "less sensitivity to and less evaluation of differences between people. . . . When essential personnel are in short supply, it is necessary to 'accept' those persons who are available and can do the job" (Barker & Gump, 1964, p. 24).

The outcome of Willems' study follows predictions from Barker's theory regarding the relation between setting size and individual behavior. Small schools produce undermanned settings; forces relevant to the undermanned settings press inhabitants to take over essential roles; the pressures include inhabitants whose qualifications make them "marginal."

If the Barker theory regarding forces is correct, not only should the outcomes just cited hold, but measurement of the forces themselves should show that more pressures to setting participation operated in the smaller schools. Further, one would expect that forces upon small school marginal students would be quite extensive as compared to large school marginals. The more optimally manned large-school settings do not need the marginal student's effort; these settings will not call upon him for participation.

The portion of the Willems' data most central to the issue of whether settings and their inhabitants are pressing students is the data on *strictly induced forces*. These forces were represented by those statements which indicated an environmental feedback encouraging participation and discouraging nonparticipation. Examples of such statements are:

"I could see the dance would need girls."
"I was supposed to sell concessions."
"If you are in choir, you are expected to go."

Data on these induced forces clearly confirm predictions:

1. Small school students report three times as many such forces as large school students.
2. Small school marginal students report six times as many induced forces as large school marginals. On the dimension of forces, as on that of performance, the large school marginals displayed particularly depressed scores.

The Willems' data indicate how effects, which originate in larger contexts and impinge upon individuals, can be predicted and confirmed through use of behavior settings as intervening situations. Larger school contexts provided settings of certain qualities; these qualities affected inhabitants to produce certain behaviors and cognitions (experienced forces). The function of person variables differed according to the kind of context and kind of variable. A marginality variable was crucially handicapping in the large context and not in the small; the person variable of audience sensitivity was irrelevant in both.

Willems investigated an array of settings and/or persons who occupied different setting positions. Except for attention to the performer-nonperformer positions, Willems did not consider the interior structure of settings and how variations here shape individual behavior. Understanding of ecology-to-person connections might be advanced if study focused upon one kind of setting and upon individuals operating from one position through various subunits of that setting. The author and his associates undertook to study how teachers in the third-grade classroom behavior setting were affected by variations in that setting's internal formations.

The interior structure, the micro-ecology, of the classroom has been described in several fashions. Some accounts are physical and geographical. The parts of the classroom are said to be: the teacher's desk, children's desks, the reading corner, the cloakroom, and the sink area. This approach is objective, but sharply inconsistent with a behavioral understanding of settings; merely the milieu qualities are identified, the standing patterns of behavior, the action structures are ignored. At another extreme, the ecology of the classroom has been equated with the acts the teachers directed toward students. This conception has the advantage of centering upon a class of pupil inputs which may be expected to make more of a difference to his behavior than milieu facts; however, it is an aborted view. Not only are the thing-place realities ignored, but the action structure which challenges and guides the student is also passed over. Naturally occurring internal differentiations, clearly existing within the classroom, are blotted out by a stream of teacher stimuli.

If one takes the time to watch a day's activities in an elementary school classroom, a compelling picture emerges of the differentiations within the day's events. A number of phenomena will be seen to change simultaneously. The *concern* of the teacher and pupils (arithmetic or milk-money), the leader role of the teacher (watch and help or check-off names), the behavior mechanisms of the pupils (studying and writing or listening for one's name), the materials of the activity (books or teacher's account ledger), and other events will stop or start more or less in concert. These starts and stops mark the boundaries of internal portions of the classroom, which have been labelled *segments*. Constituted along lines similar to the behavior setting, these segments have their own behavior patterns, their own nonpsychological milieu, and display synomorphy between milieu and behavior. They will also have an action structure which integrates inter-participant behavior. The segments differ from settings in their lack of independence from one another. As opposed to settings, segments share the same leader, the same nonleader participants, the same or adjacent sites and times, and so forth.

Segments differentiate the classroom events both cross-sectionally and longitudinally: at certain times, several segments may be in operation at once; also one segment follows another throughout the school day. The succession of segments in a third grade might run as follows.

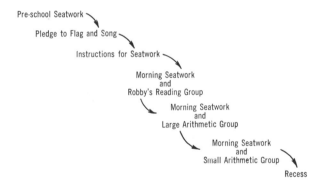

Studies so far accomplished with specially selected segments indicate that behaviors of both pupils and teachers can be markedly affected by the kind of ecological unit being inhabited. For example, pupil inattention is systematically less in seatwork than in small recitation groups (Kowatrakul, 1959; Kounin, 1966). Negative affect in teacher social action toward pupils seems to rise in segments which involve arts and crafts (Hughes, 1959). In the present study, two full days for each of six classroom teachers were recorded by on-the-scene dictation and time-lapse photography. All teacher acts toward students were dictated.

From the records and the pictures it was possible to recreate the segmental structure of the classroom. One question concerned how the teachers' acts would vary from one segment to another. There are, of course, certain kinds of teachers' acts which are almost inevitable for certain classroom activities. If the teacher establishes a drawing lesson, many of her acts must be devoted to obtaining materials, demonstrating techniques, and so forth. If the teacher is conducting a recitation, questioning acts are intrinsic to the operation of the recitation segments. There are teacher acts, however, which are not so required by the given activity. One set of such acts is criticizing and blocking. The two kinds of social actions can be seen as similar in that both are *counterforces* emitted by the teacher to stop or forestall pupil action. One can suppose that such acts are most necessary when pupil activity diverges, or threatens to diverge, from that desired by the teacher. At first it was supposed that certain segments might be especially likely to provoke teacher counterforce activity. Segments from several classroom days were displayed in sequence and the incidents of counterforce acts were coordinated to this sequence. It was clear that counterforce acts were concentrating in certain segments, but it was even more obvious that these tended to cluster about the *transitions* between segments. All teachers' first day observations were checked: in each of the six teachers, the counterforce activity was heaviest at transitions. A replication was possible: all teachers' second day observations were checked; in five of the six cases, again counterforce activity was markedly greater at transitions. Overall, counterforce activity accounted for 10 per cent of teachers' acts in the transitions and 5 per cent in the segment proper.

Full discussion of reasons for the spurt of counterforce activity requires data presentation beyond the scope of this paper; however, it is clear that the reasons must deal with ecological factors. The fashion has been to blame the negative behavior indicated by counterforce activity upon the teacher's personality, or upon her authoritarian philosophy; in the present study, one may assume that a variety of personalities and philosophies operated and yet all teachers seemed compelled in the same direction. Manifestly, the understanding of the behavior of the teacher in her classroom setting must rest upon knowledge of the behavior-demand qualities of segments of that setting.

A final example of research employing the behavior setting as the key concept involves community change. Transformations in communities frequently have been tracked and represented by use of demographic and economic data. However, there is little systematic information regarding how demographic, economic, or other forces relating to the larger context operate in the immediate environments of people. Barker and Schoggen (1966) have been able to represent and compare two communities at two different time periods in terms of the kinds of behavioral spaces available and the use of these by the towns' entire populations. Through enumeration and discription of behavior settings, all of the nonfamilial scenes and happenings of the two towns became available for analysis. Data generated by this research are rich and challenging; we must limit our attention to a few salient points relating to a single theme: changes in religious settings and activities in the American town.

A picture of a church as an environment-offering institution can be developed out of a description of its settings. The relative extent to which the settings are inhabited can be added to the picture. Degree of habitation is expressed as occupancy time, the number of person-hours the town's inhabitants spend in a behavior setting.

A major church setting was the Sunday Morning Worship Service; prominent as this setting was, it accounted for less than half of the time that the town's residents spent in church activities. The remainder of church occupancy time was devoted to Sunday School, religious study groups and religious fellowship groups, weddings and funerals, and an assortment of lesser settings.

Equipped with knowledge of the kinds of settings that constitute the town's religious institutions and with occupancy-time data, the social scientist can present changes in religious environments in a quite objective fashion. What happened in the sphere of church-generated settings over the nine years from 1954 to 1963?

The amount of time spent in church environments by town residents decreased by 21 per cent (from 42,000 hours to 33,000 hours). During this period the town's population increased by 16 per cent and their time devoted to town settings increased 21 per cent (from 900,000 to 1,100,000 hours). Clearly, the loss of time in church settings could not be considered a part of a general reduction in public behavior.

More is involved in the changed picture than simple shrinkage of time spent in church settings. The shape of these institutions appears to have changed. Such a modification appears when the proportion of occupancy time invested in settings of different types is examined.

Sunday Morning Worship Services did not decline in participation; these were as well supported in 1963 as in 1954. Occupancy time in religious study groups increased by 34 per cent but decreased in religious fellowship groups by 85 per cent. (Time spent in the religious study groups was far from compensating for the time lost in the fellowship area.) Sunday School occupancy time decreased by 35 per cent. In general, it appears that time spent beyond the traditional morning service was sharply curtailed. By 1963, the churches were less successful in claiming the interests and efforts of townspeople for church affairs beyond the traditional minimum – the Sunday Morning Service.

Parenthetically, it is interesting to note that different conclusions can be derived when the investigation is concerned with one, as opposed to all, of the institution's behavioral areas. Use of attendance at Sunday Morning Services as an index of church importance in the community affairs yields inferences quite contrary to those derived from the inspection of occupancy time in the total span of church settings.

Consideration of the forces possibly responsible for the alterations in church environments goes beyond our limit; however, two factors can be touched upon.

Influences from the churches' national organizations have discouraged establishments of the more social and money-raising affairs; group study of religious sources and issues have been encouraged. This outside force perhaps accelerated the decline of social fellowship occasions and was probably responsible for the increase in the religious study groups. Secondly, a number of new settings in the community appeared to compete with the churches for inhabitants' time. Some of these, such as the golf course, conflicted directly with Sunday church occasions; others provided social and recreational possibilities which might have detracted from the churches' weekday enterprises.

This discussion began by proposing that an environmental unit labelled *behavior setting* could serve as a useful intervening situation between persons and larger contexts. The nature of the setting unit was illustrated and defined. The utility of the setting conception was exemplified in the outline of three research efforts. Salient qualities of the behavior setting, distinguishing it from some other extra-individual units employed by social science, are the following:

1. The behavior setting has a locus in time and space. One can point at a setting; he can go into it.
2. The setting exhibits a pattern of congruencies, of synomorphies, between physical and temporal milieu elements and aspects of behavior. At the level of setting environment, aspects or behavior and milieu are seen – not as in interaction – but as new units interdependent with one another.
3. The setting has a boundary; this boundary is relatively close-in, relatively proximate to inhabitants; the setting is an enclosure of here-and-now size.

The behavior setting conception is the result of a research orientation which assumes that behaviors and environments form a patterned reality. This reality exists independently of those organizations imposed by scientific investigation; its nature is more adequately comprehended if one listens to the phenomenon before applying traditional conceptualization.

An implication of the listening stance relates to determination of units. It is assumed that behavior or environments will offer some, but not infinite, alternatives for the drawing of unit boundaries. The common assertion that unitization depends upon the interests of the investigator is a partial truth. Arbitrary boundary demarcation can yield pieces instead of units. Further, the nature of what is to be included in the units is to be decided by respecting that which listening produces from the phenomenon rather than by logic of pre-established categories. Anthropocentric psychology considers man and his behavior as forming one realm, his environments another; "parts" of the environment are stated as physical, social, and cultural. To mix behavior and environment, to combine the physical and social into units, is considered the mixing of incommensurate realms. But listening suggests that environments do not come boxed into physical, social, and cultural environments. Our conceptual heritage comes this way, but not our environments. The research outlook described here suggests that it is more appropriate to assert that environments come as arrays and sequences of behavior settings.

Bibliography

Ashton, Margaret. An ecological study of the stream of behavior. Unpublished master's thesis, University of Kansas, 1964.

Barker, R. G. Explorations in ecological psychology. *American Psychologist*. 1965, 20, 1–14.

Barker, R. G., & Gump, P. *Big school, small school*. Palo Alto: Stanford University Press, 1964.

Barker, R. G., & Schoggen, P. A quantitative study of environmental change over a decade within an American and an English town. Final report to The National Science Foundation, 1966.

Barker, R. G., & Wright, H. F. *Midwest and its children*. New York: Harper and Row, 1955.

Gump, P., & Kounin, J. S. Issues raised by ecological and "classical" research efforts. *Merrill-Palmer Quarterly of Behavior and Development*, 1959, 60, 6, 145–152.

Gump, P., Schoggen, P., & Redl, F. The behavior of the same child in different milieus. In R. G. Barker (Ed.), *The stream of behavior*. New York: Appleton-Century-Crofts, 1963. Pp. 169–202.

Gump, P., & Sutton-Smith, B. Activity-setting and social interaction: A field study. *American Journal of Orthopsychiatry*, 1955, 755–760.

Hughes, Marie M., & Associates. Assessment of quality of teaching in elementary schools. Unpublished research report, University of Utah, 1959.

Kounin, J. S., Friesen, W. V., & Norton, A. Evangeline. Managing emotionally disturbed children in regular classrooms. *Journal of Educational Psychology,* 1966, **57**, 1–13.

Kowatrakul, S. Some behaviors of elementary school children related to classroom activities and subject areas. *Journal of Educational Psychology,* 1959, **50**, 121–128.

Raush, H. L., Dittmann, A. T., & Taylor, T. J. Person, setting and change in social interaction. *Human Relations,* 1959, **12**, 361–378.

———. Person, setting and change in social interaction: II. A normal control study. *Human Relations,* 1960, **13**, 305–332.

Taylor, F. V. Human engineering and psychology. In Koch, S. (Ed.), *Psychology: A study of a science.* Vol. 5. *The process areas, the person and some applied fields.* . . . New York: McGraw-Hill, 1963. Pp. 831–907.

Willems, E. P. Participation in behavior settings in relation to three variables: Size of behavior settings, marginality of persons, and sensitivity to audiences. Unpublished doctoral thesis, University of Kansas, 1965.

A Summing Up—
Toward a
More Coherent
Future of Research[1]

BERNARD P. INDIK

*Institute of Management
and Labor Relations
Rutgers — The State University*

At the outset of our adventure into a large and relatively uncharted area we noted a number of basic issues. One of the first of these issues is how we should divide the areas of inquiry so as to allow most adequately for clarity of understanding, theoretical accuracy, and empirical testability. My initial suggestion was to divide our area of interest into several levels of analysis: people, in groups, in organizations functioning in sociocultural contexts. Each of these levels can be divided into structural and dynamic subclasses of variables.

Sells has suggested that a taxonomy of organizations might focus on their general system characteristics — including goals, personnel composition, organizational structure, technology, and environment. He then proposed to apply his system in an analysis of the multiman, extended duration spaceship social system problem, and his study of the similarities and differences among sixty campus student organizations. His results show the interdependence of organizations and their members and the total physical, social, and cultural environments.

McGrath and Altman (1966) have proposed earlier that a small number of basic dimensions of data were sufficient to describe the essential properties of small group variables and their relationships to each other. They included: (1) *object* (member, group or environment); (2) *mode* (static or dynamic properties of objects); (3) *descriptive-evaluative* judgments made about objects; (4) *source* of data (member, group, and experimenter); and (5) *viewpoint* from

[1] This chapter was written while the author was working, in part, under Contract Nonr-0001, Group Psychology Branch, Office of Naval Research, Washington, D. C. Reproduction, translation, publication, use, and disposal in whole or in part by or for the United States Government is permitted.

which the data object was described (subjective, projective, or objective). This system was tested through the notion of operational concordance, that is, the more similar two variables were in the above operational properties, the greater the likelihood of their being empirically associated. Their work essentially confirms the concordance hypothesis (McGrath and Altman, 1966). This classification system, however, is concerned with principles which are nearly devoid of substantive content and are particularly describable in methods of measurement terms. Could it be that the invariances found (the consistencies) are mainly to be attributed to that which we have been noting as "methods" variance? Altman further points out the need for systems that have both formal and substantive bases.

Altman focused on the various important choicepoints that any developer of a classification system must consider and turned to studies in other fields which have attempted to deal with these questions to see what might be gleaned from the natural sciences and library sciences that we may find useful. From these considerations he noted that attention must be given to classifying three aspects of research knowledge: (1) behavior, (2) antecedent and general situational conditions, and (3) forms of relationship among behaviors as well as between behavior and situational conditions. This is, of course, related to the question of the appropriate unit of classification. The level of analysis, of course, should be appropriate to the intent and purpose of the taxonomy, and the classification system should consider one or two levels of behavior above and below that of primary interest.

Altman also pointed out that there has been little interest in taxonomies of social and work situation characteristics. He further notes that without a general taxonomy of situations, the synthesis of research information is limited to relating behavioral events to a fragmented nonsystematic listing of situational characteristics. Another point also made by Altman is: "What form should relationship statements take, and what criteria should be used to determine whether a relationship is valid and reliable?" He noted that it may be fallacious to impose the same statistical requirements on all types of relationships.

Besides the questions related to the unit of study, Altman called for considering as important the dynamic versus static properties of units as was illustrated by both McGrath and Altman (1966) and Indik (1963). Furthermore, energy transformation processes such as operator-operand linkages, involving energy expenditures of physical and psychological types (cognitive, social-emotional, perceptual, and motor), demand attention. The magnitude or intensity of energy transformation processes as the operator deals with the operand is an important cross-cutting attribute of the relationship. Furthermore,

underlying basic dimensions might include distribution in time, distribution in space of expeditures of energy, and the characteristics of
the total environmental milieu (the ecological setting). The question
of the dilemma regarding the number of dimensions and the relative
importance or relative weight of those dimensions is also suggested, but
no answer is as yet apparent. Seemingly, this is an empirical question.
Finally, Altman turns to the question of testing the adequacy of any
classification system and notes Deutsch's (1966) important work in
this area.

This summary of the first three chapters makes clear that many of
the problems perceived by students of individual behavior, group
dynamics, and organizational behavior are really quite similar. First,
we are all interested in studying social systems; it seems to me that
individuals as well as groups and organizations may be viewed as social
systems. Secondly, we all seem to be interested in how the structure of
these particular systems influences the dynamic operation of the respective systems or settings. We are becoming more concerned that the
analysis of the given system or setting should concern itself not only
with its internal component structure, its operational processing and
product outcome, but with its relationships to its external context. It is
then in order for us to develop a more adequate approach to the understanding of this complex material. The organization and systematiza-
tion of the magnitude of data available are a challenge to our intellect
and creative rationality.

Both Sells and the present author separately suggest how a basic
kind of outline of a classification scheme might be approached. Neither
of us is completely satisfied with what we now have proposed. We
needed a place to start, and so reasonable attempts were made. Several
of the papers in this volume explore various aspects of the proposed
systems of classification. We shall learn how to modify our initial points
of view from this and future research.

The series of papers following the Altman paper deal with the
specific subareas of interest and examine in greater detail the various
panels that were proposed earlier. Popenoe explores the sociocultural
environment of individuals in groups in organizations. He is particularly partial to Sorokin's point of view of how culture, society, and
personality can be analyzed. Further, Popenoe feels that groups, as
distinguished from organizations, were not sufficiently different in fundamental dimensions as to warrant separate categories. Berrien also
points out the similarity in dimensions appearing in my classification
scheme at the levels of groups and organizations and argued for a
general systems approach that encompassed the common features of
groups and organizations. While there are similarities, the distinction

between groups and organizations is important and necessary both conceptually and empirically in order to allow for differential explanations of relations or conflict between groups within organizations, individuals and organizations, and organizations and their environments. Further, empirically, organizations exist as a supersystem in which groups and individuals as subsystems are structured and function in an interactive way. Also, it should be noted that the structure of organizations is more formalized than that of groups and frequently contains a varying number of groups within its boundaries. Weick offers the suggestion that the distinction between any two levels of complexity, whether group versus organization or individual versus group, can be identified by the existence of some new emergent feature in the output of the next higher level system. Such a position is consonant with Berrien's. From this point of view, the group versus organization distinction becomes an empirical question, unrelated to the descriptive dimensions of structure or function.

Organizations are a particularly relevant level of concern also since they seem to be particularly important in constraining, conditioning, and controlling human behavior in our modern industrial society. Etzioni's paper describes some of the forms of control that organizations exercise over individual behavior and the mechanisms of compliance that individuals manifest in reaction to various types of control over their behavior. He further notes many of the ways in which the forms of control (power) used are related to other organizational variables. While power is a central variable, some people would feel that primary concern with this variable is too narrow a focus for adequate organizational level analysis since many other variables are also central and important. That is, the control-compliance association is a relationship of importance. However, he notes that "while the two factors (control and compliance) affect each other, each is affected by other factors, and hence they may vary independently and no one-to-one relationship is expected." Etzioni also uses this complex dimension as a lever to explore relationships of this variable to other variables. The complexity of the findings presently available to test his theoretical propositions shows the value of these organization level variables as emergent properties to be considered theoretically at the organizational level of analysis.

The question may be raised here as in other substantive areas. Why base our theories on specific variables of a first level of abstraction (like the kind of control-compliance relationship), when these variables clearly do not show a consistant and invariant relationship to each other? On the other hand, if we focus on the next higher level of abstraction as per Indik (1963) or McGrath and Altman (1966), we find that much more consistent and invariant findings occur. Maybe it is at this relatively more generic level that the lawfulness we seek is to be found.

It is, however, interesting to note that most of the findings suggested by the theory explored by Etzioni are supported by the data he presents. There is even a partially supportive psychological concomitant theory proposed by Katz and Kahn (1966). They propose that there are four motive patterns that can evoke the behavior required in organizations.

Katz and Kahn (1966)	Etzioni (1961)
1. Legal compliance	1. Coercive power — alienative involvement
2. Instrumental satisfaction	2. Remunerative power — calculative involvement
3. Internalization of organizational goals	3. Normative power — moral involvement
4. Self-expression	4. (none comparable)

Equally interesting in this comparison is that Etzioni (1961) started from a sociological point of view and had to develop psychological linkages, whereas Katz and Kahn (1966) started from a psychological point of view and have moved to a general systems approach, in order to find a more adequate and justified total viewpoint.

Berrien's paper picks up the general systems theory point of view and explores our present understanding of this theoretical point of view with reference to groups. It is clear from the outset that this theory is a dynamic one. It is intended to explain the processes that operate in groups and the relationship of groups to their surrounding supersystems. It is a sad commentary on the present state of our knowledge that most of the evidence that Berrien has brought to bear on his theoretical point of view is of an anecdotal or case-study variety. Where are the experiments that provide the documented evidence for or against the hypotheses suggested by this paper? They are now few and far between. We might ask why? Berrien suggests two reasons. First, the approach is too recent, and second, the requisite research designs involve frequent or continuous measurement over an extended period of time. Might I suggest a third reason: the methodology for assessing the variables to be considered has not yet been fully worked out. Procedures for continuous measurement are not only more difficult, but to satisfy the requirements of the theory, but they should not interfere with the process that is under study (Indik and Tyler 1963).

Finally, let me note that theory itself is not always an explicit guide to the empirical variables to be measured. Take the term "group need satisfaction." Conceptually one may be able to define it, but empirically how can one be sure that all of it is measured in any group? Different members may receive gratification of many different needs from their interactions within a given group at a given point in time, not to mention the satisfaction of different needs at different points in time in the same group. This is more than a purely methodological problem. This problem is more nearly comparable to measuring group aggression. It is the type of problem that at this time complicates adequate empirical testing of this theory.

Berrien also makes some interesting suggestions with reference to re-ordering the classification system that I have proposed so that it is more compatible with the general systems approach. It seems to me that this direction ought to be pursued, for at the present writing I can suggest only the few very general hypotheses that appear in the earlier paper in this volume. It would be quite valuable to join the classification scheme to a more explicit theoretical approach that more specifically suggests the functional relationships among the variables considered; however more work needs to be done before we reach this point.

Popenoe's work takes the analytic framework of Sorokin as a major point of departure. A theory of social systems at the level of socio-cultural units such as communities and societies, says Popenoe, must be modified in some considerable way, and the theories built around the specific properties and hierarchical levels of organized groups do not apply to communities and societies. He exemplifies this point in his discussions of territorial-ecological analysis at the community level and of cultural integration at both the community and societal levels. It is of particular importance, he notes, that the utility of a general systems approach decreases with the increasing levels of hierarchy to be studied. He feels that there is a need for an analysis paralleling Sorokin's at the sociocultural level of reality that will enable integration of the larger cultural world with the organized group and personality system. He can only make some very general suggestions as to the structure of this type of integration, and little specific guidance is available at present, except for his noting some of the categories of variables that should be considered. It seems that, unlike most of the other contributors to this volume, he favors the theoretical approach at the general level which leads to the specific variables, whereas the more generally accepted approached exemplified by Sells, Altman, and myself has tended to start with the specific variables and then look for the generic attributes of their relationships. Both strategies are probably necessary at this point.

Golembiewski's chapter adds to our knowledge in the area of how some of the variables that fall at the various levels considered fit together. In dealing with how groups relate to their supersystems (organizations), he notes five linkages: the first is called "structural integration," which is described as the congruence of formal status and informal rank. Second, the functional roles of leadership is asserted to be a strong linkage of the group to the larger system. Third, he considers the properties of tasks as an important but relatively unexplored linkage between the group and the organization. Fourth, he mentions the structure of the managerial units as an important linkage variable. Fifth, he note differences in technology which he considers as important linkage variables. As an added bonus, he presents birth order as a variable that links the group to the personality or individual level of analysis. He considers the fund of new research dealing with the importance of this variable and its ties with the individual level of analysis.

Williams' work picks up the thread of how individual-level variables are relevant to behavior of individuals in organizations. He emphasized particularly developmental personality dimensions of three quite different modes. First was a cognitive (perceptual and learning) mode including dimensions described as concrete versus abstract, rigid versus flexible, intolerant of ambiguity versus tolerant of ambiguity, looking for immediate gratification versus looking for delayed gratification, and regularly reinforced versus aperiodically reinforced. Second, he considered values, beliefs, and motives, which can be characterized as pessimistic versus optimistic, past or present orientated versus future orientated, dominated by fear of failure versus the need to achieve, and security seeking versus risk taking. Third, he viewed the interpersonal mode, including dimensions described as mistrustful versus trusting, autocratic-authoritarian versus democratic-nonauthoritarian, traditional versus modern, and prejudiced versus nonprejudiced.

Through the use of the above dimensions he discusses the relationship between personality characteristics and variables at the level of the organization. The lack of an explicit and empirically demonstrated developmental theory, either at the personality level or organization level, suggested to him that a number of dimensions might be simultaneously investigated at both levels at the same time. This approach defers the question of what current variables should be considered and what variables are appropriate and inappropriate at the personality and organizational levels of analysis. His approach also bypasses the question of how we parsimoniously divide up the myriad variables that might be selected. Do we use the criteria of their being mutually exclusive of each other and exhaustive of the domain, or do we temporarily select that list of variables that looks to be relevant, and hope that future research will provide the evidence by which parsimony will be instituted as a criterion? This is a tactical question.

The Seashore and Yuchtman chapter struggles with one of the most perplexing problems in the study of organizations: How should we conceptualize and measure organizational performance? The approach to this problem that Seashore and Yuchtman take is that no one criterion (except the unmeasurable ultimate criterion) can reasonably be used by itself to represent organizational performance. One must account for, or at least consider, a full roster of penultimate criteria variables. Theoretically, this scheme emphasizes that organizational performance is extremely complex and probably involves hundreds of variables. However, it is necessary to consider both the elements of universality and elements of uniqueness among these variables. They acknowledge that organizational performance fluctuates with time and that few variables can be expected to reveal much consistency over time, even though the network of variables may have rather stable features. Further, they assume that the ultimate goal of the organization is not a part of the actual process of the organization's life and thus is an unmeasurable construct. It follows, they say, that effectiveness can be assessed then only in terms of the position of an organization on all the penultimate dimensions.

The Seashore and Yuchtman chapter reports in detail on an empirical test of their suppositions by data obtained from seventy-five insurance sales agencies. The data are, of course, restricted. Their findings refer to organizations of relatively uniform size that have similar formal goals and that use similar methods and resources to produce the end products or outcomes of these kinds of organizations. Further, all the data used in analysis were basically "hard" indices of performance. They, of course, were not able to measure all performance variables, but selected 76 variables, eliminating others on the grounds of duplication, unreliability of measurement, or insufficient variability or dubious accuracy.

Factor analyses of these performance variables showed some considerable consistency across time and led to the following tentative conclusions. First, Seashore and Yuchtman essentially reject all conceptual schemes that link organizational effectiveness solely and only to values of some one or another goal element in the environment. They instead suggest that standards of effectiveness are to be sought with reference to the organization itself. Second, they argue that one needs to avoid the conceptual trap of imputing goals to organizations, for organizations do not try to do anything. They exist and function. Their third point is that the ten factors extracted for these sales organizations probably contain some basic dimensions having general meaning for all organizations and others that are unique to these and similar organizations.

We can also say that other performance dimensions that were not measured by at least two variables and which could not have therefore come out in their analysis might well be either general in nature or specific to the kind of organization that they were studying. It does seem relevant to follow their final suggestion, though, which is to apply similar procedures to other populations or organizations. A comparative understanding of different sorts of organizations is necessary to determine which of these underlying dimensions are universal, and which are specie-specific to particular types of organizations. It also seems reasonable to suggest that performance measures not just be limited to "hard" measures but include other dimensions that are less measurable but equally important when analysis of organizational performance is the major consideration.

The series of papers dealing with substantive issues having to do with individuals, groups, and organizations leads us to the position that it is necessary in dealing with these problems to be equally concerned with methodological issues. McGrath and Weick turn their attention to some of the important methodological questions. McGrath's major point is illustrated by his several different kinds of analytic schemes. He uses facet analysis, as an input design, to provide a useful mechanism for building analysis frameworks for the study of the behavior of individuals in small groups or organizations. Facet analysis does seem to be a very technically difficult approach to use, because it attempts to be as complete as possible. It attempts to consider all relevant properties in an exhaustive way, and it tends to ask for measurement of all persons on each property. Next it is necessary to categorize all persons on each property, such that each property has a set of mutually exclusive values and that these values are logically separated and multifaceted. This of course makes for a very cumbersome method of approach, but it is thorough. However, one needs to consider that the more measures taken the more likely the measurement process will interfere with the process that is being measured. Further, the analysis problem becomes large and the measurement problem tedious and difficult to say the least. There needs to be an empirically based guideline developed in order to cut down judiciously the number of dimensions approached in this manner.

Weick, on the other hand, spends most of his effort dealing with ways in which experimental methodology can be applied to the problems discussed in the earlier papers. Some of his most insightful points refer to the basic questions that have plagued social science for many years. How may it be established that entities such as groups and organizations exist? If they do, what are their key properties? Further, in what ways do properties of these entities at different levels interact?

Questions also arise from Weick's analysis concerning the priorities among levels as determinants of behavior, the interaction among levels in the determination of behavior, and the idea that as conditions change, different levels assume more or less importance as determinants of action. Weick also suggests that as stimulus situations become more ambiguous, persons tend to behave in terms of that level which provides the clearest prescription for action. Another question is: What conditions expand or contract the range of dimensions which control behavior?

Weick proposed several experimental approaches which should help to develop answers to these questions; however, the questions he raises do, by and large, remain unanswered at this time. Hopefully, the future pattern of research will enable us to find the answers to these questions.

Gump's contribution to this book is substantial, for he has broadened our perspectives on several counts. We had conceived of the idea of considering people, groups, organizations, and their sociocultural environment as the major components of the analytic framework. Gump points out that persons exist in "settings" (their proximate situations) and that they also upon analysis exist in larger contexts which enclose "a span of people and their behavior, together with the places and things which enable behavior." He further points out that understanding the impact of the larger context on the individual requires knowledge of the parts, the inhabited subunits of the context. Here we can agree. The point of departure comes with Gump's preference for the concept "setting" and "larger contexts" as contrasted with the more usual concepts of "groups," "organizations," and the sociocultural environment. He argues that, on two counts, his concepts are more appropriate. First, settings are observational rather than analytic. Second, if one follows the flow of behavior as individuals change settings, it is clear that setting shifts are accompanied by behavior shifts.

Gump notes that "settings" have time and place aspects, as well as behavioral aspects. Behavior settings are neither entirely social nor entirely physical. The setting shows a pattern between physical and temporal milieu components and aspects of behavior. The setting also generally has a quite easily recognized boundary. Finally, Gump suggests "that environments do not come boxed into physical, social, and cultural environments. Our conceptual heritage comes this way but not our environments." The implication from Gump is clear that for him it is more accurate to assert that environments come as arrays and sequences of behavior settings.

Some Central Issues as Yet Unresolved

It can be seen from the above summaries and the papers that preceded them that there are a number of important issues which need to be considered in order to present some closure and set the stage for the future. First of all, let us focus on what the appropriate analysis units are. Initially, I argued for the analysis frame of the individual, group, organization, and sociocultural context. Popenoe has argued that the distinction between group and organization is not central enough. More basic argument has come from Gump, who feels that the distinctions to be made should be among people, settings, and larger contexts. However we decide to resolve this question, it needs solution so that we may focus on some other important problems.

Another central problem is semantic confusion. The same terms seem to have different meanings, and different terms have the same meanings. Even more confusing, some terms have no clear meanings. Clarification is necessary. There ought to be some common agreement on at least essential terms both conceptually and in terms of empirical measurement. Further, there ought to be a readily available source that shows the definitions presently held and the evidence (reliability and validity) that the measurement instruments do in fact measure the conceptually defined dimensions. In a crude way we have attempted to do this very recently (Indik, Hockmeyer, and Castore, 1968). The likelihood is very strong that considerable modification will be necessary; however, we need some first steps in this direction before much more progress can be made.

We also need to consider that most of our methods of analysis are tied to a rather static analysis methodology and that what is needed is a more dynamic analysis mode. It is also clear that not only is multivariate analysis necessary but multilevel multivariate analysis techniques also, because of the natural complexity of dimensions that affect the variability of behavior of people.

Weick has suggested another related problem: that sometimes variables at one level (the group) are more important to understanding behavioral variability while at other times variables at another level (the organization) are more controlling. The problem is that we don't quite know when which level is more relevant. Another kind of problem is the question of how we know when we have fully developed an appropriate number of variables that are exhaustive and parsimonious. Even with Deutsch's excellent recent paper (1966) the practical problem is not solved although a fine guide is available.

A not unrelated issue is how should we conceive of task variables. That is, how do task variables fit into our consideration of behavior in organizations? In my original chapter of this book, I tried to summarize many of the aptitude and skill dimensions that have been studied by psychologists and the present state of thinking on these problems. Further, I did note in panel six those attributes of performance that I see as central. This book, however, has not focused particularly on task variables, as they have been analyzed in detail in studies like Fleishman, (1967), Mangelsdorf (1965), or Miller (1965). We have been more concerned with the social constraints and controls over behavior variance that come from groups, organizations, and their sociocultural environments.

Several rather interrelated factors affect the consistency of behavior of members of organizations. The first and probably most significant is the set of formal role definitions that seems to be characteristic of most large complex organizations. These role definitions specify and define the range of legitimate behaviors of individuals who occupy their specific designated roles. It is important for the consistency and continued existence of the organization that the role definitions are clear among the members and are meshed together so that the organization itself is able to function. These role definitions maintain the continued consistency of the organization and are quite functional, generally, so that predictability of individual role occupant behavior is very high. Thus, the set of mutual role expectations among the members of the system can be consistent and be depended upon for job performance. In effect these role definitions generally specify the range of behaviors that is acceptable with reference to the occupants of each particular role. Most of the behaviors of individuals in organizations are quite easily predictable once it is known what the formal role definitions of the individuals include, and what reciprocal role expectations are existent.

A second important influence is the authority relation system that is built into the organization. This is very much like the pecking order among a flock of chickens. It is generally quite clear who is able to influence whom in the organization if one knows what the formal-informal relations are in that system, and if the pattern is rather clear and consistent over the range of relationships tending to occur among the individuals involved. Interestingly enough, this seems to operate to constrain behavior much more within organizational families than among members of different subunits of the same organization. It is certainly more consistent, more legitimate within an organization, for an individual who has authority in his own area — say, the superintendent of a production department — to influence the behavior of some member of his department than somebody in the sales department. First of all, he is not as likely to attempt to influence the sales operation at all in terms of individual behavior, though he may deal with the manager of the sales operation, but he does not deal with the men who are subordinate to the sales manager. On the other hand, the sales manager is not at all likely to deal with any submember within the production operation; he is much more likely to operate through his own department, or through some contact with the production manager. Here what we have is a pattern of relations within one's organizational family that is quite consistent and pervasive, but with inter-organizational unit relationships generally existing only between those at the top of those families in terms of authority.

Another important constraint on behavior in organizations is that set of relationships and expectations between members of the system built not on the formal role definitions or specified authority relations, but through the development of normative relations. By this it is clear that there are informal processes that develop over time that relate one individual to another, and that can, through existing reciprocal role relations, function to influence and to some degree control the behavior of reciprocal members of an interrelated group. Another important factor, frequently not considered, but also quite influential in the pattern of how individuals are related in social systems, is the technology of the system and its related effect on spatial arrangements. These factors influence not only who will have contact with whom, but also major aspects of the ways in which the organizational behavior will be interrelated. Individuals who tend to be spatially close together are more likely to interact with each other. Certainly those who are technologically interconnected in a spatial sense are also more likely to be interrelated in terms of their interaction. Finally, the allocation of rewards in the system provides for consistency of behavior.

We are then faced with the problems associated with the question of how to handle dynamic multiple causation among variables where the interrelationships are interactive. Multivariate techniques as presently developed can only partially handle the problem. It seems clear that future work must accept and account for a more complex model of how behavior variance may be explained. We have only just begun to face up to the complexity of our future tasks.

It is also clear that we have in many ways posed only some of the questions that we need to approach in the future. We have suggested that though the state of our knowledge is limited, in some areas we have considerable empirical evidence and some understanding. However, the complexity of the task is more ahead of us than behind us.

Finally — in our rush to analyze the problems that we face — we have quite possibly lost some of the gestalt of the problems. The human being as we know him is not really any set of trait attributes but a complex whole that is in some way more than the combination of his parts. We have been willing though, at this point, to oversimplify our analysis in order to obtain insights that will in the future enable us to reconstitute the whole more adequately and understand those factors that influence his behavior.

Bibliography

Deutsch, K. W. Communication codes for organizing information. *Behavioral Science*, 1966, 11, 1–18.

Etzioni, A. *A comparative analysis of complex organizations.* New York: The Free Press, 1961.

Fleishman, E. A. Development of a behavior taxonomy for describing human tasks: A correlational-experimental approach. *Journal of Applied Psychology*, 1967, 51, 1–10.

Indik, B. P. The study of organizational and relevant small group and individual dimensions. New Brunswick, N. J.: Rutgers — The State University, Technical Report 13, 1963, Contract Nonr-404(10).

———, Hockmeyer, M., & Castore, C. A compendium of measures of individuals, groups and organizations relevant to the study of organizational behavior. New Brunswick, N. J.: Rutgers — The State University, 1968.

Indik, B. P., & Tyler, J. Homeostatis theory of small groups VIII: Longitudinal study. New Brunswick, N. J.: Rutgers — The State University, Technical Report 11, 1963, Contract Nonr-404(10).

Katz, D., & Kahn, R. L. *The social psychology of organizations.* New York: John Wiley & Sons, 1966.

Mangelsdorf, J. E. Empirical measurement: Rational approach. In Van Cott, H. P. (Chm.), *Task taxonomy and its implication for military requirements.* Symposium presented at American Psychological Association, Chicago, September 1965.

McGrath, J. E., & Altman, I. *Small group research: Synthesis and critique of the field.* New York: Holt, Rinehart & Winston, 1966.

Miller, R. B. Task analysis and task taxonomy: Inventive approach. In Van Cott, H. P. (Chm.), *Task taxonomy and its implication for military requirements.* Symposium presented at American Psychological Association, Chicago, September 1965.

PEOPLE, } GROUPS, AND } ORGANIZATIONS { INDEXES

Author Index

Subject Index